Towards Development Economics

Towards Development Economics

Indian Contributions 1900–1945

edited by

J. Krishnamurty

OXFORD
UNIVERSITY PRESS

OXFORD
UNIVERSITY PRESS

YMCA Library Building, Jai Singh Road, New Delhi 110 001

Oxford University Press is a department of the University of Oxford. It furthers the University's objective of excellence in research, scholarship, and education by publishing worldwide in

Oxford New York

Auckland Cape Town Dar es Salaam Hong Kong Karachi Kuala Lumpur Madrid Melbourne Mexico City Nairobi New Delhi Shanghai Taipei Toronto

With offices in

Argentina Austria Brazil Chile Czech Republic France Greece Guatemala Hungary Italy Japan Poland Portugal Singapore South Korea Switzerland Thailand Turkey Ukraine Vietnam

Oxford is a registered trademark of Oxford University Press in the UK and in certain other countries

Published in India
by Oxford University Press, New Delhi

First published 2009

ISBN-13: 978-019-569817-6
ISBN-10: 019-569817-7

Typeset in AGaramond by Le Studio Graphique, Gurgaon 122 001
Printed in India at De Unique, New Delhi 110 018
Published by Oxford University Press
YMCA Library Building, Jai Singh Road, New Delhi 110 001

Contents

Preface

Out of interest and as a post-retirement activity I began studying the lives and careers of the first generation of Indian professional economists. In the course of this work, I read the major works of a large number of Indian economists of the pre-Independence period, and came across several which are unknown to modern economists and historians. Struck by the range, quality, and relative inaccessibility of much of this work, I decided to collect a baker's dozen of 13 papers written by twentieth century Indian economists over the period before Independence. I felt the need to provide short biographies of each of these economists, since such biographies either do not exist or are seriously inaccurate. Short introductions, notes on each selected contribution and a bibliography have been added.

I hope this volume will prove a useful sampler and stimulate others to look at the works of this group of economists. It also complements the research I am doing on early Indian professional economists, documenting their lives and their work, tracing the development of economics as a profession in India, and assessing the contributions of Indian economists to research, teaching, and public policy.

As an independent researcher, living for much of the time away from libraries and archives relevant to Indian studies, and with limited opportunities to interact with scholars with similar interests, I have been fortunate to have the generous support of many friends and well-wishers, as well as libraries, archives, and research institutions in different parts of the world. I am particularly thankful to the following for facilitating access to material and/or advice, comments, and encouragement: Priya Adarkar, the late Raj Chandavarkar, N.K. Chowdhury, Partha Dasgupta, Geoff Harcourt, Sumita Kale, Sunanda Krishnamurty, Tirthankar Roy, Leena Vakil, David Washbrook, and J.C. Whitaker. I am also indebted to the authorities and staff of the following institutions for providing access to their resources: the National Archives of India, New Delhi; the Nehru Memorial Museum and Library, New Delhi; the Gokhale Institute of Economics and Politics, Pune; the British Library, London; the Indian Institute Library, Oxford; the Regenstein Library, Chicago; Columbia University Library, New York; St John's College, Cambridge; the South Asian Studies Centre, Cambridge; and St Antony's College, Oxford.

As a student and researcher, I had the good fortune to interact with some of the greatest economists and teachers of my time. I dedicate this volume to the three to whom I believe I owe the most: the late K.C. Nag at St Stephen's College, and K.N. Raj and the late Dharma Kumar at the Delhi School of Economics.

At a personal level I am indebted to my wife, Sunanda, and our daughters, Parvati and Arundhati, who have been a constant source of encouragement.

The staff of Oxford University Press, New Delhi, deserves a special word of thanks for assisting in the finalization of the manuscript for publication.

Geneva
30 November 2008

J. KRISHNAMURTY

Acknowledgements

Grateful acknowledgement is made to the following individuals, journals, and institutions for granting permission to reprint copyright material.

Palgrave Macmillan, Houndmills, Basingstoke, Hampshire, UK, for the extract from L.C. Jain (1929), *Indigenous Banking in India*, Macmillan and Co Ltd., London (Chapter VIII, pp. 226–46).

Ms Leena Vakil for the essay by C.N. Vakil (1930), 'The Economic Basis of the Communal Tension in India', reprinted in his book *Poverty and Planning*, Allied Publishers, Bombay, 1963.

The *International Labour Review* for the essay by Rajani Kanta Das (1931), 'Woman Labour in India', Volume 24, pp. 376–97 and 536–62.

Professor L. Subramaniam and Mr L. Swaminathan for the extract from P.S. Lokanathan (1935), *Industrial Organization in India*, George Allen and Unwin, London, pp. 13–40.

The Managing Editor, *Indian Journal of Economics*, Allahabad University, for the following:

- Radhakamal Mukherjee (1933–34), 'The Broken Balance of Population, Land and Water', Volume 14, pp. 255–66.
- Gyanchand (1934–35), 'The Essentials of Economic Planning for India', Volume 15, pp. 409–22.
- P.J. Thomas (1935), 'A Plan for Economic Recovery', Volume 15, pp. 447–57.
- V.K.R.V. Rao (1937–38), 'The Problem of Unemployment in India', Volume 18, pp. 627–34.

Ms Priya Adarkar for B.P. Adarkar (1941), 'Protection in India: A Bird's-eye View', from his book *Indian Fiscal Policy*, Kitabistan, Allahabad.

The article by V.G. Kale (1917), 'The Present Economic Condition of India' was published in his *Indian Industrial and Economic Problems*, Natesan, Madras. It is no longer subject to copyright as he died in 1946.

Brij Narain's essay, 'Indian versus Western Industrialism' was published in a collection of his papers, *Essays on Indian Economic Problems*, in 1919. Brij Narain died in 1947 and the paper is no longer under copyright.

J.C. Coyajee's article 'Arguments for Protection' appeared in *Indian Fiscal Problem*, being a course of seven lectures delivered at Patna University in August, 1923, published in 1924. It is no longer under copyright as Coyajee died in 1943.

The article by B.R. Ambedkar, 'Small Holdings in India and Their Remedies', appeared in the *Journal of the Indian Economic Society*, Volume I, 1918. By 1925, the Society had ceased to exist. Hence, it is no longer under copyright.

For permission to publish photos I am indebted to the following:

The Kale family, Pune, for the photos of V.G. Kale and of V.G. Kale with D.G. Karve (the latter appears on the back cover of the book).

The Institute for Social and Economic Change, Bangalore, for the photo of V.K.R.V. Rao.

The ILO Archives for the photo of Rajani Kanta Das.

Dr Koustubh Panda for the photo of J.C. Coyajee from *Nostalgia: An Illustrated History of Hindu-Presidency College, 1817–1992*, by Koustubh Panda et al., Sulagna Mukherjee, Calcutta, 1993.

Professor N.K. Chowdhury of Patna University for his photo of a portrait of Gyanchand.

Professor Ajit Kumar Singh, Director, Giri Institute of Development Studies, Lucknow, for the photo of Radhakamal Mukherjee.

The Director of the Indian Institute of Economics, Hyderabad, for the photo of L.C. Jain, which appeared in S. Kesava Iyengar (ed.) (1953), *Indian Economists at Home and Abroad*, published by the Institute.

Professor L. Subramaniam and Mr L. Swaminathan for the photo of P.S. Lokanathan.

Ms Leena Vakil for the photo of C.N. Vakil.

Ms Priya Adarkar for the photo of B.P. Adarkar.

It has not been possible to obtain permission from the Institute for Techno Economic Studies, Chennai, for the photo of P.J. Thomas which appeared in P.V. Rajkumar et al. (1978), *Economics is Not All: Thoughts and*

Tributes: Dr B Natarajan 67th Birthday Commemoration Volume, published by the Institute. Efforts to contact the Institute were unsuccessful.

Every attempt has been made to trace copyright holders and obtain permission. Any omission brought to my attention will be remedied in future editions, if any.

Introduction

'There's a point about those wretched Indians,' he explained, 'that I ryahly must clyah up. I think I may find it in Pramathanatha Banerjea's book. Or it may be dealt with by Radhakumud Mookerji.'

Aldous Huxley.[1]

The Big Names in Indian Economics Before Independence

Few Indians today have heard of Pramathanath Banerjea or Radhakumud Mookerji or would be able to name the major professional economists of pre-Independence India. Yet colonial India produced several economists of note. These economists contributed to the development of an economics profession, to a body of economic research and analysis, and to the training of large numbers of students who joined government service and the professions.

The present volume seeks to showcase Indian contributions to development economics, well before the subject became a major part of mainstream economics in the UK and the US. The aim is not an encyclopaedia but a sampler of writings that reflect, the wide variety of views and approaches to the problem of Indian development. For reasons of space and focus, it does not deal with Indian contributions to general economic theory. The major Indian writers on theoretical issues before Independence, A.K. Dasgupta, J.K. Mehta, B.R. Shenoy, and B.P. Adarkar, made important contributions to economic theory and monetary economics.

The work of Indian economists was not generally appreciated by the colonial government. In the late 1930s, the Finance Member of the Viceroy's Executive Council, Sir James Grigg, argued that there were no suitable Indian economists for the post of economic adviser to the government. Indian economists, in his view, were at best 'school masters' (Chandavarkar 1989,

p. 117). More recently, the Australian economist, H.W. Arndt also dismissed the work of Indian economists before 1945.[2] He based his conclusion on the views of an Indian economist, D.H. Bhutani (Bhutani 1941–42, p. 280) who claimed that the Indian contribution to economics was negligible, and that Indians lacked the 'apparatus of mind' that made the economist; that they had not developed 'techniques of analysis', and that the 'sources of our inspiration are foreign'.

While I believe that the papers published in this volume will help to negate these assessments, I do not wish to exaggerate Indian contributions, prior to Independence, to economics in general and to development economics in particular. The output of Indian economists varied greatly in volume and quality, and much of it was of poor quality. One must remember that it was a new profession where standards were in the process of being set and access to resources and facilities was limited. It would naturally take time before a body of high class work could emerge. Given this, I believe that some really good work was done, and it is still worth reading today.

How large was the economics profession before Independence? Over 170 Indian economists were listed by the *Indian Journal of Economics* in 1923–24.[3] Again, a list published by the same journal in 1941–42[4] listed 159 names, which is certainly an underestimation of the size of the profession. The size of the profession was certainly large for an underdeveloped country under colonial rule. The volume and range of work was also impressive, although the quality varied a great deal.[5]

Apart from several good articles published in the *Indian Journal of Economics* from 1916 and several books published by Indian publishers, Indians began to publish articles and books abroad as well. P.P. Pillai published a paper on the Indian iron and steel industry in the *Economica* in 1923—perhaps the earliest article published by an Indian professional economist in a foreign technical journal (Pillai 1923). This was followed by P.A. Wadia's paper on protection in the *Economic Journal* in 1924 (Wadia 1924). Over the years, several others published important papers in the *Economic Journal*, including V.K.R.V. Rao, P.J. Thomas, S. Kesava Iyengar, and B.P. Adarkar. B.R. Shenoy published two papers on monetary economics in the *Quarterly Journal of Economics* in the early 1930s (Shenoy 1932; 1934). Several Indian economists, including Brij Narain, Benoy Kumar Sarkar, and V.G. Kale, contributed papers to the *Review of World Economics* (*Weltwirtschaftliches Archiv*), published by the Kiel Institute for the World Economy in Germany.

While some Indian economists, whether by choice or necessity, published their books with relatively less known Indian publishers, others published their books with reputed British publishers (who often had Indian branches or collaborators) like Macmillan, P.S. King, George Allen and Unwin, Routledge, and Oxford University Press. A few published their books in other countries, such as Italy and Germany.

Several economists of the pre-Independence period are remembered today for their contributions to public life. Thus B.R. Ambedkar is famous as a leader of Dalits and the father of the Indian Constitution; K.T. Shah is remembered as the dynamic Secretary of the National Planning Committee of the Congress party; John Matthai as a post-Independence Finance Minister; D.R. Gadgil as Vice-Chairman of the Planning Commission; V.K.R.V. Rao as Vice-Chancellor of Delhi University, founder of several economic research centres, and Education Minister; P.S. Lokanathan as Executive Secretary of the Economic Commission for Asia and the Far East and later Director of the National Council of Applied Economic Research; and B.P. Adarkar as a pioneer in Indian social insurance.

Some economists have been recently rediscovered. Perhaps the most important is Radhakamal Mukherjee, the pioneer in the 1930s of environmental economics (see Guha 1992; also see Gottlieb 1971). Again, the works of some economists like Gyanchand (on population), Lokanathan (on managing agencies), or Gadgil (on the industrial evolution of India), continue to be frequently cited. On the other hand, economists like Brij Narain, Jehangir Coyajee, Manohar Lal, Rajani Kanta Das, P.J. Thomas, and L.C. Jain are not widely known today.

If I had to make a list of eminent Indian professional economists of the pre-Independence period, I would certainly include B.P. Adarkar, B.R. Ambedkar, Brij Narain, Jehangir Coyajee, Rajani Kanta Das, A.K. Dasgupta, H.L. Dey, D.R. Gadgil, Gyanchand, V.G. Kale, S. Kesava Iyengar, L.C. Jain, J.C. Kumarappa, P.S. Lokanathan, John Matthai, J.K. Mehta, Radhakamal Mukherjee, S.G. Panandikar, N.G. Ranga, V.K.R.V. Rao, Benoy Kumar Sarkar, K.T. Shah, B.R. Shenoy, P.J. Thomas, and C.N. Vakil.

Training

We tend to imagine that front-ranking Indian economists of the pre-Independence era were trained in Great Britain, principally at Cambridge, Oxford, or London. This is certainly true of several of them. Manohar Lal,[6]

Jehangir Coyajee, D.R. Gadgil, V.K.R.V. Rao and B.P. Adarkar were trained in Cambridge; B.R. Ambedkar, Gyanchand, L.C. Jain, P.S. Lokanathan, John Matthai, K.T. Shah and C.N. Vakil in London; and P.J. Thomas and N.G. Ranga in Oxford. Relatively few were trained in the US: B.R. Ambedkar at Columbia (as well as London) and R.K. Das at Madison, Wisconsin. A few others did their degrees from Germany, including Zakir Hussain (later President of India) from Bonn and L.K. Hyder from Heidelberg. But these Indian economists often owed much to their Indian education prior to departure and their Indian experience on their return.

Several famous Indian economists, including Brij Narain, V.G. Kale, J.K. Mehta, and Radhakamal Mukherjee, did not have foreign degrees. Brij Narain and Radhakamal Mukherjee studied at Calcutta University, Kale studied in Poona, and Mehta in Allahabad. Indian economists usually had MA degrees in economics, but, as was the case in other parts of the world, only some had doctoral degrees. Reputed economists like Jehangir Coyajee, V.G. Kale, Brij Narain, K.T. Shah, C.N. Vakil, B.P. Adarkar and D.R. Gadgil did not have Ph.D. degrees.

Work Settings

Initially, Indian economists worked in colleges all over the country. From 1908, universities began to establish departments of economics geared to postgraduate teaching and research and these provided opportunities to the growing numbers of professional economists. The important departments were in Calcutta (from 1908), Madras (from 1916), Allahabad (from 1916), and Bombay from (1921). University departments also developed in Banaras, Punjab, Nagpur, and other places.

There was a national labour market in economists at this time and many universities recruited the best available, irrespective of which region they came from. Thus Calcutta's first university professor, Manohar Lal, was from the Punjab and Jehangir Coyajee of Presidency College, Calcutta, was from Bombay Presidency. Lucknow's Radhakamal Mukherjee was from Bengal, Patna's Gyanchand was from the Punjab and Dacca's S.G. Panandikar from Bombay. Several expatriates taught in different universities and colleges, including (to mention just a few) Americans like C.D. Thomson and Clark Warburton in Allahabad, and British economists like Gilbert Slater in Madras, H. Stanley Jevons in Allahabad, and C.J. Hamilton in Calcutta and Patna.

From the mid-1920s Indian economists served on government committees and commissions and, especially from the 1930s, some worked for the government on a more or less continuing basis. Important examples include V.G. Kale, who was Member of the first Tariff Board from 1923 to 1925; John Matthai, who was Member (1925–31), later President (1931–34), of the Tariff Board and Director General of Commercial Intelligence and Statistics (1935–40); Coyajee, who served on the Indian Fiscal Commission (1921–22) and on the Royal Commission on Indian Currency (1924–25); L.K. Hyder who was Member of the Taxation Inquiry Committee (1924), and the Royal Commission on Indian Agriculture (1928); and P.J. Thomas, who worked for the Bowley–Robertson Committee in developing a scheme for an economic census. Several economists, including V.G. Kale, Radhakamal Mukherjee, and L.C. Jain, were associated with the Provincial Banking Inquiries in the late 1920s and early 1930s. By the late 1930s, the extent to which Indian economists participated in government work was quite significant.

Major Contributions

Professional Indian economists produced a body of scholarly work before Independence, which in turn generated much discussion among their compatriots and others. Following Ranade, there was an unsuccessful attempt to develop a truly 'Indian' economics. This was a daunting task and perhaps for that reason it did not succeed. Increasingly the emphasis was on using economic analysis, developed abroad, to explain the Indian economic situation, development prospects, and options.

While it would be difficult to characterize Indian work in economics in any simple way, some features may be identified. First, India's current situation was generally regarded by Indian economists as bad, marked by widespread poverty, illiteracy and lack of modern skills, shortage of capital, low rates of investment, and social institutions and practices inimical to development. Second, the potential for development existed, provided appropriate development policies were followed. However, there were considerable differences of opinion on the path to development. Some favoured agriculture-led growth, while others favoured industrialization of the modern kind.[7] Indian economists felt that new development-oriented policies were needed on education and skill development and productivity enhancement; public health and sanitation; banking and credit systems;

economic diversification, involving promotion of industry by state policies, tariffs, subsidies, and other measures and promotion of agriculture by reform of landholdings and reduction of pressure on land (through industrialization); reorientation of public revenue and expenditure policies to reflect Indian development needs; and reform of existing social and economic institutions.

These policy priorities emerged from the studies and analyses done by economists of that period. These included studies on issues that had been in the forefront of the national movement, like financial policies, protection, and exchange rate policies. Others were on new and relatively under-researched subjects like village society and economic systems, employment and labour market conditions, traditional credit systems, indigenously developed systems of industrial management, national income, macroeconomic policy, and economic planning. Among the major contributors to this kind of policy work were not only all the economists whose work figures in this volume, but many others whose work could not be included.

To give an idea of the pioneering work that led to major realignments in Indian economic policy thinking, I would just briefly mention a few examples.

The importance of institutions: Much attention was devoted to detailed studies of the rural economy to understand how it functioned. One of the earliest Indian works was by Radhakamal Mukherjee in 1916. But his generally favourable assessment of the traditional village economy was seriously questioned by Brij Narain in 1919. While it was part of the received wisdom that moneylenders were a major problem, L.C. Jain in 1929 was bold enough to argue that indigenous bankers had an important role to play in what we would today call the unorganized money and capital market. Again, Lokanathan in 1935 examined in depth another unique institution, the system of managing agents in industry, and came up with important findings. A common thread in the conclusions of both Jain and Lokanathan was that traditional or pre-existing institutions need not be jettisoned, but could be adapted to serve new and emerging needs. This may be contrasted with the positions of some who believed that institutions would need to be overhauled and of others who wanted to preserve the village economy at all cost.

Employment and economic diversification: Indian economists consistently believed that the Indian economy needed to be diversified. Coyajee used it as an argument for tariff protection. Ambedkar in 1918 used it to argue that industrialization was essential for successful land reform by reducing the intolerable pressure of numbers on the land. This idea that excess population had to be taken off the land was also behind Rao's adaptation of the concept of disguised employment to India in 1938. Again, the solution was sought by many in modern industrialization, but there were others like Kumarappa (1945), who favoured the Gandhian approach to development and yet others like Gyanchand (1935), who feared that its benefits would not trickle down.

Economic policy: Most Indian economists were struck by the exploitative character of colonial rule and were well aware that developing and developed countries generally followed promotional and interventionist economic polices with great success. Hence issues of monetary and fiscal policy, including exchange rates, currency systems, tariffs, and budgetary policies, held centre stage. A common feeling among Indian economists was that economic policies must reflect national self-interest; also, the data required to debate government policies was available. Thomas (1935), and later Adarkar (1941), introduced Keynesian economics into the debate. There were also attempts to improve estimates of macroeconomic aggregates like national income and expenditure. Despite the pioneering work of Rao (1940), and others, the real constraint was the unwillingness of the colonial government to spend more on data collection, partly out of fears that the results would provide further ammunition to the nationalists.

Keeping in mind the fact that India was a colony, the development of economics as a profession and a discipline in a relatively short time is unique in the annals of history. Yet, an 'Indian economics' in the sense that M.G. Ranade had visualized it, never came about. Indian economists did not change the foundations of economics in India; they did, however, produce new work which led to a deeper understanding of Indian problems. While Indian thinking on policy questions was influenced by the new work that was coming out, its incorporation into concrete policy responses could not take place on any significant scale until Independence.

Indian economists before Independence were development economists of necessity; widespread poverty and general economic backwardness in India and the lack of coherent development policies on the part of the colonial rulers[8] drove them to apply the economic ideas prevalent in the West, particularly in continental Europe and the United States. They also developed a tradition of careful empirical work drawing upon, and adapting,

Western methods. This facilitated a better understanding of how the economy actually functioned and what the constraints to development were. As the individual papers included in this volume show, they anticipated later thinking on development economics in several important respects.

Selection Criteria for the Volume

Selecting papers for inclusion in this volume posed many problems. Several criteria were adopted: first, the paper must still have some relevance and evoke interest among scholars today; second, the topic covered or its treatment must show originality or be ahead of its time; third, the paper must make good reading for a professional economist or a reader with a social science background; fourth, the writings of different 'generations' of pre-Independence economists should be included; and fifth, no author should have more than one paper in the volume. A further constraint was that the volume could not exceed a certain size, and this last constraint proved to be the most serious one. I had, in several instances, to make difficult choices.

The bibliography at the end of the volume is partly intended to make up for the inevitable arbitrariness of any selection process. It includes references to works that had to be omitted but warrant reading, and to some that I would not select but others might.

The papers are presented in chronological order. This may help to provide an idea of the way Indian economic thinking was developing. Most of the authors, with the exception of L.C. Jain, B.P. Adarkar, and V.K.R.V. Rao, were born before 1900; most began their careers before the early 1920s, only V.K.R.V. Rao and B.P. Adarkar began their careers around 1930; and most of the authors remained professionally active after Independence, with the important exceptions of V.G. Kale, Jehangir Coyajee, Brij Narain, and B.R. Ambedkar. It may be added that several economists who joined the profession before Independence made, or continued to make, important contributions after Independence. For obvious reasons their post-Independence writings cannot be taken into account in this volume.

Before each paper, there is an introductory note providing some biographical details, placing in context the contributions, and assessing their originality and contemporary relevance. Photos of most of the authors have been included. Editorial changes to the papers have been kept to the minimum so that they retain their original flavour. Non-Indian readers may note that 1 lakh is 100,000 and 1 crore is 100 lakh (or lacs), and a rupee comprises of 16 annas.

Together the contributions included in this volume help us to go back in time to share the thoughts and ideas of some great Indian economists of the pre-Independence period. We find that they were good scholars; widely read and receptive to new ideas and perspectives. They took up new issues, or examined old ones afresh, with a view to understanding them fully and coming up with policy prescriptions. On several subjects like the nature of underdevelopment and alternative paths to development, surplus labour and disguised unemployment, the limitations of 'trickle-down' theory, environmental economics, women in development, employment and conflict, trade policy, and the role of the state they were at least abreast, if not ahead, of Western thinkers. While some examples of their anticipation of modern economic concepts and ideas are provided in the commentaries on the individual papers, a discerning reader is sure to find many more such examples.

Notes

1. Aldous Huxley, *Point Counter Point*. NY, Doubleday, Doran and Company, Garden City, 1928, p. 263.
2. See Arndt (1972, p. 21–22), for a summary dismissal of the contribution of Indian and other non-Western economists before 1945.
3. See *Indian Journal of Economics* (1923–24), pp. 218–23 and p. 328.
4. See *Indian Journal of Economics* (1941–42), pp. 864–73. Perhaps enthusiasm to register had waned over the years.
5. While there were several publications in Indian languages, especially Bengali, Hindi, and Marathi, I am not in a position to evaluate them.
6. The first Minto Professor of Economics, Manohar Lal, had been a student of Marshall and came first in the moral sciences tripos in Cambridge in 1902. His publications were, however, few.
7. See for example, H.L. Dey in Mukherjee and Dey (1939), p. 357, who argued that only a flourishing agriculture could provide the basis for a large, secure, and expanding market for factory products. Brij Narain was one of many who placed their faith in modern industrial development to transform the economy (see Chapter 3).
8. An account of recent Indian economic history cannot be provided within the confines of this short introduction. Interested readers should read Tirthankar Roy (2000).

Source: Courtesy Sumita Kale.

V.G. Kale (1876–1946)

One of India's earliest professional economists, Vaman Govind Kale was educated entirely in India. He was born in Sangli in present-day Maharashtra in 1876 and studied in Fergusson College, Poona, obtaining his BA degree in 1903. After obtaining his MA degree, he began teaching history, English, and economics at Fergusson College, where he continued for most of his professional life. He formally retired in 1932. Apart from his formal education, Kale benefited from staying for some time with Mr Justice Ranade, while he served as his reader and writer. From 1923 to 1925 he was a member of the first Indian Tariff Board. He played an important role in the founding of the Indian Economic Association in 1917 and was elected President of the Indian Economic Conference for 1929.

Kale was a member of the Indian Council of States from 1921 to 1923 and active in public affairs. He held important posts in the Poona Central Cooperative Bank, the Commonwealth Insurance Company, the Maharatta Chamber of Commerce and Industry, the Brihan Maharashtra Sugar Syndicate, and the Bank of Maharashtra. He was also a member of the Bombay Provincial Banking Enquiry Committee of 1929–1930.

Perhaps the most important of the many books he published was his textbook, *Indian Economics*. First published in 1917, it went into several editions. His collection of papers entitled *Indian Industrial and Economic Problems* (1917), from which the piece I have selected is drawn, provides a good idea of the range of his work. Three other publications are worthy of special mention: *Economics of Protection in India*, published in 1929; 'Some Observations on the Economics of Education', published in the *Journal of the Indian Economic Society* in 1918; and 'Prospects for Technically Trained Indians', submitted to the Industrial Conference of 1912 and published in his *Indian Industrial and Economic Problems* in 1917. The first, a book, presents a very balanced and well-informed discussion of protection, while the latter papers are among the earliest pieces on the economics of education and human resource development, visualizing education and training as investments in development. He published a large number of papers, reviews, reports, and books in several languages, including English, Marathi, and German. They covered topics in a variety of areas, including economic history, protection, monetary theory, trade theory, banking, cooperatives, and industrial development. Professor Kale died in 1946.

Major Biographical Sources: Material provided by the Kale family in Pune (courtesy Sumita Kale); P.J. Thomas, 'The Late Professor V.G. Kale', *Indian Journal of Economics*, vol. 27, 1947, pp. 333–4.

'The Present Economic Condition of India'* was written in 1909, although it was published in a volume in 1917. Apart from providing a good example of the quality of thinking and writing of early Indian professional economists, it is also a good starting point for this volume as it sketches the economic situation early in the twentieth century and reflects the hopes and aspirations of Indians that their country could start on the path to development like the West and Japan.

Kale favoured industrialization, preferably without the evils it produced in the West. He dismissed arguments that India should remain agricultural, stating: 'We must advance, we must imitate, we must assimilate.' Giving the examples of sugar and cotton textiles, he conceded that 'agricultural improvement is essential for the growth of the manufacturing industry'. But he felt that manufactures should grow at the same time. Kale did not feel labour supply was a serious constraint and argued for diversity of occupations so that 'the surplus population may be drawn from agricultural pursuits and led to find their means of subsistence in manufactures or some such employment'. While he argued against sending out raw materials, which would be reimported as finished goods, he was opposed to autarky: 'By manufacturing locally articles for which we enjoy special facilities, and exchanging them for such as we cannot make with advantage, we shall profit ourselves and contribute economic gain to the world.'

Kale acknowledged that the state in India was helping to promote development, but he felt much more was needed. In Germany, America, Japan, and even England 'the State has completely identified itself with the people in the promotion of industries'. In India, too, measures by the state like bounties and drawbacks, protective tariffs, and technical education were needed. In Kale's words: 'The State here must make it its serious business to see that Indian resources are developed in the interests of India and its people.... It has been done in Japan, in America, in Germany, and in England. Why not then in India?'

Kale made the case for state intervention without suggesting that the colonial state had done nothing, or that promoting industrial development in India would be inimical to its interests. The tone of his argument is not strident, but reasoned and persuasive.

* V.G. Kale (1909): 'The Present Economic Condition of India', from V.G. Kale, *Indian Industrial and Economic Problems*, G.A. Natesan, Madras, 1917, pp. 38–60.

1

The Present Economic Condition of India*

V.G. Kale

In the paper, which I read last year before the Madras Session of the Industrial Conference, entitled 'Twenty-five Years' Survey of Indian Industries', I attempted to form an estimate of the progress we have made during the last twenty-five years in the industrial field and tried to direct attention to certain industries, which await development. I propose, in this paper, to take a rapid survey of the general economic situation in India at the present day, to determine what stage we have reached in economic growth and indicate the directions in which further effort has to be made. Last year I quoted facts and figures to show that from being merely a rural country with its vast population subsisting mainly on agriculture and the production of raw materials, India is slowly but surely taking to manufactures on modern lines. Various causes have contributed to bring about this welcome result. The rapid rise of Japan from a backward country like India to position of eminence in commerce and industry, the comparative helplessness and poverty to which this country seemed to be reduced, and a close study of the industrial history of England, and especially of America and Germany, gave rise to a conviction in the minds of people here, that the salvation of the land lay entirely in its industrial regeneration and development. It was felt as an irony of fate that while other nations with a smaller population and with a scanty supply of raw materials, which they had to import from outside, were dumping their manufactured goods on the Indian market, and thus growing fat on the gains made by commerce and industry, India, which at one time supplied the people of Europe with its far-famed shawls, carpets and cotton fabrics and exported large quantities

* Paper submitted to the Indian Industrial Conference, Lahore, 1909.

of other articles of manufacture to foreign lands, should be reduced to the condition of a helpless customer for other people's goods. Memories of past prosperity and despair of the future combined to nerve men to a resolution to do something to reoccupy the ground which was fast slipping from under their feet. But in these times of mechanical inventions and scientific progress, it is easier to talk about industrial regeneration and development than actually to move an inch in the desired direction, especially in a country like ours, full of ignorance, conservatism and poverty. The conviction had, however, gained ground that the history of industrially advanced countries of the West might repeat itself here and that a sympathetic Government and a people awakened to a sense of their duty to themselves, might co-operate to place India on the path of speedy advancement. Though Government have been doing much latterly to assist the growth of indigenous industries, it will not be ungenerous or unjust to say that they have not been able, owing to their peculiar situation, to do what other states have done for their people. The Free Trade policy of England, the old attitude of people there towards 'plantations' and dependencies, still survives, and it is no wonder, if India is by many looked upon as a rich field for the exploitation of European capitalists and manufacturers. In determining the place of India in the British Empire, it is usual to put the commercial and the monetary advantage derived therefrom in the forefront. Though people in India have been roused to a sense of the grave economic situation of the country and are straining every flabby nerve of theirs to flog the dead and dying industries into life, they cannot be unaware of the stupendous task that lies before them. The whole world around them armed with the most modern and scientific processes of manufacture, with enormous quantities of capital to finance industries, fortified with high protective tariffs and ever ready and able to take the least advantage that may offer itself, is a giant competitor, with which this pigmy people with little capital, no scientific and technical knowledge and no protection for industries, have to wrestle, and one may imagine what the issue of the contest is likely to be. The situation is indeed so gloomy that one is tempted, through sheer despair, to give up everything for lost. A mighty economic revolution has been slowly working in the land doing havoc with the time-honoured old order of things. The very foundations are being undermined and their tenacity is giving way to new forces. There is undermining going on here and there, and new foundations are being laid in places on which a new structure is to be reared. But, for the time, the old ruins distress the eye more glaringly than do the new works greet the sight. Like England and other countries, India has been a land of domestic industries, all of which have either crumbled to dust or are fast falling to pieces. The hand-loom weaving industry is almost gone—past recall, and the attempts to prop it up by means of improved crutches are not likely to be much of a success. The same dismal fate has overtaken other industries, which at one time were so flourishing. Old industries, connected with sugar, paper, glass, silk, iron—where are they? Almost all of them killed or in the process of being killed by foreign competition broad-based on modern appliances and up-to-date methods. Other nations, which have had a start over us, have occupied entrenched positions from which they look down complacently on us ineffectually toiling below. Latest methods and machinery, which modern science can devise, have long been in use there, and everyday improvements are made therein which leave us still further in the back-ground. Hardly do we think of adopting a new process in manufacture, when we hear that in the go-ahead nations of the West, it has been already replaced by another, still more economical and remunerative. We started paper-mills on modern lines and for the first few years we competed successfully with the foreign article. But soon wood pulp to be utilised in the manufacture of paper in Western countries and our indigenous industry carried on on the old elementary prime formula, the paper is made of rags and straw, began to decline. The imports of paper and paste-board into India were valued at some 44½ crores of rupees, the average of the three years, 1890–91 to 1892–93. They continuously declined during the next seven or eight years till in the triennium ending in 1898–99 the figure came to 36½ lacs. This decline in the imports of foreign paper is explained by the successful competition of the indigenous paper-mills. But from the year 1900 an upward tendency became visible, and the imports increased, till at last in 1907–08 they were valued at about one crore. From the year 1901 the Indian mills could not hold their ground against the foreign competition which was assisted by wood-pulp. The history of the sugar industry has the same dismal tale to tell. We have got a few sugar factories and refineries and new ones on modern lines are also being started. But we are told that unless we adopt the central factory system, which has proved such a success in Mauritius and Formosa, our prospects must be anything but cheerful. The general impression that a study of the indigenous industries, old and new, leaves on one's mind is, to put it briefly, that it is an unequal fight in which we are engaged. But fight we must. The cessation of efforts would be suicidal.

I am not pessimist and hold that we are slowly but steadily progressing. But we have got to realise what is exactly the situation in which we are placed and what is the nature and extent of the obstacles we have to surmount. An easy-going optimism is not better than a despairing pessimism. The situation must be rightly understood before we essay to face the odds that are against us. And however gloomy the prospect, we must work with a singleness of purpose and a firm faith in our destiny.

The decay of old industries has thrown thousands of artisans and craftsmen out of work. Some new industries have been and are being started, but they cannot provide work to the unemployed. The period of an industrial revolution or transition is always a time of distress. People are swept off their old moorings and drift aimlessly along the hard times without support. No doubt, labour is in great demand just at present, and whatever of it is available in the various industries, is well paid. Prices have risen and along with them wages. It is a remarkable feature of the present economic situation that manual labour of every kind fetches very high wages and a common cooly or cook is better paid than a clerk. But domestic industries having disappeared, and the centres of industry having shifted, the lack-works accustomed to their old environments and attached to their old localities do not easily migrate to places where labour is in great request. It is well-known that man is of all baggages the most difficult to move, and it is not very easy for people to reconcile themselves to a change of environment and employment. When the period of transition is over, things will soon adjust themselves, but, for the time being, there will be distress and hardship which can only be relieved by a further expansion of trade and industries. I have said above that the development of indigenous industries and the attainment of wealth and prosperity by their means, has become the settled ambition of the people of this country. But it may be asked if the establishment of national industries is such a difficult job as already described, why waste efforts upon it? India is essentially an agricultural country, with three-fourths of its people living upon agricultural alone. Devote all your energies to its improvement; develop it to the highest degree attainable. Leave other countries which have already occupied an impregnable position in manufacturing activities, to that business. They will require food, they will want raw materials, and must look up to you for the supply of the same. For instance England must have cotton for her mills and wheat for her belly and must import them from outside. The very rumour that the supply of American wheat was inadequate and that it was being cornered by Mr Patten made the heart of England flutter with anxiety and suspense. A similar rumour with regard to cotton sent a shiver into the manufacturing centres of that country, and short work was at once resolved upon in the cotton mills. India has thus a splendid opportunity of becoming an indispensable feeder of manufacturing countries and can occupy the same vantage ground in the production of food and raw materials, as they occupy in manufactures. Those who have an intimate knowledge of the social and economic condition of the West tell us that even there there is now a reaction against city life, full of hurry and bustle, smoke and squalour, wretchedness and poverty, which come in the train of the modern factory system, and that 'Back to land' is the cry often heard at present in some of those countries. A warning is given to us and we are advised to think seriously before we plunge headlong into the life of manufacturing nations on modern lines. India has been, from time out of mind, a happy land of village communities and republics, leading the life of Arcadian simplicity, and its adoption of Western methods must bring upon it all the evils of industrialism, the over-crowded cities with their few millionaires and myriads of toiling work-people, the struggles between the employers and the employees, with their problems of unemployment, old age pensions, Poor Laws, Factory Legislation, and Socialism. Sir George Birdwood in one of his speeches asked the other day, 'Is Europe going to make Asia an East End?' The gruesome picture often presented to us of European industrialism is such as to make us pause and think. But we who know India, know that Arcadian simplicity and rural bliss are now things of the past among us, to be found henceforth only in Utopias or the day dreams of the poet. Japan, a country of the Orient, has shaken off its old garb and put on a Western raiment. Even the sleepy Celestial Empire has been awakened from its slumber of ages and is going in for European civilisation. The countries of what is called the Middle East are slowly preparing to follow. Can India be a solitary exception? Of course, not. Our lot has been thrown in with the greatest of the nations of the earth. Our contact with England, the peace she has given to this country and the other blessings she has brought us here have already changed the face of Indian society. Our hopes, our aspirations, to take our proper rank among the nations of the world, have once for all fixed the lines of our march and there is no returning or lagging behind. We may indeed try, if possible, to avoid the evils that have been disgracing industrialism in the West. But we cannot remain where we were or what we are. We must advance, we must imitate, we must assimilate.

Many friends of India, taking a deep interest in the well being of its people, hold that instead of frittering away their energies on the pursuit of manufactures, success in which is doubtful, and even if attained, would entail a heavy price, Indians should devote their energies to the development of agriculture, the premier industry of the land, which, on account of its supreme importance, needs all the attention that can be paid to it. H.E. Sir George Clarke, the popular Governor of Bombay, seems to share this view. In a speech that His Excellency made at the time of opening the Agricultural Conference recently held in Poona—a speech which furnishes much food for reflection to the Indian mind—he made a pointed reference to this subject. One of the points emphasised by His Excellency was that agriculture is and must remain by far the most important of all Indian industries and an essential basis of India's prosperity. The argument may be thus briefly summarised. India's increasing millions will have to be fed and a point may be reached when the growth of other staples will have to be checked unless the production of the necessaries of life can be increased. European countries are becoming more and more dependent for their food supply. India not only feeds herself but derives a large share of income from the produce of land. It is supremely important, therefore, that this position should be maintained. A sudden expansion of manufactures on a large scale would be disadvantageous. There is already a shortage of labour in certain localities and a further demand upon it would deplete the numbers required for the vital interests of agriculture. A rapid transference of country-dwellers to town-life would be an evil. The foreign demand for the produce of land must not be lost. Some of the important points contained in the above have been already dealt with. It remains to determine exactly what should be our attitude towards agriculture and manufactures. Here we have to bear in mind three important facts. A majority of Indian population subsists on agriculture. Nearly three-fourths of our exports consist of land produce. And Indian agriculture is in a most backward condition. The more advanced nations have come to apply up-to-date methods and scientific processes to all agricultural operations and the production of the fruits of the earth per acre is much larger in other countries than in India. The development of agriculture is therefore a very important direction in which we must make serious efforts, if not for the purpose of increased exports of food and raw materials, at least for the sake of meeting the growing demand for the same in the country itself. One of the causes that have been assigned for the high prices of food grains prevailing at present is that the production of these grains has not been keeping pace with the increasing demand for them. Again, agricultural improvement is essential for the growth of the manufacturing industry. Let us take the sugar industry as an illustration. In spite of the frantic efforts latterly made to check the imports and consumption of foreign sugar by all available means, the country's sugar bill is every day going up by leaps and bounds. Last year, our imports of foreign sugar were valued at nearly eleven crores of rupees, which means an increase of 100 per cent in less than ten years. Now one of the causes that hamper the indigenous sugar industry is the poor outturn of raw sugar per acre, which is more than three times as small as that elsewhere. To come in a line with Mauritius, Java and other places in this respect means agricultural improvement, the use of scientific processes in the cultivation of sugarcane, better manures and up-to-date methods all round. The textile industry is making a commendable progress, but we want cotton of a finer quality to be produced in the country and this also points to improvements in agriculture. Our tobacco industry is also handicapped by the poor quality of the stuff we produce. The same remark applies to other agricultural products and industries depending upon agriculture. Here then is a vast field for work. The greater the value we may coax mother earth into yielding to us, the better will it be for the poor cultivators and the country generally. The spread of primary education, the establishment of co-operative societies and agricultural banks, the diffusion of useful information regarding improved methods among the ignorant peasants, the supply of better manures and more extended irrigation works, are the directions in which effort has to be made, and we must congratulate Government on the particular attention that is being paid to this subject, and the special endeavours that are being made by the Agricultural Departments in the various provinces in this behalf. Educated people and Zamindars must co-operate with Government in this matter and not leave the poor and ignorant ryot to his own crude efforts.

Admitting then the supreme importance of the agricultural industry and the infinite scope that there is for its development and the growth of the industries dependent thereon, one may ask, can we not attempt the pursuit of manufactures at the same time? Shall we follow agriculture to the exclusion of other industries? The idea of confining our attention exclusively or more prominently to agriculture militates against the present mood of the people and runs counter to their most cherished ambition. They aspire to make India a manufacturing country, not entirely so like England but it seems to be their determined attitude to attain a position of some importance in that line consistently with the maintenance of agriculture. There is no reason to suppose that this is an impracticable or unprofitable ideal. To-day there may be a shortage of labour in certain localities, the centres of manufacturing activity. But the vast and increasing population of the country may be relied upon for an adequate supply of labour for new industries that may be started and we need not cripple agriculture by drawing off labourers working in it. The pressure of the population upon the soil is so great and the openings so few that with almost all the professions overcrowded and no scope in industry and commerce, agriculture and Government or private service are the only refuge of the unemployed. Far from agriculture requiring all the available labour, the Famine Commission has recorded its opinion that the poverty of the people and the risks to which they are exposed in seasons of scarcity are mainly accounted for by the fact that unfortunately agriculture forms almost the sole occupation of the mass of the population, and one of the remedies to meet this evil effectively must be the introduction of a diversity of occupation, through which the surplus population may be drawn from agricultural pursuits and led to find their means of subsistence in manufactures or some such employment. Inland and overland emigration have been proposed as measures of relief to this congestion of population in agriculture, and thousands of Indian coolies have found their way to Mauritius, South Africa, and other places, to work there on plantations and in mines as ordinary labourers and in some cases as carpenters, masons, gardeners, and so forth. I need not here allude to the treatment that these Indian emigrants receive in their temporary foreign homes. My point in alluding to this subject is to show that there is an inexhaustible supply of labour in the country and if it is properly recruited and trained, it will be available to satisfy the demand of all the industries we may start or expand. In fact, from inquiries made in the United Provinces and Bengal regarding the supply of industrial labour, it has been discovered that there is no real deficiency in the amount of labour potentially available, and it is reported that no difficulty need be anticipated on that score. We shall also be indirectly relieving the pressure of population and guarding against poverty and distress if new industries provide work for people now solely dependent upon agriculture. As manufactures steadily advance, people will take kindly to the new system that is slowly coming into vogue.

It has been remarked with some amount of truth that the commerce of India in pre-British times was mere bagatelle in comparison with what has been developed in our own times. A glance at the figures of annual exports and imports is sufficient to prove this. The establishment of peace, the spread of railways, the post and the telegraph, which have linked together not only the distant parts of the country but the various countries of the world to one another, have led to the development of an enormous international trade. Formerly the country was self-sufficient; it supplied almost all its wants and those of other countries also. Now it cannot remain isolated and self-satisfied. New tastes and habits have created a demand for many foreign articles and the decay of our old industries has forced us to look to other countries for the supply of articles which were at one time our own proud monopoly. Though we need not and cannot hope to be self-reliant in the matter of every article among our imports, we may surely aspire to supply some of our main wants by indigenous manufactures by giving a new lease of life to old industries and starting new ones. Thus in the matter of cloth, sugar, paper, tobacco, oils, leather, matches, glass, silk, wool and other industries large and small, we have infinite scope. Instead of sending all our raw materials to foreign countries to be manufactured there, and returned to us as finished articles, we may be able to manufacture our own goods and pocket all the profit that goes at present to other people. The success of the cotton industry and its ever-increasing prosperity are there to guide and cheer us, and though it may take us years and years to reach the goal, a beginning, however small, must be made in time. By manufacturing locally articles for which we enjoy special facilities, and exchanging them for such as we cannot make with advantage, we shall profit ourselves and contribute an economic gain to the world. We cannot any more allow ourselves to be charged with foolishly remaining idle while we have abundance of natural wealth under our feet and all around us.

But our difficulties? Well, they are many, and I have indicated some of them above. The first and the foremost is that about capital. In spite of the fabulous hoards, which are said to be lying idle and useless, it has to be admitted that there is no capital in this country, adequate to the financing of the larger industries on the starting of which the heart of people is set. The word 'poverty' is writ large on the face of the country and it is superfluous to prove what is patent. The new spirit of self-help and self-improvement that is abroad, and the general desire to promote the economic growth of the country, that is visible on all hands, are slowly inducing what little capital there may be to come out of strong boxes and run into more useful channels. We learn from the latest report on Joint Stock Companies registered in India, that during the year 1907–08, 269 of these concerns were started with a nominal capital amounting to some 16 crores and that in that year there was a net increases of 139 in the number of companies with an increase of 13 crores in the nominal and of 6 crores in the paid-up capital of the same. At the close of 1907–08 the working companies had paid up capital of the amount of 50 crores, an increase of 6½ crores over the year previous. During the last decade the increase in the paid-up capital has been 45.9 per cent. These figures make it evident that Indian capital is slowly leaving its shyness and is being induced to come out in driblets. The indigenous insurance companies, banking firms, glass works, sugar factories, cotton and oil mills, match, soap and cap factories and other manufacturing concerns that are being started in various parts of the country, point in the same direction. There is a steady improvement in the economic condition and the next generation will see an industrial progress which the last whole century could not bring about. But the figures of export and production values that are usually quoted to illustrate the industrial prosperity of India, do not reflect the true state of things. The growth of tea and coffee plantations, of coal and gold mines, of jute factories, of the kerosine oil industry and of industries concerned with minerals generally, which has been very remarkable during the last few years is no compliment to Indian capital, Indian talent, or Indian enterprise. Excepting the cotton industry, which is mostly in the hands of Indians and is worked with Indian capital, almost all the so-called indigenous industries, which are taken to estimate the industrial development of India, are not indigenous in the real sense of the word. Most of these are worked with European capital and by European agency. The only profit that India makes from them is wages which the labourers engaged in them get for their manual labour. Take the tea industry for example. The total area under cultivation increased from 540,533 acres in 1907 to 548,127 acres in 1908 and the total number of plantations from 5,811 to 5,839. The total production of tea was some 247 million pounds, of which about 234 millions valued at 10.39 crores of rupees were exported; which seems to be the highest figure on record. The industry employed more than five lakhs of labourers, being an increase of 30 thousand over the previous year. The capital of the Joint Stock Companies engaged in the production of tea amounts to nearly Rs 24 crores, viz., companies registered in India Rs 3.36 crores, companies registered in London Rs 20.22 crores. Now here is an important industry carried on in India, employing five lakhs of men and with a capital of Rs 24 crores, an industry bigger than even the cotton industry. But the most remarkable thing about it is that it is almost wholly controlled by Europeans and nearly 83 per cent of its capital comes from companies registered in London. There were in 1907–08 some 50 jute mills in India employing 188,000 persons. The paid-up capital of 49 of these was £8,664,000. In 1908–09 the exports of raw jute were estimated at about 20 crores of rupees while jute manufactures were exported to the value of 15¾ crores. The whole of this important industry is in the hands of non-Indians. The same remark applies to the output of Indian minerals, the total value of which raised during 1908 was returned as £7,823,745 against £7,079,708 in 1907, an increase of 10.5 per cent. In his Presidential address at the Madras Conference, Rao Bahadur Mudholkar adverted to this feature of India's industrial development and showed how the precious resources of the country are being exploited by outsiders, while we are getting only the wages for Indian labour employed to raise the minerals. Not one of the gold-mining companies is Indian, and the value of the gold produced last year was more than three crores. All the profit made in this industry goes clean out of the country. On account of their scientific knowledge, long experience, and enormous capital, foreigners can easily take advantage of the many natural facilities, which India offers and the children of the soil have only to look at them with despair. The fault is partly ours inasmuch as we do not possess the necessary enterprise and knowledge, and cannot command the requisite capital. How can a backward people labouring under every disadvantage be expected all at once to be ready to compete with the fully equipped foreign exploiter? Of what earthly use is it to the Indians—taking the word in its widest significance—if millions of pounds worth of minerals are annually extracted out of the soil and carried away without giving them any moral or material gain? We cannot certainly be expected to congratulate ourselves on the growth and prosperity of industries in which our only gain is wages of labour of the lowest kind. Such industries are Swadeshi by courtesy. The whole question is rather a ticklish one and Government is perhaps helpless in the matter. But so are people too and more so than Government. Rao Bahadur Mudholkar was handled rather roughly by certain critics for his unpalatable but true remarks on the point. As he said, this is not a question of race or creed; it is a question in which the most vital national interests are at stake, and as trustees of those interests, the Indian Government have a duty to perform by the people. The conservation of the natural resources of this country is the first duty of a paternal Government such as our British Rulers ought to show themselves. The Geological Department is making a survey of the whole country and publishing useful information as to the openings there are for capital and enterprise. But we are not in a position to profit by it. It is therefore necessary that larger numbers of Indian students must receive instruction in mining and metallurgy, licenses and mining leases must be altogether withheld from or more sparingly given to non-Indians, and Indian enterprise and capital ought to be encouraged. Our motive in seeking industrial development is the desire to promote the growth of national wealth and national income. But much of our present economic development is development by proxy. We have a very small share in it and the profits our industries do not remain to fructify in the pockets of the people.

British capital investments in this country are estimated by some at about 700 crores of rupees, distributed among various industries and other concerns. I am not one of those who would taboo all foreign capital. I would rather welcome it provided it is handled by our own people. It is said that the burden of the interest charges that India has to bear is already very large, and we cannot afford to increase this burden by borrowing European capital any further. But if we ourselves borrow foreign capital for the exploitation of our national resources, the burden of the interest charged thereon will be more than counter-balanced by the profits that will find their way into our pockets and the increase of national wealth that will ensue. So long as no Indian capital is coming forth in the desired quantities, we must borrow cheap foreign capital. But the industries thus financed by foreign capital must be entirely in the hands of Indians. The enterprise and the management must be Indian, all the profits derived therefrom must also be Indian. Let us try by all means to get as much indigenous capital as possible. But large concerns—and concerns have to be on a large scale to be remunerative—require enormous capital, which we cannot hope to get locally for a long time to come. At present we put all European managed industries whether coal or gold mines, woollen or jute mills, tea or coffee plantations, in the Swadeshi category, and this is good so far as it goes. But our next step must be to make them genuinely Swadeshi. Irrespective of creed or colour, they are the sons of India who have made this country their home, who have a stake in it, and who share its poverty and prosperity. To the wealth of these ought our industrial growth to contribute. European talent, enterprise and capital have done and are doing the work of pioneers in many a difficult industrial and commercial line, and they are deservedly reaping the fruit of their exertions. We are much indebted to them for their having shown us the way and fired us with a zeal to follow their foot-steps. We owe it to ourselves to acknowledge the service they have rendered to us, and our success depends upon how we profit by the lesson they have taught us.

There is an Indian proverb which says that the times are always what the sovereign makes them. This adage reflects the notorious dependence of Orientals upon the State. India has been ever foreign to the democratic and representative institutions like those now predominant in the countries of the West. But what people are there on the earth who have not been helped into their commercial and industrial prosperity by the State? In Germany, America, Japan and even in England, the State has completely identified itself with the people in the promotion of industries. In England there was a reaction against too much State interference and in favour of *laissez faire* and individualism. But there is now a swing of the pendulum in the opposite direction, and a tendency towards State protection and State Socialism is clearly discernible almost in all countries of the West. By means of bounties and drawbacks, protective tariffs and technical education, and in a hundred other ways the governments of other countries are promoting the growth of national industries and national wealth. We in India expect our State to do the same thing for us. Our educated people are often taunted with their too much dependence on Government and their extreme fondness for Government service. Whether the taunt is merited or not, we have the example of other States before us and we know what they are doing for their people. I do not wish to exaggerate, and it would be doing injustice to Government if I were not to acknowledge freely what the Indian State is actually doing to promote nascent industries. Evidences are not wanting to show that Government have become alive to their duties, and the economic development of the country is being assisted by them in various ways such as industrial conferences, exhibitions, experiments and demonstrations, surveys and scholarships, and the introduction of better types of implements and machines. What little has been done is nothing, however, in comparison with what has and ought to be done. The people, though they have not done all that is expected of them, have risen to the occasion, and mutual response and co-operation may be calculated to do the needful in the near future. Government in India has, however, to devise its measures for the good of its people with one eye upon London and the other on Calcutta. And the two eyes do not often see things in the same light. It is a delicate task, to reconcile two often-conflicting interests. But the firmness and liberality which have been just displayed in the matter of the Reforms may, with advantage, be extended to the sphere of industry. Public opinion in India has become uncompromisingly protectionist and expects Government too to accept that creed. India will be willing to join in the scheme of Tariff Reform which is to embrace the whole British Empire, provided she receives her due share of advantages. The Government of India is sure to stand by the people in this respect. Circumstanced as we are, our purpose will not be served by mere palliative and temporary measures. The State here must make it its serious business to see that Indian resources are developed in the interests of India and its people. It must give us all the facilities we want; nay much more. It must stimulate interest, spread broad-cast primary, technical and scientific education, send young men in their hundreds and thousands to foreign countries to learn various industries there, help capitalists and enthusiastic men to start new industries and protect them against outside competition. For Indian people this is presumably not too much to expect of their Government. It has been done in Japan, in America, in Germany, and in England. Why then not in India?

In short, the situation is this. An economic revolution is in progress in the land. The old national industries are dead or dying. New ones have not yet taken their place. the competition around us is keen and killing. We lack enterprise, capital, experience, scientific knowledge and sufficient State protection. Agriculture is in the most backward condition. There is congestion of labour in agriculture which must be relieved by employment in manufactures. Poverty and ignorance stalk over the land. Conscious of their helplessness, and yet awakened to a sense of their duty, people are doing what they can to relieve the gloom that surrounds them. A ray of hope cheers their way and the Government is showing its interest in their efforts to revive old and start new industries. Most of the credit of the little progress that official reports and statistics show, belongs to European capital and enterprise. Most of what are called flourishing Indian industries, with the growth of which India is usually credited, are in European hands, the fruit of their labour. The profits made from them naturally go out of the country and India is none the richer for them. People in India expect their Government to be national and do for them what other States have done and are doing for their own people. New India is Protectionist and wishes Government to adopt the same faith. The complete identification of the rulers and the ruled is the keynote of success. Single-handed, the people can do nothing. Nor have they done, it must be confessed, all that they should have. The little work that has been done only emphasises the vastness and the extreme difficulty of the whole problem. Some efforts are being made both by Government and people; but infinitely much more remains to be accomplished. The future depends upon how we help ourselves and induce Government to help us.

B.R. Ambedkar
(1891–1956)

Bhimrao Ramji Ambedkar was born in 1891 in Mhow in present-day Madhya Pradesh. He belonged to the Hindu Mahar caste, who were treated as untouchables and subjected to intense social and economic discrimination. He overcame many obstacles to succeed as an economist and a public figure. While the many biographies that have been written mention his achievements as an economist, these achievements tend to get overshadowed by his contributions to politics and social and economic change. In the present note I will focus on his work as an economist and leave it to the interested reader to look at the several biographies of Ambedkar that are available for an account of his considerable achievements in other fields.

Ambedkar was educated at Elphinstone College, Bombay, and obtained his BA degree in 1912 in political science and economics. With financial assistance from the Maharaja of Baroda he was able to proceed to the US where he obtained his Master's degree in 1915 from Columbia University. In June 1916, Ambedkar left New York for London. He was admitted that year to Gray's Inn and the London School of Economics and Political Science and began working for a DSc degree. In 1917 he was recalled to Baroda to serve the state, but had to leave soon due to harassment and caste discrimination. In 1918 he was selected as a professor of political economy at Sydenham College, Bombay, where he again experienced discrimination. With assistance from the Maharaja of Kolhapur he went back to London in 1920 to resume work for his D.Sc. with Edwin Canaan at the London School of Economics. In 1923 he was awarded the London D.Sc. degree and obtained his law degree from Gray's Inn. Ambedkar had begun work much earlier on a Ph.D. in Columbia with Edwin Seligman, but was formally awarded the degree only in 1927. In 1923 Ambedkar returned to India and began his legal practice soon thereafter.

Ambedkar's publications on economics were concentrated over about one decade, between about 1918 and 1925. These include his book based on his London D.Sc. thesis, *The Problem of the Rupee: Its Origin and Solution*, published in 1923 and *The Evolution of Provincial Finance in British India*, published in 1925 based on his work towards the Columbia Ph.D. degree. These, along with his evidence to the Royal Commission on Indian Currency and Finance in 1925, show that he was not only an excellent analyst and powerful writer, but he was also trenchant in his criticisms and not afraid to contradict others. These attributes may also explain why his London D.Sc. thesis was sent by back for revision by an examiner who did not agree with him. Again his supervisor, Edwin Canaan, in his Introduction to *The Problem of the Rupee*, states that he disagrees with many of Ambedkar's criticisms, but admits that 'he hits some nails very squarely on the head'.

Perhaps less noticed is the paper I have selected for the present volume, which addresses the problems of agricultural transformation in a most original way. S. Ambirajan, in an excellent review of Ambedkar's contributions to economics, rightly notes that there 'is an almost prophetic statement made by him' on surplus labour in Indian agriculture, 'long before modern theorists of development systematised notions of disguised unemployment or under-employment'.

Sadly for the economics profession, Ambedkar decided in the late 1920s, in his own words, to 'changeover from economics to law and politics'. Recent work suggests that he continued his interest in economic problems. Ambedkar served on the Viceroy's Executive Council from 1942 to 1946 and made major contributions to labour, water, and power policies. Later, as Law Minister in independent India, he piloted the Constitution through Parliament and drafted the Hindu Code Bill. He died in 1956.

Major Biographical Sources: W.N. Kuber, *Ambedkar: A Critical Study*, New Delhi, People's Publishing House, 1973; Dhananjay Keer, *Dr Ambedkar: Life and Mission*, Bombay, Popular Prakashan, 1971; S. Ambirajan, 'Ambedkar's Contributions to Economics', *Economic and Political Weekly*, vol. 34, no. 46/47, 20 November, 1999, pp. 3280–7; and Sukhadeo Thorat, *Ambedkar's Role in Economic Planning, Water and Power Policy*, New Delhi, Shipra, 2006. Material has also been obtained from the Columbia University Archives, Seligman Collection, and the Nehru Memorial Museum and Library, Ambedkar Papers.

This paper, which appeared in 1918, was written by Ambedkar to attack a common view of the time that the problem facing Indian agriculture was primarily that of small and fragmented holdings.* Different proposals were being made to address the problem through legal and administrative measures. Ambedkar felt that the underlying economic forces made such solutions unworkable.

Ambedkar argued that undue attention had been focused on excessive subdivision and fragmentation of agricultural holdings as the cause of low productivity. This in turn raised the question of what should be the size of the so-called economic holding. He rejected the idea of defining such a holding as one which met the needs of the household, arguing that this ignored the question of productivity. The economic holding had to be judged as a production, not consumption unit. It was not a question of the amount of land alone; it was dependent upon the relation between the piece of land and other factors of production. This led to his major conclusion that the remedy for the ills of agriculture was increase in capital, which, in turn, required more saving though the creation of surplus.

* B.R. Ambedkar (1918): 'Small Holdings in India and Their Remedies', *Journal of the Indian Economic Society*, vol. I, 1918. [From V.W. Moon (ed.) (1979), *Babasaheb Ambedkar—Writings and Speeches*, vol. 6, Bombay, Government of Maharashtra, pp. 454–79.]

The Indian problem was an acute shortage of cultivated land per head, which meant that a large part of the employable population did not have productive employment. Sir James Caird, as Ambedkar acknowledged, was the first to notice the existence of idle labour in India, arguing that not more than one-third of the population could be productively employed. Ambedkar noted that the numbers idle had probably risen due to 'a decreasing proportion of land under cultivation' and progressive ruralization.

Excess population put pressure on land, leading to subdivision. People cultivated small holdings because, in their constrained situation, this was the most profitable thing to do. Ambedkar argued that 'bad social economy' was responsible for the ills of agriculture. Heavy dependence on agriculture led to small and scattered farms, and idle labour 'makes ours a country without capital'. It was the problem of surplus or idle labour that had to be addressed and the solution lay in industrialization. This would reduce pressure on land and increase capital formation.

In this paper, Ambedkar outlined very clearly a concept of surplus labour:

> If we succeed in sponging off this labour in non-agricultural channels of production, we will at one stroke lessen the pressure and destroy the premium on land in India. Besides, this labour when productively employed will cease to live by predation as it does to-day, and will not only earn its keep but will give us a surplus; and more surplus is more capital (p. 477).

The above argument implied that the transfer of labour to non-agricultural production would not reduce agricultural production—a central tenet of the surplus labour/disguised unemployment argument—but he did not state this explicitly.

Ambedkar initiated the debate over size and productivity in Indian agriculture which became active in the 1950s, when surveys suggested that small holdings were not necessarily less productive than large ones and a variety of arguments and evidence was presented to answer this question.

The policies needed to promote industrialization were not discussed in this paper, perhaps because the focus was on attacking simplistic solutions to the problem of Indian agriculture.

2

Small Holdings in India and Their Remedies

B.R. Ambedkar

Importance of Agriculture

A study of the economic ways of getting a living will ever remain important. These ways generally take the form of industries or services. Confining ourselves to industries, they may be divided into primary and secondary. The primary industries are concerned with extracting useful material from the earth, the soil or water and take the form of hunting, fishing, stock-raising, lumbering and mining. These primary or extractive industries are fundamental in two ways: (1) They extract from the physical world useful materials which become the original sources of man's subsistence; (2) They provide raw materials for the secondary or manufacturing industries, for, manufactures, in the language of Dr Franklin, are simply, 'substance metamorphosed'. From a national point of view as well, the importance of primary industries is beyond question. But important as are the primary industries, farming is by far the most important of them all. It is most ancient and abiding of all industries, primary or secondary: while the fact that it is concerned with the production of food is enough to make its problems demand our most serious thought. But when a country, like India, depends almost wholly upon farming its importance cannot be exaggerated. The problems of agricultural economy dealing directly with agricultural production are what to produce, the proper proportion of the factors of production, the size of holdings, the tenures of land etc. In this paper it is attempted to deal only with the problem of the size of holdings as it affects the productivity of agriculture.

Small Holdings in India

It may be said that some countries are predominantly countries of small holdings while in others it is the large holdings that prevail. According to Adam Smith it is adoption of the law of primogeniture chiefly due to the exigencies of a military life that leads to the creation and preservation of large holdings. While it is the adoption of the law of equal sub-division necessitated by the comparatively peaceful career of a nation that gives rise to small holdings, he says:

When land like moveables is considered as the means only of subsistence and enjoyment, the natural law of succession divides it like them among all the children of the family; of all of whom the subsistence and enjoyment may be supposed equally dear to the father, [thus tending to have small holdings]. But when land was considered as the means, not of subsistence merely, but of power and protection it was thought better that it should descend undivided to one. In those disorderly times...to divide it was to ruin it, and to expose every part of it to be opposed and swallowed up by its neighhours. The law of primogeniture, therefore came to take place in the succession of landed estates [thus tending to preserve large holdings].[1]

England is, therefore, a country of large holdings. Post-revolutionary France is a country of small holdings. So are Holland and Denmark. Turning to India, we find holdings of the following size held separate and direct for the years 1896–97 and 1900–01.

Table 2.1 Average area of holdings in acres

Years	*Assam*	*Bombay*	*Central Provinces*	*Madras*
1896–97	3.37	24.07	17	7
1900–01	3.02	23.9	48	7

Data, more recent, more exact, though from a more restricted area, is available from the Baroda State.[2] Statistics of land holdings in the State are summarized in bighas in Table 2.2.[3]

Another investigation conducted by Dr H.S. Mann and his colleagues indicates more specifically the fact of small holdings in the village of Pimpala Saudagar near Poona. The size of holdings in that village is indicated by Table 2.3.[4]

From these tables it can be easily seen that the average size of holdings varies from 23.9 acres in the Bombay Presidency to an acre or two in Pimpala Saudagar.

TABLE 2.2

Name of the district	*Total agricultural land*	*Survey no. into which it is divided*	*Number of khatedars*	*Average under khatedars*	*Average area per survey no.*
Baroda	17,17,319	4,30,601	107,638	15–19–2	4
Kadi	25,13,982	5,89,687	141,145	17–16–5	4.25
Naosari	10,46,176	2,16,748	52,652	19–17–8	4
Amveli	9,72,040	55,635	17,214	36–9–7	3.25
Total	82,49,517	12,92,671	318,649	17–10–10	3.87

(8 bighas = 5 acres)

TABLE 2.3

	Over 20 acres	*10 to 20 acres*	*5 to 10 acres*	*3 to 5 acres*	*2 to 3 acres*	*1 to 2 acres*	*30 to 40 gunthas*	*20 to 30 gunthas*	*15 to 20 gunthas*	*10 to 15 gunthas*	*5 to 10 gunthas*	*Below 5 gunthas*
Number of plots of each size	1	7	21	25	67	164	75	136	71	57	59	25

(40 gunthas = 1 acre)

Note: In this table the modal holding is between 1 and 2 acres. A mode is a statistical average indicating the point of largest frequency in an array of instances.

This diminutive size of holdings is said to be greatly harmful to Indian agriculture. The evils of small holdings no doubt, are many. But it would have been no slight mitigation of them if the small holdings were *compact* holdings. Unfortunately they are not. A holding of a farmer though compact for purpose of revenue is for purpose of tillage composed of various small strips of land scattered all over the village and interspersed by those belonging to others. How the fields are scattered can only be shown graphically by a map. Herein we shall have to remain content, since we cannot give a map, with knowing how many separate plots are contained in a holding. The number of separate plots in each holding will show how greatly fragmented it is. We have no figures at all for the whole of India bearing on this aspect of the question. But the Hon'ble Mr G.F. Keatinge in his note[5] submitted to Government in 1916 has collected figures of typical cases from all the districts of the Bombay Presidency. Table 2.4 is constructed to present his data in an intelligible form.

These small and scattered holdings have given a real cause for anxiety regarding our great national industry. Comparative statistics go to swell this feeling by laying bare two very noteworthy but equally sad facts regarding economic life in India: (1) that it is largely an agricultural country (see Table 2.5); and (2) that its agricultural productivity is the lowest (see Table 2.6).

Both these truths are painful enough to have startled many people into inquiring the causes of this low productivity. As a result, attention has now been concentrated on the excessive sub-division and fragmentation of agricultural holdings. Enlarge and consolidate the holdings, it is confidently argued, and the increase in agricultural productivity will follow in its wake!!

CONSOLIDATION

Consolidation of holdings is a practical problem while the enlargement of them is a theoretical one, demanding a discussion of the principle which can be said to govern their size. Postponing the consideration of the theoretical question of enlargement, we find that the problem of consolidation raises the following two issues: (1) how to unite such small and scattered holdings as the existing ones, and (2) once consolidated how to perpetuate them at that size. Let us consider them each in turn. Sub-division of land need not involve what is called the fragmentation of land. But unfortunately it does, for, every heir desires to secure a share from each of the survey numbers composing the entire lands of the deceased instead of so arranging the distribution that each may get as many whole numbers as possible, i.e. the heirs instead of sharing the lands *by* survey numbers, claim to share *in* each survey number, thus causing fragmentation. Though fragmentation does subserve the ends of distributive justice it renders farming in India considerably inefficient as it once did in Europe. It involves waste of labour and cattle power, waste in hedges and boundary marks, and waste of manure. It renders impracticable the watching of crops, sinking of wells and the use of labour saving implements. It makes difficult changes in cultivation, the making of roads, water channels, etc., and it increases the cost of production. These disadvantages of fragmentation are to be recounted only to lend their support to the process of restripping or consolidation. The methods of 'restripping' are many, though all are not equally efficacious. Voluntary exchanges can hardly be relied upon for much. But a restricted

Table 2.4

Case II V. Shirgaon T. Ratnagiri D. Ratnagiri			Case V V. Badlapur T. Kalyan D. Thana			Case VI V. Kara T. Mawal D. Poona			Case VII V. Althan T. Ghorssi D. Surat			Case IX Surat District			Case X Kaira District			Case XII V. Lhasurna T. Koregaon D. Satara		
Area of a holding		*No. of separate plots*	*Area of a holding*		*No. of separate plots*	*Area of a holding*		*No. of separate plots*	*Area of a holding*		*No. of separate plots*	*Area of a holding*		*No. of separate plots*	*Area of a holding*		*No. of separate plots*	*Area of a holding*		*No. of separate plots*
A.	g.		A.	g.		A.	g.		A.	g.		A.	g.		A.	g.		A.	g.	
	34.50	3	48	6	53	60	0	27		0	9	1	0	14	62	13	27		38	6
	33	2	67	0	38	2	27	8	85	0	8	13	0	18	65	34	23		23	7
	20	3	1	9	6	2	31	5	26	9	8	22	0	20	36	16	16		36	3
1	14	5	6	30	8	16	6	7	–		–	3	6	4	7	9	5		22	10
1	30	5	24	0	17	2	35	6	–		–	5	0	7	5	26	5	–		–
1	10.75	4	–		–	–		–	–		–	1	26	9	13	16	6	–		–
6	33	9	–		–	–		–	–		–	0	26	9	28	4	15	–		–
3	29.75	7	–		–	–		–	–		–	–		–	12	10	8	–		–
2	20.50	2	–		–	–		–	–		–	–		–	12	7	3	–		–
	35.75	3	–		–	–		–	–		–	–		–	5	26	5	–		–
–		–	–		–	–		–	–		–	–		–	5	34	5	–		–
–		–	–		–	–		–	–		–	–		–	3	39	3	–		–

(A = acre; g = guntha; V = village; T = taluka; D = district)

Table 2.5 Occupational statistics

	England and Wales	*Ireland*	*Austria*	*Belgium*	*Bulgaria*	*Denmark*	*France*	*Germany*	*Holland*	*Hungary*	*Italy*	*Russia*	*Switzerland*	*India*	*USA*
Percentage of Agricultural Population	15.3	44.7	60.9	20.7	82.6	48.2	42.7	35.2	30.7	69.7	59.4	58.3	30.9	71.5	33.3

Table 2.6 Produce in lbs per acre

												Indian Provinces				
	UK	*Canada*	*New Zealand*	*Austria*	*Egypt*	*France*	*Germany*	*Hungary*	*Japan*	*USA*	*Turkey*	*UP*	*NWP*	*Punjab*	*Bombay*	*U. Burma*
Wheat	1973	1054	1723	1150	1634	1172	1796	1056	1176	–	1318	850	555	555	510	322
Maize	–	3487	3191	1135	2059	1097	–	1489	1525	–	1372	1100	735	766	–	–

sale of the right of occupancy may be expected to do a good deal. For, under it, when survey numbers are put to auction on account of their being relinquished by the holders or taken in attachment for arrears of assessments, only those may be allowed to bid in the auction for the sale of the right of occupancy whose lands are contiguous to the land hammered out. Again as further helping the process of reunion, the right of pre-emption may be given to farmers whose neighbour wishes to sell his land. These methods, it must be admitted, can achieve the desired result in a very small measure. The evils of fragmentation are very great and must be met by a comprehensive scheme of consolidation. It is, therefore, advocated[6] that if two-thirds of the Khatedars, dealing more than half of the village lands, apply, Government should undertake compulsorily to restrip the scattered fields of the village. This compulsory restripping is to be executed on two principles, (1) of 'Economic Unit' and (2) of 'Original Ownership'. Regarding the merits of these two principles the Baroda Committee observes:[7]

In the first value of each holding is ascertained, then the original boundaries are removed, roads are marked out, lands required for public purposes are set apart, and the rest of the land is parcelled out into new plots. Each of these new plots must be of such a size as, having regard to the local conditions of soil, tillage etc. to form an economic field, i.e., a parcel of land necessary to keep fully engaged and support one family. These new plots may be sold by auction among the old occupants, restriction being placed on purchase so as to prevent a large number of cultivators from being ousted. The purchase money may then be divided in a certain proportion among the original owners of pieces, a portion being reserved for expenses, in which Government would also contribute a share. Another mode would be acquire all the land of the village then to sell it in newly constituted plots by auction as is done by City Improvement Trusts or by Government when laying out new roads in Cities or when extending a town. But we do not recommend its adoption in the improvement of agricultural land. It may result in land speculation and the small holders may be ousted in such numbers as to cause a real hardship.

According to the second method when the restripping has been decided, a list of Khatedars and their holdings is made, and the latter are valued at their market price by Panchas. Then the land is redistributed and each khatedar is given new land in proportion to his original holding and as far as possible of the same value, difference to be adjusted by cash payment. In this method no khatedar is deprived of his land. Each is accommodated and in the place of his original small and scattered fields gets one plot of almost their aggregate size. It is only a few people whose holding may be very small and whom it would not be expedient to keep on as farmers, that may have to lose their small pieces. But they too would benefit as they would get their full value in money.

The Baroda Committee prefers the second method because:

It takes as its starting principle, that nobody (except perhaps a few, holding plots of insignificant sizes) is going to be driven off the land. It will give even the smallest man, chance to better his condition. Each land holder receives a new compact piece of land proportionate to the value of his old small and scattered field. In this way the previous sub-divisions together with their attendant evils totally disappear.[8]

Regarding consolidation, Prof. H.S. Jevons says:

The principles which should guide the choice of a method of carrying out the re-organization of villages on the lines above described are the following. In the first place compulsion should be avoided as far as possible and the principle adopted that no charges should be imposed upon any area unless the owners of more than one-half of that area desire the change. Should this condition be satisfied for an area...it would seem expedient that legal power should be taken to compel the minority to accept the redistribution of holdings under the supervision of Government. In the second place...the expense of the operation should be kept as low as possible....In the third place considerable elasticity should be permitted in the methods of carrying through the re-organization in the different places during the first few years, as the whole undertaking would be in an experimental stage so that different methods might be tried, and the best be ultimately selected for a permanent set of regulations. Fourthly, the possible necessity for a considerable change of the existing tenancy law in the re-organised villages must be faced....For the sake of completeness I may add as a fifth principle the obvious condition that redistribution of land must be made upon the most equitable basis possible, and that liberal compensation should be given to those, if any, who may be excluded from a former cultivating ownership.[9]

As for procedure in the compulsory consolidation of holdings both Prof. Jevons and the Baroda Committee propose the appointment of Commissioners to hear applications for consolidation and to carry it out, leaving to any objector the right to petition the Court to stay the proceedings in case he felt that an injustice was being done to him.

The problem of perpetuating such a consolidated holding will next demand the care of the legislator. It is accepted without question by many that the law of inheritance that prevails among the Hindus and the Mahomedans is responsible for the sub-division of land. On the death of a Hindu or a Mahomedan his heirs are entitled without let or hindrance to equal shares in the property of the deceased. Now a consolidated holding subject to the operation of such a law of inheritance will certainly not endure for long. It will be the task of Sisyphus over again if, after consolidation, the law of inheritance were to remain unaltered.

But how is the existing law of inheritance to be changed? If it is not to be the law of equal sub-division shall we have the law of primogeniture?[10]

The Baroda Committe thinks that:

It is not necessary that it should be introduced. All that is wanted is, that there should not be sub-divisions of land beyond a certain limit, which may be fixed for the sake of good agriculture. There is no objection to a holding being sub-divided, so long as by so doing each of the parts does not become less than the limit fixed for the sub-division of land. But when a holding reaches a stage to render further sub-division uneconomic, the other members of the family may not be allowed to force further sub-division of the holding. Instead of being sub-divided, it may be either cultivated in common or be given to one of the members of the family as a whole, and that member made to pay amounts equal to the value of their shares as compensation to the other members.[11]

The principle of not dividing immovable property among the heirs, when division would result in inconveniently small shares, but of giving to the highest bidder among the shares or in case none of them is willing to have it, to outside bidders, and dividing the money realized in proportion to the recognized shares, has been accepted in the Indian Partition Act, No. 4 of 1893, Section 2 of which runs thus:

Whenever in any suit for partition, in which, if instituted prior to the commencement of this Act, a decree for partition might have been made, it appears to the Court that, by reason of the nature of the property to which the suit relates, or of the number of the shareholders therein or of any other special circumstance, a division of the property cannot reasonably or conveniently be made and that a sale of the property and distribution of proceeds would be more beneficial for all the share-holders, the Court may, if it thinks fit, on the request of any such share-holder interested individually or collectively to the extent of one moiety or upwards direct a sale of the property and a distribution of the proceeds.

Granting the advisability of thus changing the law of inheritance it only requires to amend the Civil Procedure Code so as to make it obligatory on the Courts to refuse partition whenever it would reduce a field beyond the economic limit fixed in advance.

Another method of dealing with the problem is advocated by the Hon. Mr G.F. Keatinge, Director of Agriculture, Bombay Presidency. In the Statement of Objects and Reasons appended to his draft bill he says:

4. ...The object of this bill is to enable such landowners as may wish to do so to check the further sub-division of their lands and to enable them, when it is otherwise possible, to effect a permanent consolidation of their holdings; and also to enable

the executive government to secure the same results in respect of unoccupied land. The legislation proposed is purely enabling, and it will be operative in the case of any holding only upon the expressed wish of any person possessing an interest in that holding.

5. The scheme embodied in this bill for securing these objects is briefly as follows. In order to be constituted an economic holding a plot of land must be entered as such in a register prescribed by rules. If the land is occupied, it will rest with some person having an interest in the land to make an application to the Collector to have the land registered as an economic holding....Unless the Collector considers that there are sufficient grounds for rejecting the application, he holds a careful enquiry in which he follows a procedure similar to that prescribed in the Land Acquisition Act, 1894. If the proceedings show that all persons interested agree, that land is registered. Land vesting absolutely in Government may be registered without inquiry. The holding must in any case be registered in one name only, and the act of registration annuls all the interest of all other persons, except the registered owner, in the holding. Therefore the owner cannot divide the plot but must so long as he owns it, keep it entire. He may sell, mortgage or otherwise dispose of it as an entire unit, but not dispose of part of it or do anything that might result in splitting up the holding. On the death of the holder, if he has not disposed of the land by will it will devolve upon a single heir. If the provisions of the bill are contravened (for instance if the holder mortgages a part of his holding and the mortgagee obtains a decree for possession), the Collector is empowered to send a certificate to the Court, and the Court will set aside its decree or order. The Collector may also evict a person in wrongful possession. When a plot has been once constituted an economic holding, the registration cannot be cancelled except with the consent of the Collector; the grounds on which cancellation will be allowed, will be laid down by rule and it is proposed that it shall be permitted chiefly in cases where economic considerations indicate that it is expedient.

Summing up this discussion of the two issues of consolidation, it must be said that the problem has not been viewed as a whole by all its advocates. The Baroda Committee alone endeavours to consolidate as well as to preserve the consolidated holding. Prof. Jevons makes no provision to conserve the results of consolidation. Mr Keatinge does not deal with consolidation at all. He is concerned only with the prevention of *further* fragmentation. But fragmentation, there will be in a holding even after it is entered as an economic holding. By his measure he will only succeed in preserving the holdings as they will be found at the time of registration, i.e., he will not allow them to be reduced in size. But they will be small and scattered all the same. Mr Keatinge, notwithstanding his legislation, leaves the situation more or less as it exists. Real consolidation is, however, aimed at by

Prof. Jevons and the Baroda Committee. The principles they advocate for the purpose are almost the same; and so are their procedures for carrying it out.

As for the preservation of consolidated holdings Mr Keatinge as well as the Baroda Committee establish the one-man rule of succession. The Baroda Committee would adopt this rule only when division of land would result in uneconomic holdings and then too would compel the successor to buy off the claims of the other dispossessed heirs. Mr Keatinge would let the dispossessed heirs off without compensation.

A more serious criticism against these projects of consolidation consists in the fact they have failed to recognize that a consolidated holding must be an enlarged holding as well. If it is said that Indian agriculture suffers from *small* and *scattered* holdings we must not only consolidate, but also enlarge them. It must be borne in mind that consolidation may obviate the evils of scattered holdings, but it will not obviate the evils of small holding. The Committee as well as Mr Keatinge have entirely lost sight of this aspect of the question. Prof. Jevons, alone of the advocates, keeps it constantly before his mind that consolidation must bring about in its train the enlargement of holdings.

ENLARGEMENT

Granted that enlargement of holdings is as important as their consolidation we will now turn to the discussion of regulating their size. It is desired by all interested in our agriculture that our holdings should be economic holdings. We would have been more thankful to the inventors of this new, precise and scientific terminology had they given us a precise and scientific definition of an economic holding. On the other hand, it is believed that a large holding is somehow an economic holding. It may be said that even Prof. Jevons has fallen a victim to this notion. For when discussing what the size of a holding should be he dogmatically states that in the consolidated village the mode should be between 29 and 30 acres.[12] But why should the mode be at this point and not at 100 or say 200? We might imagine Prof. Jevons to reply that his modal point is placed at that particular acreage because it would produce enough for a farmer to sustain a higher standard of living. Raising the general standard of living in India is the one string on which Prof. Jevons harps even to weariness throughout his pamphlet.[13] The error underlying this doctrine, we shall consider later on. It is enough to say that he does not give any sound economic reason for his modal farm.

The case with the Baroda Committee is much worse, Prof. Jevons at least sticks to one definition of an ideal economic holding; but the Report of the Baroda Committee suffers from a plurality of definitions. While commenting on the size of an average holding in the state as is summarized in the above table, it should be noted that the Committee, though it desired consolidation, was perfectly satisfied with the existing size of the holding as is clear, from the following:

> If the average holding of a Khatedar was a compact field of those figures, the situation would be an ideal one and would not leave much to be desired.[14]

But absent-minded as it were, the Committee, without any searching analysis of the question it was appointed to investigate and report upon, lays down that:

> An ideal economic holding would consist of 30 to 50 bighas of fair land in one block with at least one good irrigation well and a house situated in the holding.[15]

If the size of existing holdings is an ideal size why should they be enlarged? To this, the Committee gives no answer. But this is not all. The Committee does not even adhere to the *quantitative* limit it has already set down to its ideal economic holding. When it comes to discuss the project of re-arrangement of the scattered fields of the village on the principle of 'Economic Unit' it presents a third ideal of an economic holding. To realize this ideal it says:

> Each of these new plots must be of such a size, as having regard to the local conditions of soil, tillage, etc., to form an Economic field, i.e., a parcel of land necessary to keep fully engaged and support one family.[16]

Thus with perfect equanimity the Baroda Committee holds, not too fast, to three notions of an ideal economic holding. No wonder then that the Report of the Committee is a model of confused reasoning though it is a valuable repository of facts bearing on the subject.

According to the Hon. Mr Keatinge an economic holding is:

> a holding which allows a man chance of producing sufficient to support himself and his family in reasonable comfort, after paying his necessary expenses.[17]

His definition of an economic holding will be accepted, we may expect, by the Baroda Committee: for, it does not differ from its own, given above as third in order. Assuming they agree, we may now proceed to see how far tenable this definition is.

It is plain that these definitions including that of Prof. Jevons view an economic holding from the stand-point of consumption rather than of production. In this lies their error; for consumption is not the correct standard by which to judge the economic character of holding. It would be perverse accounting to condemn a farm as not paying because its total output does not support the family of the farmer though as a *pro-rata* return for each of his investments it is the highest. The family of a farmer can only be looked upon in the light of so much labour corps at his disposal. It may well be that some portion of this labour corps is superfluous, though it has to be supported merely in obedience to social custom as is the case in India. But if our social custom compels a farmer to support some of his family members even when he cannot effectively make any use of them on his farm we must be careful not to find fault with the produce of the farm because it does not suffice to provide for the workers as well as the dependants that may happen to compose the family. The adoption of such an accounting system will declare many enterprises as failure when they will be the most successful. There can be no true economic relation between the family of the entrepreneur and the total out-turn of his farm or industry. True economic relation can subsist only between the total out-turn and the investments. If the total out-turn pays for all the investments no producer in his senses will ever contemplate closing his industry because the total out-turn does not support his family. This is evident; for though production is for the purpose of consumption it is for the consumption only of those who help to produce. It follows, then, that if the relation between out-turn and investments is a true economic relation, we can only speak of a farm as economic, i.e., paying in the sense of production and not in the sense of consumption. Any definition, therefore, that leans on consumption mistakes the nature of an economic holding which is essentially an enterprise in production.

Before going further, we must clear the ground by a few preliminary remarks to facilitate the understanding of an economic holding from the standpoint of production.

It must be premised at the outset that in a competitive society the daily transactions of its members, as consumers or producers, are controlled by a price regime. It is production, then, in a price regime that we have to analyse here for our purpose. In the main the modern process of production is captained by the entrepreneur, is guided and supervised by him and is worked out through him. All employers of labour or hirers of instrumental goods are entrepreneurs. His computations run, as they must, in a pecuniary society, in terms of price-outlay as over against price-product, no matter whether the prospective product is offered for sale or not. The entrepreneur, in producing for gain, apportions his outlays in varieties of investments. These investments, the same as factors of production or costs to the entrepreneur, have by tradition been confined to wages (labour) profits, rent (land) and interest (capital). Industrial facts do not support this classification. There are many other factors, it is contended, which as they share in the distributive process must have functioned in the productive process, in some way immediate or remote. But it is immaterial how many factors there are and whether they differ in kind or degree. What is important for the purpose of production is the process of combining them.

This combination of necessary factors of production is governed by a law called the law of proportion. It lays down that disadvantage is bound to attend upon a wrong proportion among the various factors of production employed in a concern. Enlarged, the principle means that as a certain volume of one factor has the capacity to work only with a certain volume of another to give maximum efficiency to both, an excess or defect in the volume of one in comparison with those of the others will tell on the total output by curtailing the efficiency of all. Having regard then to this interdependence of factors, and economically efficient combination of them compels the producer if he were to vary the one to vary the rest correspondingly. Neither can it be otherwise. For, the chief object of an efficient production consists in making every factor in the concern contribute its highest; and it can do that only when it can co-operate with its fellow of the required capacity. Thus, there is an ideal of proportions that ought to subsist among the various factors combined, though the ideal will vary with the changes in the proportions.[18]

These proportions it must be acknowledged are affected by the principle of substitution chiefly brought into play owing to variations in the prices of the factors. But this principle of substitution is too limited in its application to invalidate the law of proportion which is the law governing all economic production and which no producer can hope to ignore with impunity.[19]

Bringing to bear the above remarks regarding production on the definition of an economic holding, we can postulate that if agriculture is to be treated as an economic enterprise, then by itself, there could be no such thing as a large or a small holding. To a farmer a holding is too small or too large for the other factors of production at his disposal necessary for carrying on the cultivation of his holding as an economic enterprise. Mere size of land is empty of all economic connotation. Consequently, it cannot possibly be the language of economic science to say that a large holding is economic while a small holding is uneconomic. It is the right or wrong proportion of other factors of production to a unit of land that renders the latter economic or uneconomic. Thus a small farm may be economic as well as a large farm; for, economic or uneconomic does not depend upon the size of land but upon the due proportion among all the factors including land.

An economic holding, therefore, if it is not to be a hollow concept, consists in a combination of land, capital and labour, etc., in a proportion such that the *pro rata* contribution of each in conjunction with the rest is the highest. In other words to create an economic holding it will not do for a farmer solely to manipulate his piece of land. He must also have the other instruments of production required for the efficient cultivation of his holding and must maintain a due proportion of all the factors for, without it, there can be no efficient production. If his equipment shrinks, his holding must also shrink. If his equipment augments, his holding must also augment. The point is that his equipment and his holding must not be *out* of proportion to each other. They must be *in* proportion and must vary, if need be, in proportion.

The line of argument followed above is not without support from actual practice. It is happy from an economist's point of view, to find it recognized and adopted in India itself by the fathers of the Survey and Settlement System in the Bombay Presidency. The famous Joint Report (1840) contains an illuminating discussion of the problem. The question before the officers deputed to introduce the Survey System in the Deccan was how to levy the assessment. Was it to be a field assessment or an assessment to be placed on the whole lands of the village or on the entire holdings of individuals or co-parceners, whether proprietors or occupants? That after much deliberation the system of field assessment was finally adopted is known to many. But as the reasons that led to its adoption are known only to a few the following explanatory parts from the Joint Report will be found to be both interesting and instructive:

Para 6. That one manifest advantage of breaking up the assessment of a village into portions so minute [as indicated by a survey number] is the facility it affords to the cultivators of contracting or enlarging his farm from year to year, according to the fluctuating amount of agricultural capital at their disposal which is of incalculable importance to farmers possessed of so limited resources as those of the cultivating classes throughout India.

Para 7. The loss of a few bullocks by disease or other causes may quite incapacitate a ryot from cultivating profitably the extent of land he had previously in village and, without the privilege of contracting his farm, and consequent liabilities on occasion of such loss, his ruin would be very shortly consummated.[20]

Judging in the light of this conclusion the proposal to regulate the size of holdings appears ill-considered and futile. For as Prof. Richard T. Ely observes:[21]

Obviously no simple answer can be given to the question [as to what should be the size of a farm]. The value of land or the rent it will bring is perhaps the most important factor....In addition to the factor of rent the amount of capital that he can command, the kind of farming in which he is most skilled, the character of the labour he can secure, the proximity of markets, and the adequacy of transportation facilities, all must be taken into account by the farmer in determining how large a farm he will attempt to manage and how intensively he will farm it.

This question is primarily one of private profit which the individual must decide for himself, but the legislator and the scientific student can be of some assistance in helping to develop that most difficult branch of commercial science—farm accounting—and in keeping the farmer alive to those changes in prices, wages, and transportation charges to which the farm organization must adjust itself.

To those who have the temerity to fix the size of a holding Prof. Ely's well-considered opinion will bring home that in spite of good intentions their vicarious mission will end in disaster: for none but the cultivator can decide what should be the size of his holding. They would do well to remember that the size of his holdings will vary in time. Consequent to the changes in his equipment with which he has to adjust the size of his farm, at one point in time he will decide in favour of a small, as at another he will decide in favour of a large holding. He would therefore be a poor economist who would legally fix the size of the holding which in the interest of economic production must be left to vary when variation is demanded. By fixing the size of a holding he can only make it a large holding but not an economic holding. For an economic holding is not a matter of the size of land alone but is a matter of the adjustment of a piece of land to the necessary equipment for its efficient cultivation.

Critique of the Remedies

The proposal to enlarge the existing holdings which is brought forward as a cure to the ills of our agriculture can be entertained only if it is shown that farms have diminished in size while the agricultural stock has increased in amount. Facts regarding the size of farms have already been recorded. It only remains to see if the agricultural stock has increased. Mr K.L. Datta in his exhaustive survey says:[22]

178. Most of the Indian witnesses, whom we examined, appeared to be under the belief that there has been a decrease in the supply of agricultural products, owing to the inefficient tillage of land. It was said that land is not now cultivated as carefully and efficiently as before, owing to the *scarcity and dearness of plough, cattle and labour.* In order to effect a saving in the cost of cultivation, cultivators do not also plough their lands as often as they did before, and manuring and weeding, as also the amount of irrigating where wells are used for the purpose, have all been reduced.
179. As regards the scarcity of plough cattle...(the) figures bear testimony to the deplorable effects of famine, the inevitable result of which has always been to reduce the number of cattle, though the deficiency is generally made good in a few years if otherwise favourable. The number of plough cattle in the latest year (1908–09) included in the statement was lower than in the commencement (1893–94) in some of the circles namely Assam, Bundelkhund, Agra Provinces—North and West, Gujarat, Deccan, Berar, Madras-North and Madras-West. Although great reliance cannot be placed on these statistics, they can be accepted as showing that in some areas at any rate has been a dearth of plough cattle.

Regarding the existence of capital Mr Elliot James says:

The ryots have a keen eye to the results of a good system of farming as exhibited on model farms, but they cannot derive much good from the knowledge though they may take it in and thoroughly understand that superior tillage and proper manuring mean a greater outturn in crops. Their great want is *capital.*[23]

The farmer knows, says the same author, that his agricultural equipment is inefficient and antiquated but he cannot substitute better ones in its place for:

A superior class of cattle and superior farm implements mean to him so much outlay of what he has not—Money.

Similar facts for the Baroda State have been collected in another connection by Mr M.B. Nanavati, Director of Commerce and Industry. But unfortunately he did not bring his knowledge of such facts to bear upon the conclusions of the Committee for the consolidation of holdings in the State of which he was also a member, apparently thinking that the size of a holding bore no relation to the instruments of production. He bemoans that:

The farmers are not fully equipped with draught-cattle. They have today (1913) 8,34,901 bullocks, etc., for use on farms, that is one pair for 36 bighas of land. On an average a pair of good bullocks can cultivate 25 bighas of land. But the present breed has much deteriorated and one pair is supposed to cultivate 20 bighas at the most, while the present actual averages comes to about 36 bighas. Under the circumstances it is not likely that ploughing can be deep. It must be like scratching the surface. The small cultivators do not possess any draught-cattle or at the most a single one and cultivate land in co-operation with their friends similarly situated. As for farm implements there are 1,54,364 ploughs in the State, i.e., one for two khatedars. It must be understood here that the number of cultivators and tenants is much more than three lakhs. Every one of them needs full equipment. Therefore actually the average must be much smaller than shown above.[24]

In fact the equipment for agricultural production in the State has considerably deteriorated since 1898 as shown by Table 2.7:

TABLE 2.7

Year	*Plough*	*Carts*	*Plough cattle*	*Other domestics*
1898	1,75,989	–	4,15,089	5,70,517
1910	1,51,664	68,946	3,34,801	5,09,416

Given this state of affairs can we not say with more propriety that not only the existing equipment is inadequate for the enlarged holdings but that the existing holdings, small as they are, are too big for the available instruments of production other than land? *Facts such as these interpreted in the light of our theory force upon us the conclusion that the existing holdings are uneconomic, not, however, in the sense that they are too small but that they are too large*. Shall we therefore argue that the existing holdings should be further reduced in size with a view to render them economic in the sense in which we have used the term? Unwary readers might suppose that this is the only logical and inevitable conclusion—a conclusion that is in strange contrast with the main trend of opinion in this country. Contrary, no doubt, the conclusion is; but it is by no means inevitable. For, from our premises we can with perfect logic and even with more cogency argue for increase in agricultural stock and implements which in turn will necessitate enlarged holdings which will be economic holdings as well.

Consequently the remedy for the ills of agriculture in India does not lie primarily in the matter of enlarging holdings but in the matter of increasing capital and capital goods. That capital arises from saving and that saving is possible where there is surplus is a commonplace of political economy.

Does our agriculture—the main stay of our population—give us any surplus? We agree with the answer which is unanimously in the negative. We also approve of the remedies that are advocated for turning the deficit economy into a surplus economy, namely by enlarging and consolidating the holdings. What we demur to is the method of realizing this object. For we most strongly hold that *the evil of small holdings in India is not fundamental but is derived from the parent evil of the mal-adjustment in her social economy*. Consequently if we wish to effect a permanent cure we must go to the parent malady.

But before doing that we will show how we suffer by a bad social economy. It has become a tried statement that India is largely an agricultural country. But what is scarcely known is *that notwithstanding the vastness of land under tillage, so little land is cultivated in proportion to her population*.

Mulhall's figures for the year 1895 clearly demonstrate the point.

TABLE 2.8 Acres per inhabitant in 1895

Great Britain	*Ireland*	*France*	*Germany*	*Russia*	*Austria*	*Italy*	*Spain and Portugal*	*USA*	*India*
0.91	3.30	2.30	1.70	5.60	2.05	1.75	2.90	8.90	1.0

That since 1895 the situation, however, has gone from bad to worse figures eloquently bear out (see Table 2.9).

Now, what does this extraordinary phenomenon mean? A large agricultural population with the lowest proportion of land in actual

TABLE 2.9

	1881	*1891*	*1901*	*1911*
Bengal	1.5	0.8	1.12	–
Bombay	1.7	1.6	1.41	1.3
Madras	1.3	0.3	0.68	0.79
Assam	–	0.5	0.78	0.85
Punjab	1.2	1.3	1.05	1.11
Oudh	0.81	0.7 }	0.73	0.75
NWP	–	0.8 }		
Burmah	–	1.5	1.08	1.09
Central P.	1.67	2.4	1.8	1.79
B. India	1.04	1.0	0.86	0.88

cultivation means a large part of the agricultural population is superfluous and idle. How much idle labour there is on Indian farms it is not possible to know accurately. Sir James Caird who was the first to notice the existence of this idle labour estimated in 1884 that:

A square mile of land in England cultivated highly gives employment to 50 persons, in the proportion 25 men, young and old, and 25 women and boys. If four times that number, or 200, were allowed for each square mile of cultivated land in India, it would take up only one-third of the population.[25]

Out of the total population of 254 millions in 1881 nearly two-thirds were returned as agricultural. Allowing, as per estimate, one-third to be taken up, we can safely say that a population of equal magnitude was lying idle instead of performing any sort of productive labour. With the increasing ruralization of India and a continually decreasing proportion of land under cultivation, the volume of idle labour must have increased to an enormous extent.

The economic effects of this idle labour are two-fold. Firstly, it adds to the tremendous amount of pressure that our agricultural population exerts on land. A quantitative statement will serve to bring home to our mind how high the pressure is:

TABLE 2.10 Mean density per square mile in 1911

	Oudh and NWP	*Bengal*	*Madras*	*Punjab*	*Bombay*	*Assam*	*Berar and CP*	*Coorg*	*British Burma*
of Total Area	427	551	291	177	145	115	122	111	53
of Cultivated Area	829	1162	785	453	444	766	360	792	575

Such high pressure of population on land is probably unknown in any other part of the world. The effect of it is, of course, obvious.

Notwithstanding what others have said, this enormous pressure is the chief cause of the subdivision of land. It is the failure to grasp the working of this pressure on land that makes the law of inheritance such a great grievance. To say that the law of inheritance causes sub-division of land is to give a false view by inverting the real situation. The mere existence of the law cannot be complained of as a grievance. The grievance consists in the fact that it is invoked. But why is it invoked even when it is injurious? Simply because it is profitable. There is nothing strange in this. When farming is the *only* occupation, to get a small piece of land is better than to have none. Thus the grievance lies in the circumstances which put a premium on these small pieces of land. The premium, is no doubt, due to the large population depending solely on agriculture to eke out its living. Naturally a population that has *little else to prefer to agriculture* will try to invoke every possible cause to get a piece of land however small. It is not therefore the law of inheritance that is the evil, but it is the high pressure on land which brings it into operation. People cultivate the small piece not because their standard of living is low as Prof. Jevons seems to think[26] but because it is the only profitable thing for them to do at present. If they had something more profitable to do they would never prefer the small piece. It is therefore easy to understand how the universal prevalence of the small farms or *petit culture* is due to this enormous pressure on land.

In spite of the vehement struggle that our agricultural population maintains in trying to engage itself productively as cultivators of a farm however small, it is true that judged by the standard of Sir James Caird a large portion of it is bound to remain idle. Idle labour and idle capital differ in a very important particular. Capital *exists*, but labour *lives*. That is to say capital when idle does not earn, but does not also consume much to keep itself. But labour, earning or not consumes in order to live. Idle labour is, therefore, a calamity; for if it cannot live by production as it should, it will live by predation as it must. This idle labour has been the canker of India gnawing at its vitals. Instead of contributing to our national dividend it is eating up what little there is of it. Thus the depression of our national dividend is another important effect of this idle labour. The income of a society as of an individual proceeds (1) from the efforts made, and (2) from possessions used. It may be safely asserted that the aggregate income of any individual or society must be derived either from the proceeds of the current labour or from productive possession already acquired. All that society can have today it must acquire today or must take out of its past product. Judging by this criterion a large portion of our society makes very little current effort; nor does it have any very extensive possessions from which to derive its substance. No doubt then that our economic organization is conspicuous by want of capital. Capital is but crystallized surplus; and surplus depends upon the proceeds of effort. But where there is no effort there is no earning, no surplus, and no capital.

We have thus shown how our bad social economy is responsible for the ills of our agriculture. We have also proved how our entire dependence on agriculture leads to small and scattered farms. How a large portion of our population which our agriculture cannot productively employ is obliged to remain idle has been made clear. We have also shown how the existence of this idle labour makes ours a country without capital. This being our analysis of the problem, it will be easy to see why the remedies for consolidation and enlargement under the existing social economy are bound to fail.

Those who look on small holdings as the fundamental evil naturally advocate their enlargement. This, however, is a faulty political economy and as Thomas Arnold once said 'a faulty political economy is the fruitful parent of crime'. Apart from the fact that merely to enlarge the holding is not to make it economic, this project of artificial enlargement is fraught with many social ills. The future in the shape of an army of landless and dispossessed men that it is bound to give rise to is neither cheerful from the individual, nor agreeable from the national, point of view. But even if we enlarged the existing holdings and procured enough capital and capital goods to make them economic, we will not only be not advocating the proper remedy but will end in aggravating the evils by adding to our stock of idle labour; for capitalistic agriculture will not need as many hands as are now required by our present day methods of cultivation.

But if enlargement is not possible, can we not have consolidation? It can be shown that under the existing social economy even consolidation is not possible. The remedy for preventing sub-division and fragmentation of consolidated holdings cannot be expected to bring real relief. Instead it will only serve to be a legal eyewash. This becomes easy of comprehension if we realize at the start what the one man rule of succession means in actual practice. For this we shall have to note the changes it will introduce in the survey records. At present according to the Bombay Land Revenue Code Chapter I, Section 3, clause (6):

> 'Survey Number' means a portion of land of which the area and other particulars are separately entered, under an indicative number in the survey records of the village, town or city in which it is situated, and includes a recognized share of a survey number. Again by clause(7):
>
> 'Recognized share of a survey number' means a sub-division of a survey number separately assessed and registered.

After the adoption of the one man rule of succession a survey number will be made to cover a piece of land which will be of the size fixed for an ideal economic holding. Secondly, it will be necessary to refuse separate registration to any sub-division of such a survey number; i.e., in order that a piece of land should be registered with a separate and a distinct survey number it must not be below the economic limit. Then too this survey number covering a piece of land large enough to be styled economic will be registered in the name of one person. This is precisely what will happen if we put into practice the project of the Baroda Committee. Mr Keatinge instead of having one survey number covering a large and compact holding will have in the name of one person many survey numbers covering a unit of land composed of small and scattered fields. Abandoning Mr Keatinge's scheme as serving no practical purpose *the one man rule of succession to a consolidated holding means in practice refusal to recognize legally a piece of land if it were below a certain size.* Now this refusal to recognize smaller pieces of land, it is claimed, will prevent the sub-division of a consolidated holding. Sub-division of land may be due to many causes the operation of which is rendered economic or uneconomic by the nature of the occasion which evokes it. Not to allow sub-division on any ground, as does Mr Keatinge, is to cause a serious depreciation of the value of land. But if sub-division is needed as when the stock has depleted, not to grant it is to create an uneconomic situation—a result just opposite of what is intended to be achieved, apart from this to prevent sub-division legally is not to prevent it actually, if necessitated by the weight of economic circumstances. Granting the pressure of population on land and the scanty agricultural equipment—evils to which the authors of consolidation and enlargement have paid no attention—we must look forward to the sub-division of holdings. If we legislate in the face of this inevitable tendency and refuse to record on our survey roll holdings below a certain limit required for a separate survey number we will not only fail to cure what we must know we cannot, at least by this means, but will help to create a register that will be false to the true situation.

This being our criticism of the means for preventing sub-division and fragmentation it will not take us long to state our view as regards the project of consolidation. Consolidation and its conservation are so intimately connected that the one cannot be thought of without the other. Now if we cannot conserve a consolidated holding, is it worth our while to consolidate, however feasible the project may be? This work of Sysiphus will not fail to fall to our lot unless we make effective changes in our social economy.

As the evils of this surplus and idle labour which will be added on to by the consolidation and enlargement of holdings are likely to outweigh their advantages, the proposals do not find much favour at the hands of Prof. Gilbert Slater.[27]

As against Prof. Slater we hold that the evils are avoidable and it is because we are anxious to avoid them that we wish to advocate different remedies for bringing about the enlargement of holdings. Consequently, we maintain that our efforts should be primarily directed towards this idle labour.[28]

If we succeed in sponging off this labour in non-agricultural channels of production we will at one stroke lessen the pressure and destroy the premium that at present weighs heavily on land in India. Besides, this labour when productively employed will cease to live by predation as it does to-day, and will not only earn its keep but will give us surplus; and more surplus is more capital. In short, strange though it may seem, *industrialization of India is the soundest remedy for the agricultural problems of India*. The cumulative effects of industrialization, namely, a lessening pressure and an increasing amount of capital and capital goods will forcibly create the economic necessity of enlarging the holding. Not only this, but industrialization by destroying the premium on land will give rise to few occasions for its sub-division and fragmentation. Industrialization is a natural and powerful remedy and is to be preferred to such ill-conceived projects as we have considered above. By legislation we will get a sham economic holding at the cost of many social ills. But by industrialization a large economic holding will force itself upon us as a pure gain.

Our remedy for the enlargement as for the consolidation of holdings as well as the preservation of consolidated holdings reduces itself to this: We prefer to cure agriculture by the reflex effects of industrialization. Lest this might be deemed visionary we proceed to give evidence in support of our view. How agriculture improves by the reflex effects of industrialization has been studied in the United States in the year 1883. We shall quote *in extenso* the summary given by the *London Times*:

The statistician of the Agricultural Department of the United States has shown in a recent report that the value of farm lands decreases in exact proportion as the ratio of agriculture to other industries increases. That is, where all the labour is devoted to agriculture, the land is worth less than where only half of the people are farm labourers; and where only a quarter of them are so engaged the farms and their product are still more valuable. It is, in fact, proved by statistics that diversified industries are of the greatest value to a state, and that the presence of a manufactory near a farm increases the value of the farm and its crops. It is further established that, dividing the United States into four sections or classes, with reference to the ratio of agricultural workers to the whole population, and putting those States having less than 30 per cent of agriculture and of agricultural labourers in the first class, all having over 30 and less than 50 in the second, those between 50 and 70 in the third, and those having 70 or more in the fourth, the value of farms is in inverse ratio to the agricultural population, and that where as in the purely agricultural section, the fourth class, the value of farms per acre is only $ 5.28, in the next class it is $ 13.03, in the third $ 22.21, and in manufacturing districts $ 40.91. This shows an enormous advantage for a mixed district. Yet not only is the land more valuable the production per acre is greater, and the wages paid to farm hands larger. Manufactures and varied industries thus not only benefit the manufacturers, but are of equal benefit and advantage to the farmers as well.

This will show that ours is a proven remedy. It can be laid down without fear of challenge that industrialization will foster the enlargement of holdings and that it will be the most effective barrier against sub-division and fragmentation. Agreeing in this, it may be observed that industrialization will not be a sufficient remedy for consolidation. That it will require *direct* remedies may be true. But it is also true that industrialization, though it may not bring about consolidation, will facilitate consolidation. It is an incontrovertible truth that so long as there is the premium on land consolidation will not be easy, no matter on how equitable principles it is proposed to be carried out. Is it a small service if industrialization lessens the premium as it inevitably must? Certainly not. Consideration of another aspect of consolidation as well points to the same conclusion: that industrialization must precede consolidation. It should never be forgotten that unless we have constructed an effective barrier against the future sub-division and fragmentation of a consolidated holding it is idle to lay out plans for consolidation. Such a barrier can only be found in industrialization; for it alone can reduce the extreme pressure which, as we have shown, cause sub-division of land. Thus, if small and scattered holdings are the ills from which our agriculture is suffering to cure it of them is undeniably to industrialize.

But just where does India stand as an industrial country?

Sir Robert Giffen after a survey of the economic tendencies of various countries concludes that:

The wants of men increasing with their resources the proportion of people engaged in agriculture and mining and analogous pursuits, in every country is destined to

TABLE 2.11

	England and Wales		*Germany*		*USA*		*France*		*India*	
	Rural	*Urban*	*Rural*	*Urban*	*Rural*	*Urban*	*Rural*	*Urban*	*Rural*	*Urban*
1790	–	–	–	–	87.5	–	–	–	–	–
1840	–	–	–	–	77.5	–	75.6	24.4	–	–
1851	49.92	50.08	–	–	–	–	–	–	–	–
1871	38.20	61.80	–	36	47.6	–	–	–	–	–
1881	32.1	67.9	–	41	44.3	29.5	–	–	–	–
1891	27.95	72.05	–	47	39.2	36.1	–	–	64.4	–
1901	23.00	77.00	–	54	35.7	40.5	–	–	67.5	–
1911	19.9	78.1	–	–	33.3	46.3	57.9	42.1	71.5	–

Note: The figures for the various countries do not correspond with the years. The range of variation is 3 years.

[There appear to be some inconsistencies in the table. Ed.]

decline, and that of people engaged in miscellaneous industry—in other words in manufactures using the latter phrase in a wide sense to increase.[29]

Figures for India, however, run counter to this dictum illustrating a universal tendency observed by an expert. While other countries like the USA starting as agricultural are progressively becoming industrial, India has been gradually undergoing the woeful process of de-urbanization and swelling the volume of her rural population beyond all needs. The earlier we stem this ominous tide, the better. For notwithstanding what interested persons might say[30] no truer and more wholesome words of caution were ever uttered regarding our national economy than those by Sir Henry Cotton when he said 'There is danger of too much agriculture in India.'

Notes

1. *Wealth of Nations*. Bk. III, Ch. 11.
2. Report of the Committee appointed to make proposals on the Consolidation of Small and Scattered holdings in the Baroda State, 1917. This will be throughout referred to as RBC.
3. Ibid., p. 3.
4. *Land and Labour in a Deccan Village*, 1927, p. 48.
5. The author is thankful to him for a copy of this valuable note.
6. RBC, p. 38.

7. Ibid., p. 35.
8. Ibid.
9. *The Consolidation of Agricultural Holdings in the United Provinces*, 1918, pp. 45–6. The author is grateful to Prof. Jevons for a copy.
10. Besides these two systems of inheritance there is a third which allows a father liberty to do as he likes with a part of his estate provided he leaves sufficient for his heir to constitute what is called *pars legitima*. Under it the Germans have enacted a permissive law of *Anerbenrecht* designed to obviate the effect of the law of inheritance in causing unnecessary sub-division of land. In some aspects it anticipates the proposals of the Baroda Committee; in other those of the Hon. Mr Keatinge. For a description of it see Prof. N.G. Pierson's *Principles of Economics*, vol. II, pp. 286–90.
11. RBC, p. 26.
12. Op. cit. chart on p. 38.
13. Op. cit. Introduction.
14. Ibid., p. 4.
15. RBC, p. 31.
16. Ibid., p. 53.
17. *Rural Economy in the Bombay Deccan*, p. 51.
18. This description of the process of production is pieced together from the remarks of Prof. H.J. Davenport in his masterly treatise *The Economics of Enterprize*, New York, Macmillan, 1913. In this connection see also the able paper by Prof. Henry C. Taylor on 'Two Dimensions of Productivity' read before the 29th Annual Meeting of the American Economic Association held in December 1916 and the remarks on the same by Prof. A.A. Young. Both these will be found in the *American Economic Review* for March 1917.
19. Some economists who hold that it is the law of Diminishing Returns that governs agricultural production will demur to the universal applicability that is claimed for the Law of Proportion. Briefly stated the Law of Diminishing Returns asserts that additional 'doses' of capital and labour administered to a given piece of land will be responded to by a less and less yield. This means that if only the *non-land* expense of production is doubled there results less than a doubled product. But if this is the fact that is intended to be generalised by the Law of Diminishing Returns then there is nothing in it that is peculiar to agricultural production. If the expense to the land be doubled but the land not doubled it is certain that the extra return will fall short of the increased expense. This is simply another way of saying that if the returns are to grow all the factors must be increased in proportion. But so stated is not the law of Diminishing Returns a confused version of the Law of Proportion?
20. Survey Settlement Manual, Bombay Presidency, 1882. p. 3.
21. *Outlines of Economics*, pp. 531–2 (Italics ours).

22. Report on the Enquiry into the Rise of Prices in India, 1914, vol. 1, pp. 66–7 (Italics ours).
23. *Indian Industries*, p. 6.
24. Report on Agricultural Indebtedness in the Baroda State, para. 35.
25. *India, the Land and the People*, p. 225.
26. Op. cit., Introduction. The impression that Prof. Jevons leaves on his readers is that agriculture suffers in India because of the low standard of living. That a higher standard of life once established will necessitate a large holding because people with a high standard of life will prefer to migrate rather than accept a small holding. As his argument that holdings and standard of life are related is likely to mislead his less thoughtful readers, a word of comment is necessary. A standard of living is merely a level of consumption fixed in habit. But what determines the depth of a particular level of consumption? Undoubtedly the level of production. We may grant the truth of the statement that a rise in the standard of living works as a stimulus to higher production but it is foolish to expect mere wish to be father to the deed. It is *actual* production alone that can support rise in the standard and not wish, generated though it be either by 'travel or education'. If Prof. Jevons means that an opportunity for increased production, leading to a higher standard of life, will disfavour small holdings we are one with him. But he can make himself more intelligible by dropping standard of living and only arguing for increased production; that increased production leads to a rise in standard will be granted by all; but the reverse cannot be maintained as Prof. Jevons seems to do, for it may lead to production or predation. To speak of raising the standard of life without speaking of increased production is to give expression to a pious wish, if it does not lead to mischief.
27. 'The Village in the Melting Pot', *Journal of the Indian Economic Society*, vol. 1, no. 1, p. 10.
28. Prof. Jevons does speak of removing the surplus agricultural population to towns. The author is happy to note that Prof. Jevons had recognized that there is the evil of surplus population. What he has failed to recognize is that this evil is the faithful parent of all other evils that affect our agriculture. When it is recalled that industrialization of India is the one theme against which Prof. Jevons never fails to argue with all the aid of his knowledge and influence, his remedy of removing the surplus population to towns sounds strange; for migration to towns is simply euphemism for the industrialization of India. On the other hand Prof. Jevons has forgotten that there are few towns in India. If we believe, as does Prof. Jevons, that there is the evil of surplus population, the only logical and inevitable conclusion, however unpalatable it be, is the creation of more towns, i.e., industrialization.
29. *Essays in Finance*, 2nd Series, p. 240.

30. Professor Jevons in his paper on the 'Capitalistic Development of Agriculture' read before the Indian Industrial Conference, held at Bombay in December 1915 argues against industrialization. It can however be maintained against Prof. Jevons that it is industrialization only that can make capitalistic agriculture possible. As a needful corrective to his paper *cf.* Sir Robert Giffen's Essay IV in his *Essays in Finance*, 1st Series.

Brij Narain
(1889–1947)

Brij Narain was born in 1889 in a middle class family in West Punjab, the son of a well-known Urdu poet and short story writer. Following an MA in history from Punjab University, Lahore, he went to Calcutta in 1911 to obtain his MA in economics, studying with Professor Manohar Lal at the University of Calcutta. While he visited other countries in the course of his career, Brij Narain's training was entirely Indian.

In 1914 he joined DAV College, Lahore as professor of history and economics, and then moved to the newly started Sanatan Dharma College, Lahore, as professor of economics. He taught and conducted research from this position until his tragic death on 14 August 1947 in communal riots in Lahore at the time of Partition.

Brij Narain made many valuable contributions to Indian economics, covering several different subjects. His work displayed high standards in data collection and careful analysis. Known for his radical views, he was quite critical of Gandhi, referring contemptuously to Gandhian economics as '*Charkha* economics'. He favoured the development of modern industry, particularly heavy industry, cooperative farming, and democratic socialist planning.

Among his major contributions was the use of data from the Dutch and Portuguese archives to attack Moreland's claim that living standards in India had improved since Mughal times. Colin Clark used Brij Narain's estimates in his *Conditions of Economic Progress* in 1957. He was one of the first in India to carefully examine and interpret long-term price trends. Unlike most of his contemporaries, he favoured the use of mathematical and statistical methods in economics and produced a book in 1944, entitled *Curve Fitting for Students of Economics*.

Among his books and articles, perhaps the best known is *Indian Economic Life, Past and Present*, first published in 1929, which has been republished in the 1990s. This was widely read and reviewed. His *Charkha, Marxism, Indian Socialism* is perhaps his most polemical book. The modern reader would also find his last work, *Economic Structure of Free India*, published in 1946, still worth reading. Like Professor Kale, Brij Narain published several papers in Germany and he gave some lectures in foreign universities.

Major Biographical Sources: Asoka Mehta, *The Economic Revolution of Our Time*, Brij Narain Memorial Lecture, Punjab University, Chandigarh, 1966 (biographical note on Brij Narain); G.R. Madan, *Economic Thinking in India*, Delhi, S. Chand and Company, 1981, chapter IX.

Published in 1919, this essay attacked a view prevalent among some Europeans and Indians that Western industrialism was not suited to India.* Brij Narain's chief target was Radhakamal Mukherjee's *Foundations of Indian Economics* published in 1916. Brij Narain took care to not directly confront the views of Justice Ranade, a highly respected Indian figure of the last quarter of the nineteenth century, who had questioned the relevance to India of Western ideas of development. He argued that the situation had changed: 'Industrial India of today is not the same as the India of Ranade's time....The economic transformation of India has begun; it is going on before our eyes'. This cleared the way for his attack on Mukherjee.

According to Brij Narain, Mukherjee stressed the contrast between India and the West on three counts. First, Westerners believed in the multiplication of wants and their satisfaction. Indians sought comfort, not luxury, and believed in plain living and high thinking. The respect of man for man and self-denial characterized the Indian outlook. In his response, Brij Narain argued that the average Indian was not much more spiritualistic than an average individual in the West. 'The motives for economic activity in India are essentially the same as those which operate in western countries.' This issue was taken up many times over by Gandhians and by others in the 1950s.

Second, Mukherjee had claimed that Indian production systems in agriculture and industry were not exploitative in nature. Agriculture exploited the land, not the people. Again in the Indian industrial world there are no disputes, and relations are harmonious. Brij Narain drew attention to widespread class-based exploitation and conflict of class interests. He also noted the considerable inequalities in consumption and wealth in India.

Finally, Mukherjee had argued that in India there was more concern for distribution than for the production of wealth. Brij Narain rebutted this argument by drawing attention to widespread poverty and inequality in India.

Brij Narain summarized his position thus:

> We have tried to show that the motives which lead to the production of wealth in India are the same as in the manufacturing countries of the West; that there is the same inequality in the distribution of wealth in India; that there is the same exploitation of labour by capital; and that the economic organization of India is even more unstable than that of a manufacturing country.

He concluded: 'Industrialism alone can save India. And, our industrialism will, probably, have to be the same type as the Western industrialism.'

* Brij Narain (1919): 'Indian versus Western Industrialism', from Brij Narain, *Essays on Indian Economic Problems*, Lahore, The Punjabee Electric Press, 1919, pp. 26–40.

3

Indian versus Western Industrialism

Brij Narain

It has been explained that India is slowly changing. The Industrial India of to-day is not the same as the India of Ranade's time; as compared with the state of things 50 or 60 years ago, the change would appear to be still more remarkable. Of all our manufacturing industries the cotton industry, with its 267 mills and 6,675,000 spindles, is the most important. But in 1861 there were only a dozen cotton mills in India with 338,000 spindles. The economic transformation of India has begun; it is going on before our eyes. Labour and capital are concentrating in factories, competition between steam power and hand power is increasing. The conditions of life and work in some of our large towns already resemble those of the industrial towns of the West. Industrialism has also brought in its train industrial disputes. Its good as well as evil effects are beginning to be felt. As yet, however, the economic revolution has affected only a small portion of the industrial field. Agriculture our great industry, remains unaffected. Many manufacturing industries use hand power; the weaver is flourishing. But what is to be India's industrial goal? Will it be capitalistic farming and capitalistic industry as in the West? If so, would the change be for the better? Or shall we, for a long time to come, remain, as we are now, a predominantly agricultural people, with a small number of power industries, but a large number of cottage industries; with a small number of large towns and a small industrial population; a country exporting chiefly food grains and raw produce, and importing chiefly manufactured goods? It is legitimate to ask these questions; it is not easy to answer them.

There are some of us who are only half reconciled to the idea of Western industrialism. Western industrialism, they say, is not suited to the conditions of India. The line of industrial evolution, in the case of each country, should be adapted to the peculiar conditions, physical, moral, and social, of that country. One man's meat is another man's poison. Capitalistic industry may be a good thing for Western countries, but it does not follow that it is a good thing for us. And has not capitalism promoted class war and set man against man, master against labourer? Besides, it presupposes certain habits of mind and moral qualities which we lack. We have our own social environment, with the moral conditions which it implies. 'Western industrialism' says Professor Radhakamal Mukerjee 'presupposes the existence of other moral qualities and a different social environment. As long as there is no fundamental agreement of these in India and the West the line of economic evolution will be different.'[1]

Professor Mukerjee believes that our economic organization and social environment, together with the moral qualities on which they are based, are fundamentally different from those of the West. The more important points of contrast between Indian and Western industrialism, as indicated by Professor Mukerjee, are given below.

1. 'The Western people's attitude towards the satisfaction of wants is different. They believe in the multiplication of wants. A higher social position in the West implies a higher grade of comfort, luxuries and conventional needs. To the Indian, on the other hand, there is only one plane of living, one standard of consumption in theory. In India, comfort, and not luxury is sought for, and the ideal of comfort is the same for all classes in society. The same ideal of plain living and high thinking dominates all. The respect for man as man, and for the ideal of self denial as the means for the realization of God in man, the two striking characteristics of the Indian outlook of life, have their influence on the system of industry' (p. 324). Again,

> India can never wholly lose her discipline of the limitation of wants and the concentration of activities for the development of the soul. To India, the mystery and grandeur of the limitless vistas of the development of the soul are far more inspiring and fascinating than the mastery over external physical nature (p. 458).

2. The Indian economic organization is based on land, and the land basis is 'eupsychic'. Agriculture 'is a school of the virtues of sobriety, forethought and mutual helpfulness. Success in agriculture implies only the exploitation of nature. Urban economic prosperity on the other hand, is based on the exploitation of man. Rural economy prevents the waste of friction due to the conflicts of interest among individuals and groups, and brings about social harmony in industry. The land as the basal factor of economic life is the best insurance against class warfare and the consequent

economic instability due to the irregular and inequitable distribution of income. That is eudemic' (p. 465).

In the Indian industrial world there are no disputes, strikes or lock-outs, because, here, man is not engaged in exploiting man. 'The middleman, the trader or the money-lender in their dealings with the craftsman are always straightforward. They do not exploit the labourer but maintain him. The craftsman also looks towards them with due reverence. Indeed all the relationships which are entered into in the industrial world, for example, between debtor and creditor, employer and employed, master artisan and apprentice, artisan and trader, landlord and tenant, and their respective duties and obligations, call for a perpetual exercise of the social virtues and humanities' (p. 327).

3. 'In the West,' says Professor Mukerjee 'the problem of distribution is subordinated to the problem of the production of wealth.' In India it is otherwise. 'India is much more busy with the problem of the distribution of wealth than with the problem of production. What wealth she produces she attempts to distribute equitably amongst all classes of society, and this is the object which her socio-economic institutions like the joint family and caste, her system of land tenure and law of inheritance, her social and ethical ideals, seek to achieve' (p. 333).

Western industrialism being unsuited to Indian conditions, India will follow her own line of economic evolution. There will be no concentration of labour and capital in a few large cities as in the West. Industries will be carried on in villages as well as in towns. Cottage industries will be strengthened and further developed. Manufacture will be combined with agriculture. The small peasant proprietor will not disappear; he will, on the contrary, find his position improved. In the ideal state of things, each family in the village will be more or less self-supporting. Each will have a small plot of land and two or three looms driven by motor or electric power. That is how Professor Mukerjee proposes to combine agriculture with cottage industries.

Professor Mukerjee's description of Indian industrialism is more or less idealistic. It does not correspond to facts. The motives to economic activity in India are essentially the same as those which operate in Western countries, though Professor Mukerjee thinks they are radically different. Human nature here is fundamentally the same as in the West. Professor Mukerjee contrasts the limitation of wants which Hinduism preaches with the multiplication of wants in the West. How far is the limitation of wants practised in India?

It is true that many people in India are satisfied 'if they can get a morsel of food twice a day without being borrowers to anybody'. Their contentment, which Professor Mukerjee ascribes to racial habit, is largely the outcome of poverty. It would be interesting to know the number of people, possessing wealth and property, who strive to realize 'the ideal of self-denial as the means for the realization of God in man'. Far be it from me to deny that there are many noble men and women in India who do not care for wealth. Such men and women are to be found in every country. Economics is not directly concerned with them. It is chiefly concerned with the vast majority of the people in every country in whose case the desire for wealth is one of the strongest incentives to activity. It cannot be denied that in this desire for wealth the vast majority of the people of India, of every religion and of every class of society, find the main spring of their activity. There is only one plane of living. One standard of consumption, in India, says Professor Mukerjee; but 'in theory' as he is careful to add. As a matter of fact, there are many planes of living and many standards of consumption in India. The ideal of plain living and high thinking does not dominate all; it dominates a few individuals here and there. Professor Mukerjee's view seems to be that our economic organization is, somehow, spiritualistic, while the Western is materialistic. But it may be doubted whether an average individual in India, engaged in any industry, whether agricultural or manufacturing, is much more spiritualistic than an average individual in the West. It is all very well to talk about 'the limitless vistas of the development of the soul', in which the Indian is supposed to find his source of inspiration but one should not forget that this kind of talk is unpractial, and that it does not help much in the solution of the real problems of the country.

Professor Mukerjee thinks that in our system, based as it is on land, there is only exploitation of nature by man, and no exploitation of one class by another. Again he ignores facts. How does the absentee landlord of Bengal live? What work, pray, does he do? What about the majority of the talukdars of the United Provinces, and the rent receiving classes in other parts of India? Again, while it is true that the rise of prices has enriched large cultivators, it cannot be denied that agricultural labourers have not shared in their prosperity.

On an average the unskilled agricultural labourer earns about six annas daily; in some parts of India he earns much less. The rise of prices has reduced his real wages. While he has helped to make the fortunes of large cultivators, he himself remains sunken in poverty. Is he not exploited by those who employ him? There are no strikes and lock-outs in India, not because there is any 'real concrete equality between man and man in the Indian economic organization', but because our labour is not organized. If organizations of agricultural labourers and rural artisans were in existence at the present time, their wages would not have been so low as they are. It is wrong to think that there is no conflict of interests in the Indian system. The landlord cannot do without the labourer, nor can the capitalist employer, without the factory hand. And yet wherever labourers work for a master, whether in the factory or in the field, a conflict of interests arises and exploitation begins. It will be said that the number of labourers in India whether urban or rural, is comparatively small, and that, for the most part, people here work on their own account. That is true enough, but we are in no case justified in ignoring the Indian labourer—he forms part of our population and he is the poorest member of our community.

Wealth is produced in India by a large number of men each working independently. 'It is the production of wealth by free men'. This system has its advantages as well as its defects. The average size of the holding in India is small. The resources of the Indian cultivator are small and his power to make improvements is very limited. Almost every small cultivator is in debt. A Punjabee cultivator when asked about the cause of his indebtedness, replied that he had to repair his *kuchcha* house. How can you expect a cultivator who has no money to repair his house, to make improvements? He cannot buy agricultural machinery; and he cannot try experiments. Wealth is produced in India by free men, but the amount of wealth that is produced is small.

Nor is the Indian economic organization so stable as Professor Mukerjee seems to think. 'The Indian economic system never gets out of joint. Economic disasters are unknown in India'. One wonders if Professor Mukerjee is talking about this India of ours or some other India which his own imagination has created. Agriculture is the most precarious of all industries, since it depends on an uncertain rainfall. Our economic system gets out of joint every now and then. A famine is an economic disaster and famines are only too common in India. What Professor Mukerjee means by saying that our economic system is to be regarded 'not as the temporary equilibrium of rival forces, but rather as the permanent equilibrium when motion and energy are restricted in their operation in their proper spheres', is difficult to understand. There are, of course, no strikes and lock-outs in the agricultural industry because of the absence of combinations of labour and capital, but a study of the history of Indian famines would show how very unstable the equilibrium of economic forces is in India. Capital may pursuade labour to work by reducing the number of hours of work, or by offering a higher monetary reward for labour. But nature cannot be persuaded to work when she is not in the mood. Two or three famines, following close upon the heels of each other, would absolutely ruin the cultivator and reduce the rural labourers to beggary. It is this instability of the Indian economic organization which is the chief cause of the instability of Indian finance.

It is interesting to learn that the Indian craftsman is maintained, not exploited, by his friends the money-lender, the middleman, and the trader. The craftsman looks towards the money-lender 'with due reverence', and the money-lender, we suppose, loves him as a brother. Why is so much written about rescuing the craftsman from the clutches of the money-lender when the money-lender maintains the craftsman and the craftsman looks towards the money-lender 'with due reverence'? According to Professor Mukerjee, there is no exploitation of one class by another in the Indian system, but he must know that the rate of interest charged by money-lenders in many places, is as high as 36, 48, or even 60 per cent. There are many methods of exploitation besides wage-slavery.

In what sense can India be said to be more busy with distribution than production? Not in the sense that there is any real equality of wealth in India. An equitable distribution of wealth does not, of course, mean equality in distribution, but if wealth were distributed more equitably among all classes of the community we should hear less about Indian poverty than we do. Not that India is not poor. The official estimate of the average annual income per head of the whole Indian population in 1898 was only £2, or 2½ rupees monthly. According to Professor Slater of Madras the income per head has increased; his own estimate of the average income per head, in Madras, in 1916–17, is Rs 72. Assume that the average income per head for the whole of India has risen to Rs 72 annually, or six rupees monthly. In order that the average should be six, if many earn more than six rupees, many more must earn less than six. Inequality of income causes inequality of wealth. Before any one would persuade us to believe that the present distribution of wealth in India is equitable, he would have to convince us that the inequality of incomes in India is, in all cases, due to justifiable causes.

We have tried to show that the motives which lead to the production of wealth in India are the same as in the manufacturing countries of the West; that there is the same inequality in the distribution of wealth in India; that there is the same exploitation of labour by capital, and that the economic organization of India is even more unstable than that of a manufacturing country. We should cease to think that the Indian system, since it is based on land, is superior to the Western, or that our system is founded on justice or equality while the Western in based on exploitation and iniquity. Professor Mukerjee describes in his book the appalling poverty of the labouring classes in the West. Is the labourer in India, whether urban or rural, more prosperous? The labourer in England or America is far better housed, fed, clothed and educated than the Indian labourer. There is unemployment in Western countries, but the amount of this unemployment is small as compared with the unemployment caused by a single famine in India. It may also be pointed out that labourers in India, being spread over the whole country, will find it difficult to combine. Trade Unions are easily formed in a manufacturing country, for in such a country, labour is concentrated in towns. Trade Unions have done a good deal, both directly and indirectly, to, improve the conditions of labour. The position of the craftsman in the domestic system of industry is, generally, not a happy or a comfortable one. He depends on the money-lender and the middleman, and more often than not, he is exploited by both. As the craftsmen work in their homes, it is impossible for them to know as much about prices, wages and the conditions of the market as the middleman. A clever trader can easily play off one craftsman against another. The sweating system is the product of the domestic organization of industry. It cannot flourish where a large number of labourers work together, as in a manufacturing town.

Machinery, it is said, dehumanizes labour. It makes work mechanical and has a narrowing effect upon the mind of the worker. It may be argued, on the other hand, that with the introduction of machinery, the demand for skilled labour has increased; that some machinery is highly intricate and requires a high degree of intelligence, mental alertness and resourcefulness on the part of the operative. The objective gains of machinery are immense. Hours of work in all trades in all manufacturing countries have become shorter. Means are being devised for the settlement of industrial disputes without recourse to strikes and lock-outs. Attempts are also being made to make industrial towns healthy and beautiful. Altogether the labourer in Western countries has not much to complain of.

Those of us who are opposed to Western industrialism and who want India to pursue her ancient line of economic evolution, should remember two things—that an agricultural country means a poor country, and that the growth of civilization with all that it implies, depends upon the growth of town life, which, in its turn, depends upon the growth of industrialism. Revive the village community, if that be possible; restore the village by all means, but that is not how the problem of Indian poverty can be solved. The lesson that history teaches is, that so long as a country has remained a predominantly agricultural country, it has remained poor and in a lower stage of civilization as compared with manufacturing countries. To what does England owe her prosperity? Would the United States have become the wealthiest country in the world if they had not learnt to manufacture? What is the cause of the progress and prosperity of Japan during the last half a century? Industrialism alone can save India. And our industrialism will, probably, have to be of the same type as the Western industrialism. We shall have to fight the West with the same weapons which it employs against us. The struggle between the factory and the domestic system in India has not yet begun in right earnest. The struggle will be a long one, but it can end only in one way. With our system of manufacture, let us hope, our agriculture will also be transformed. The existing system in which land is worked by a large number of small cultivators, is uneconomical and wasteful in the extreme.

Note

1. *Foundations of Indian Economics*, p. 338.

Jehangir C. Coyajee (1875–1943)

Source: Panda, Koustubh (1993), *Nostalgia: An Illustrated History of Hindu–Presidency College, 1817–1992*, Calcutta.

Jehangir Cooverjee Coyajee was born in Rajkot in present-day Gujarat in 1875. After obtaining his degree in Persian and history from Elphinstone College, Bombay in 1898, he taught history and Persian for several years in Bombay and Junagadh. At the age of 32 he secured a Tata scholarship to study in England at Gonville and Caius College, Cambridge. He studied for the economics tripos, which he passed in the first class in 1910. His tutor, Alfred Marshall made the prophetic statement that: 'Coyajee will add one more to the now not inconsiderable number of natives of India who may claim to rank with the ablest and most thorough students of economics in any country'.

On the strong recommendation of Marshall, and two other Cambridge economists, J.M. Keynes and H.S. Foxwell, Coyajee was selected for the Indian Educational Service in 1911 and appointed professor of political economy at Presidency College, Calcutta.

Until his retirement in 1931, Coyajee taught successive batches of students at the College. He also taught general economic theory and international trade at the University Department. Many of the outstanding economists produced by Calcutta University, both at Presidency College and at the University Department were his students. These included J.C. Sinha, J.P. Niyogi and H.L. Dey. He was also acting Principal of the College for some time. After retirement, he moved to Andhra University to become Head of the department of history, economics and politics from 1932 to 1935. On his return to Bombay, Coyajee continued his work in economics and Persian. Coyajee died in Bombay in 1943.

Coyajee made a major contribution to policy as a member of the Indian Fiscal Commission, appointed in 1921. While Keynes was nominated as vice-chairman of the Commission he did not really participate in its work. We now know that the key parts of the report recommending discriminating protection were contributed by Coyajee, the only economist on the Commission. When the Royal Commission on Indian Currency and Finance was set up in 1925, Coyajee was appointed a Member and, again, contributed substantially to its findings and recommendations. He was knighted in 1928, appointed a member of the Council of State in 1930 and represented the government at the League of Nations in 1930–2.

His work for the government, while lauded by senior British officials, was attacked by nationalist Indian economists who felt that the policy of discriminating protection recommended by the Fiscal Commission did not go far enough. Again, many favoured a 1s 4d exchange rate rather than the 1s 6d rate that the Royal Commission on Currency and Finance proposed. Coyajee sought to answer critics through several articles and two books, *The Indian Fiscal System* (1924) and *Indian Currency System* (1926).

Coyajee maintained close links with British officials in India and England and corresponded with many British economists including Alfred Marshall, John Maynard Keynes, and Walter Layton. He contributed a foreword to a pro-government publication of the Bengal Publicity Board, *Current Economic Problems of India*, published in the early 1930s.

Along with C.J. Hamilton, Minto Professor of Economics at Calcutta University, Coyajee founded the *Bengal Economic Journal* in April 1916, which published several important papers in its early years. He was an active participant in the creation of the Indian Economic Association in 1917. An office-bearer of the Association for many years, Coyajee was elected its President for the Lahore Conference in 1923. In 1930 he was appointed Indian correspondent of the Royal Economic Society in recognition of his position as the doyen of Indian economists.

As a scholar and teacher Coyajee was remarkable for his analytical and drafting skills and his prodigious reading. His diaries and private papers show that he was most methodical in his work and kept himself up to date on the latest work in the US and Europe.

Major Biographical Sources: National Archives of India, Jehangir Coyajee Private Papers; Atul Chatterjee, Obituary of Coyajee in *The Economic Journal*, vol. 53, no. 212, Dec. 1943, pp. 422–56; and Jehangir C. Coyajee, 'Some Reminiscences', *Presidency College Magazine*, Silver Jubilee Number, vol. xxv, no. 2, March 1939, pp. 162–8.

I have selected a chapter from Coyajee's book on the Indian fiscal problem to give readers an idea of his skills in analysis and the range of his reading on the very controversial topic of protection for domestic industry.* By way of background, I should mention that Coyajee had prepared a note for the Indian Fiscal Commission outlining both the pros and the cons of protection, and his arguments influenced the Commission's recommendations. His position on the question of protection was clearly reiterated in this chapter.

Coyajee generally endorsed the infant industry argument, drawing support from the views of Taussig and Marshall. The second important set of arguments he made related to the issue of diversification. He quoted Alexander Hamilton, List, Wagner, and Schmoller, all of whom argued for the development of variety in occupations and fields of enterprise.

Coyajee argued that the infant industry argument was not more important as a basis for protection than the diversification argument. He quoted the Famine Commission of 1880, G.V. Joshi, R.C. Dutt, and others to argue that India needed a diversified

* Jehangir C. Coyajee (1924): 'Arguments for Protection', from Jehangir C. Coyajee, *Indian Fiscal Problem*, being a course of seven lectures delivered at Patna University in August 1923, Patna, Patna University, pp. 1–22.

economic structure for a variety of reasons, including for mitigating the effects of famine. Moreover, diversification had to be promoted keeping in mind comparative costs and it was not an argument for autarky.

While admitting that industrialization and urbanization could bring in the social evils associated with them in the West, Coyajee did not regard this as inevitable. Again, while protection may appear to be justified on revenue grounds, the short- and longer-time impacts had to be separated. Revenue from duties depended on the price elasticity of demand of the commodity. Protection, in his view, might reduce total output and tax revenue in the short run while it might increase them in the long run.

Coyajee doubted the effect of tariffs in raising wages, but believed that higher wages should result from greater efficiency and productivity. If higher nominal wages resulted from higher tariffs, not productivity, then they would result in higher prices and wage earners would lose what they had gained, through higher prices.

While he admitted that protection helped capitalists and industrialists and concentrated wealth, he felt it could have a positive effect in actualizing potential savings which existed in the form of hoards. However, he doubted if this effect would be large. (Adarkar made a similar argument. See Chapter 13.) Coyajee believed that protection was not likely to mobilize large amounts of domestic funds and dependence on foreign capital would be necessary.

Coyajee concluded that infant industries should be protected but protection should be 'used judiciously and with discrimination'. Diversification had to be guided by dynamic comparative advantage. Other factors may have more influence on the level of wages than fiscal policy, and protection could do little to raise wages except in the long run though industrial development and rising efficiency. Protection would not improve national revenues but may in the long run increase taxable capacity. Also it was not likely to generate significant amounts of capital resources in the short run.

Given that this was written in 1924, arguments on multiplier effects, such as those made by Adarkar, were understandably absent. Also, one must remember that the analysis of the effects of protection on real wages and real incomes changed considerably in the 1940s. Still, it is significant that Coyajee argued for protection, although of a discriminating kind and drew support not only from Western economic thinking of his time, but also from the work of nationalists like Ranade, Dutt, and Joshi. While Coyajee's arguments for protection provided the basis for the Fiscal Commission's recommendation for 'discriminating protection', it was sabotaged over the 1920s and 1930s by half-hearted and tardy implementation by the government.

4

Arguments for Protection

Jehangir C. Coyajee

The Indian Fiscal Commission, which was appointed to examine the tariff policy of the Government of India, has come to the conclusion that in the interest of the country, the policy of discriminating protection should be adopted. The task of carrying out such investigations affecting the whole range of the fiscal policy of a great country is one of the most difficult in the field of applied Economics. The sifting and appraising of the arguments for either system of fiscal policy is, in itself, no easy affair. Centuries of controversy have strewn the ground with weapons, good, bad and indifferent, and the reasons for a judicious and discrimination policy have to be separated from mere appeals to popular prejudice. The theoretical difficulties in the way of the Commission were not inconsiderable—to analyse the assumptions on which free-trade theory is based, to estimate how far the assumptions were justificable or not, and on the basis of this analysis to found the case for any advisable departures in the protectionist direction. Again, in studying the possible effects of a protectionist policy a proper perspective has to be maintained, and great care has to be exercised to distinguish between the immediate and long-period effects of protectionist measures. The confusion between these two sets of effects has been the source of much fallacious reasoning, as we shall notice later on. On the practical side, the difficulties of anticipating the effects of any proposed fiscal system are still greater. It is a complicated problem to examine the full case for protection as regards any single industry—to balance the sacrifice to be made and the burden to be borne both by consumers and by other industries, against the potentialities of gain to the industry in question. But the complexity of the problem is vastly increased when the possibilities of simultaneous protection to a number of industries are being contemplated.

The items of loss and gain are then so numerous and complicated that it is difficult to guess and impossible to compute the resultant balance; and yet any judgment as to a protectionist policy would be hopelessly faulty which tried to envisage its potentialities as regards individual industries, and did not try to make some estimate of the consequences both to the consumers and to the entire industrial system.

Rationale of Free-Trade

The rationale of free-trade admits of brief and clear exposition. It has been asserted, that as in every particular exchange there is necessarily a gain to each of the parties concerned, 'the sum total of such exchanges should be allowed to attain the maximum volume so as to yield a maximum satisfaction to consumers'. *Prima facie*, international trade brings a gain and any restriction on it presumably a loss. From these axioms is deduced the practical rule of free-trade that all efforts to direct the productive forces of the country in any particular direction artificially should be given up. 'The most effective way of promoting progress would seem to be to make the way, free and open for the best producer wherever he be'.

Rationale of Protection

The correct theory of protection is based upon the unfulfilled assumptions and necessary qualifications of the naive free-trade theory. As a great master has pointed out we cannot use as convertible, the two phrases 'the commodities which a country can now produce most easily', and 'the commodities which a country has the greatest potential advantages for producing'. There might be reasons for looking much beyond the present interests of the consumer and the present capacities of the local producer. The benefits of international division of labour are no doubt great; but it is only when fully developed countries compete as equals that the best form of international division of labour can be reached, and such a division is itself reached only by tentative stages. In the popular statements of free-trade theory it is further assumed that 'so long as the capital and other resources of a country can be employed with equal profit the method of application is a matter of indifference'. Finally, the transfer of capital and labour from one industry to another, as the result of the stress of foreign competition, is a much more formidable matter than has sometimes been supposed. The unfulfilled assumptions and the unemphasised qualifications of free-trade form the armoury of protection. In the considerations stated above might be recognised the leading arguments for protection.

The Young Industries Argument

In advancing and marshalling the arguments for protection the Indian Fiscal Commission has justly given the place of honour to the infant industries argument. Not only is the theoretical validity of the argument undeniable but there has been a tendency to extend the scope of its application on the part of recognised economic authorities. By parity of reasoning, the extension of protection has been recommended even to older industries which are suffering from temporary atrophy—such industries being regarded as infants *pro tempore*. The Commission has duly noted this; but there is also another proposed line of extension of the argument. As Prof. Taussig has argued, there is scope for protection to young industries even in the case of old countries which have fairly entered upon the manufacturing stage. Obviously, however, this line of reasoning should not be carried too far. The assistance to be given to infant industries must vary with the difficulties in their way; and the general industrial development of a country cannot but diminish in a great measure the initial difficulties of industries started later. With the general industrial development a class of efficient entrepreneurs must have been trained up, capital must have been accumulated and a skilled labour force brought into existence; hence, Prof. Taussig himself qualifies his remarks by adding that the opportunity for the use of protection in the case of industrially advanced countries is to be limited to 'periods of transition and of great industrial change'.

Its Increasing Scope and Importance

What should be emphasized here is, that not only the scope of the argument but the weight and importance of the considerations lying behind it have been constantly increasing with the growth of the complexity and scale of business enterprise. The advantage always enjoyed by established enterprise has been greatly increased by the growth of massive production, the massive treatment of by-products and by the internal and external economies corresponding to the expansion of business units and industries. Capital is needed on an ever increasing scale to compete with large manufacturing establishments abroad. The natural advantages of large scale production are multiplied by the powers developed through integrations and combinations.

On the other hand, the natural protection enjoyed by domestic industries is being constantly diminished by improvements in transportation and the reduction of freights. All these factors add to the difficulties of starting new industries in a country. But even this is not the full measure of the difficulties under which infant industries labour in our days. Neither Mill nor List knew of the present day policies of cutting out foreign rivals—export bounties open or concealed, special transportation rates for export business, and specially reduced prices of commodities sold or exported. Had those writers been living to-day, they would have been even more convinced advocates of the theory of protection to young industries. Who, for example, can doubt that if India had delayed the initiation of her cotton industry by half a century, and were starting it in these days, that nascent industry would soon have been dumped out of existence?

Then again, the case for protection to nascent industries has been to a certain extent strengthened in another direction by the growth of massive production. On this subject some dicta of Dr Marshall might be carefully studied as showing the exact limits within which the advocate of protection to infant industries can take advantage of this circumstance as favouring his contention.[1] 'It is obvious that an industry which offers large scope for the economies of massive production stands to gain much from protective duties, if they can be so arranged as to insure it the almost undisturbed possession of the home market while keeping open for it opportunities for large sales abroad: its sales at home and its sales abroad, alike increase its command over economies that help it to undersell rivals in neutral markets.' In another place he observes that 'it may be admitted that there is some force in the claim that a protective tariff is needed to aid giant businesses in establishing a complete standardization on the most advanced modern model'. While thus the argument for protection to nascent industries is strengthened, to a certain extent, it does not follow that we should benefit by extending protection to all national industries conforming to increasing returns. In the first place, we must have regard to the circumstance that 'many of the advantages which a single industry derives from a protective duty in its favour, involves loss and hindrance to other industries'. Nor can we afford to forget that economies of massive production are of many different kinds, and that while protection might influence some of these economies it might adversely affect the others. Nevertheless after making allowance for these considerations, we might recognize the existence of beneficial potentialities in the extension of protection to wisely chosen manufactures which have 'great latent powers of economy through production on a large scale'. Finally, it cannot be denied that the more any country exports 'her raw produce in return for manufactures the less benefit she will get from the Law of Increasing Return'. The application of the last remark to conditions obtaining in India is obvious.

Formulation of the Argument for Diversified Industry

We might now turn our attention to the other cogent argument on behalf of protection—that for the diversification of industries—which, during the last century or so has been formulated in many different ways and presented from many angles of vision. Alexander Hamilton had noted how diversification of industry helped to afford a more ample and various field for enterprise and to furnish greater scope for the diversity of talents and dispositions. List had argued from a different point of view for 'the principle of the variety and division of occupations and the co-operation of the national productive powers.' He pointed out the importance of such co-ordination and diversification as regards the social condition of a nation, and showed that the general well-being of a people depended upon the balance and harmony of their productive powers. The illustration by which List enforces his proposition seems to be particularly applicable to Indian conditions. 'It is', he says 'possible for a nation to possess too many philosophers, philologers, and literati and too few skilled artisans, merchants, and seamen. This is the consequence of highly advanced and learned culture which is not supported by advanced manufacturing power.' Coming to more recent times, we find that in the latter part of the nineteenth century the same argument was brought into great prominence owing to what appeared to be the excessive and one-sided industrial development of Germany. This led economists like Wagner to emphasize—and even to over-emphasize—the importance of an all-round development of a nation in industrial matters. Any other policy would be followed, says Wagner 'at the cost of a one-sided occupation of its population, the narrowing of their views, the most one-side physical and mental development, the absence of all the advantages of the universality and variety of national production, and of the favourable reaction of this upon the national life in general'. He professes to look at this question not exclusively as a problem of economic value but from the point of view of 'the abiding interest of the nation's economy, of its civilization, of the national life as a whole'. Though the views of Wagner have been denounced as pessimistic by Schmoller, who held more moderate opinions of the subject, yet Schmoller himself was in favour of employing moderate duties so as to develop both the agrarian and the industrial strength of his country.

It might have been noted that the two arguments—the infant industry argument and the argument relating to diversification and correlation of industries—are closely related, the one referring to the development and the other to the co-ordination and co-operation of productive powers. The development of any particular infant industry is one means and aspect of securing the requisite national co-ordination of industries. But in looking at diversification or co-ordination of industries, our view point is shifted to the national outlook embracing all industries and to their inter-relations. Our outlook is in fact widened and we look not only to the interactions of industries and their equilibrium but to the reaction of the whole scheme of industries on the national psychology and temperament. This wide range of the diversified industry argument imports into it considerations relating to all aspects of protection—social, psychological, and industrial. But it also makes that wide topic the breeding ground of dangerous fallacies like the home market argument, indiscriminate protection and 'autarchy'.

Like the infant industry argument the argument for diversity of industry loses much of its force in the case of the more advanced manufacturing countries. Thus, a great authority on matters of fiscal policy expresses the view that 'in view of the degree of industrial activity which is certain to appear under any circumstances in a modern country of advanced civilization, this sort of vague allegation has no probative force'. But, in the case of a country like India it is far otherwise; and the best argument for diversification of industries is furnished by the statistics of industrial employees in India which are most instructive and which show either the non-existence or the insignificant beginnings of numerous industries of the first order of national importance. These statistics bring to our mind and give a fresh significance to Dr Marshall's dictum: 'A new county may be dominantly rural, may lack the stimulus and culture of a nervous town-life, and have no access to the economies of manufacturing on a large scale: she will then derive comparatively little consolation from knowing that there are busy hives of industry and thought in remote lands.' Nor need we be afraid of applying this dictum about 'new countries' to India since the same writer has remarked on the possibilities of rejuvenation of older countries provided they listen to the gospel of self-sacrifice and of industrialization.

It has often been asserted that the basis and ground-work of Indian protectionism is the infant industry argument. That, however, is not the case. While the argument from diversity of industry has been receding in importance in the advanced Western countries it has always been to the fore in India. It required some theoretical preparation to understand the infant industry argument; but no one could fail to remark the lack of diversity of industry in this country. In fact, Ranade who opened the fiscal controversy in India, dwelt most on the 'ruralisation' or 'rustication' of India—these being only strong expressions for the lack of diversified industry. The Famine Commissioners in their Report of 1880 had argued that no remedy for the evils of famines could be complete which did not include the introduction of a diversity of occupations, through which the surplus population might be drawn from agricultural pursuits and be led to find the means of subsistence in manufactures. Ranade followed this up with the view that 'a due co-ordination of three-fold forms of industrial activity, even if it be not immediately most advantageous to individuals in any one period, is a permanent national insurance against recurrent dangers, and as such is economically the most beneficent course in the interests of the community'. He further emphasised the unfortunate effects of the lack of diversity of industry on the social and intellectual side—as transferring the monopoly not only of wealth, but what is more important, of skill, talent and activity to others. His disciple, Mr G.V. Joshi, 'regarded the dependence of the people on agriculture as the sole means of subsistence as the weakest point in India's economic position and pleaded for the co-ordination of agricultural and manufacturing industries with the direct help of the state'. This train of reasoning was reinforced by historical reminiscences of the days when India possessed a series of relatively strong domestic industries and emphasis was laid on this aspect of the matter by the late Mr Romesh Chunder Dutt and Pandit Malaviya among others. In his evidence before the Fiscal Commission, Prof. Jevons advanced and ably summarised this traditional case for India in the matter of diversification of industries. He gave a new turn to the old 'ruralisation' argument by pointing to the fact that, excepting the great ports and one or two inland industrial towns, there are no great industrial centres in India, and that the towns of Northern India have been for years in a state of industrial decay. This is a pointed restatement of Ranade's complaint as to the 'rustication' of India. What is wanted urgently is a period of industrial reconstruction in India which might stimulate the growth of new inland towns and the revival of some of the old cites. The social and educational advantages of diversified industry were also brought out clearly: 'The buzz and huzz of industries, the increased profits and earnings of the people, the changed mental outlook which is stimulated by progress and success in one's immediate locality, would have an almost unimaginable influence upon the national temperament and character. When industries become established and thriving occupations of various kinds become open to all men, and every man can take up that which suits him best, a ladder of advancement is opened and with it the buoyancy of hope, which stimulates to work and enterprise.'

It has recently been argued that the extent to which an opportunity for the employment of educated Indians would be afforded by the development of industries is often exaggerated. We can well understand that the posts of an important directive character which can be made available as the result of industrial development would not be as many as are sometimes supposed. But the mere number of the posts of directive importance is no accurate measure of the influence exerted by the industrial stimulus in affording practical training of a business character to the youth of India. The leavening influence exerted by the opening up of such employments is of many times greater value than the jobs themselves; nor can it be said with truth that it is only the employment of a directive character which will have such influence, since so far as the skilled artisan class or the class of well-paid foremen increases the practical instincts and abilities will be materially strengthened. If we compute the aggregate both of those engaged in the work of direction and of those who are doing supervising and skilled mechanical work, the potential increase of talents of a practical character appears to be of a substantial character.

While desiring to secure the diversification of national industries by all judicious means, we must not let ourselves forget that such industrialisation has got some social drawbacks and possesses a less favourable side. The Fiscal Commission was fully aware that industrial development will bring in new and pressing problems—many of them arising from the aggregation of population in large towns. Again, poverty and unemployment might assume forms hitherto unknown in India and might demand new machinery to cope with them. These do form deductions from the beneficial consequences of industrial development, but they form no argument against undertaking such development. Much could be done to avoid these evils by the utilization of resources available to us in the shape of proper town-planning, housing, general sanitation and wise factory legislation. A wise guide in the field of economics would have us take a balanced view of the matter. It is true, he would say, that industrial development leads not only to urban aggregation of multitudes, but to a constantly increasing inequality of wealth due to concentration of ownership and management in the field of manufacturing enterprise. But, on the other hand, he would remind us that, socially speaking, the operatives in the manufacturing districts of industrially developed countries are generally far from being worse off than the agricultural workers of industrially undeveloped countries. Finally, he would have us note that 'after all, the mode in which an industry is conducted, and the character of the people engaged in it are far more important than the nature of the industry itself.'

Nevertheless it is peculiarly easy to exaggerate the scope of the argument for diversification of industries and we would do well to bear in mind the *limitations of the argument*. It is too often assumed that the domestic production of an article is in itself a national benefit apart from the natural advantages which a country might possess in the matter of its production. In fact, the principle of comparative costs is in some danger of being forgotten in the jubilation resultant upon what is considered to be the acquisition of a new industry for the country. The truth is that the acquisition of industries for which a country has no comparative advantage is a diversion of labour and capital from more profitable employment and hence a waste of national resources. The principle of comparative cost defines the scope of wise diversification of industry. 'The real question', as Taussig observes, 'is which of the two ways of securing the goods in question is the better. To make a thing at home is not to our advantage if we make it at a high cost. To import it is not a source of loss when we import a thing more cheaply than we make it at home. Let us hold fast to the fundamental principle that exports are the means of producing the imports, and that only if there be real effectiveness, real success in the application of our labour and capital, does the country gain.' The greater the size of a country the stronger is the case for diversification, but the temptation to apply protection beyond the judicious limits also increases. An extensive geographical area invites a diversification of industry, since it is likely that the variety of raw materials required for any industry would be found scattered somewhere over the region. But, if these materials are located by nature very far apart from each other, the cost of assembling them might add largely to the other costs of the industry and hamper it permanently, and sometimes to too great an extent, in its competition with foreign rivals. A wise location of the industry becomes in such conditions a highly complicated problem, and sometimes the great distances involved might make the solution impossible.

It would be easy to quote warnings, even from leading economists of the protectionist school, against using protection too far in the interests of diversification of national industry. There is an obvious limit to the utilization of protection with this object. Protectionist authorities like Schüller recognize that even an advanced industrial state should not attempt to produce all the objects required for its growing consumption and that it should be always content to import numerous articles. They admit that as result of a misuse of industrial protection the gain from the increased production is much smaller than the combined loss caused on the one hand to the consumer and on the other to the export trade.

Some protectionist writers have asserted like Patten that protection is necessary to keep society in a dynamic state. So far as this assertion has any significance it must be the application of protection to young industries which alone can have the effect desired. As industrial development progresses, new industries come into existence as well as new branches or grades of old industries. Protection to these can be always given advisedly and under proper circumstances, and it is in this sense only that protection is required to keep industrial society dynamic. On the other hand, protection given indirectly to old industries or to all industries without regard to the principle of comparative advantage in production, results in industrial stagnation or in a static condition in the sense understood by Patten.

The revenue argument for protection does not appear to be a strong one and was in fact over-emphasized by the Fiscal Commission. There are two propositions which appear to be very similar but are really quite different. The first of these propositions is that a high revenue tariff incidentally affords some protection to manufactures; the other is that a high revenue can be derived from a protectionist tariff. The determining factor of the revenue-yielding capacity of a duty is the elasticity of the demand for the dutiable article. So far as protectionist considerations raise a duty above the point of maximum productivity, the result is a diminution of revenue. So far, again, as the tariff reduces the real income of the consuming classes the total revenue must be reduced. Great care has to be taken, when dealing with the revenue aspect of protection to *keep apart the short-period and the long-period effects*. It is quite possible that in the long period a successful application of protection will raise the total of the revenue-yielding capacity of the country; but no such result can be looked for within several decades; the more so that the infancy stage of industries tends to grow longer with the growing complexity and scale of industries.

Effect of Protection on the Aggregate Revenues

Those persons who believe that protection will merely transfer in the near future the field of revenue earnings from the imported goods to the wealth created in the country, are to be envied for their optimism but not for their knowledge of tariff history. They are, in fact, mixing up the short-period and long-period effects of the introduction of protection. It is true that if protection succeeds in bringing on a marked industrial development, the tax-paying capacity of the country will increase the yield from income-tax, customs, etc. But that consummation is a matter of many decades, as the experience even of great and go-ahead countries like the United States of America shows. Thus, Taussig tells us that in spite of the unsurpassed mechanical skill and natural resources of that country, the iron industry had to be protected as an infant industry for about thirty years. As the same author has shown, during the above period (1875 to 1897) protection must have enabled the American iron-masters to make profits at the expense of the consumers, and no doubt they paid over a small portion of these profits to their Government in the shape of taxes; but these profits for the three decades could not be said to have *added* to the tax-bearing capacity of the country as a whole. All such profits were made at the expense of the American purchasers of iron and steel; and, as these purchasers thus paid a heavy tax to the local producers in the shape of higher prices, the capacity of the former to pay taxes to their Government must be taken to have been correspondingly reduced. It is obvious, in short, that during the period of infancy of industries there is no possibility of any increase of the aggregate tax-paying capacity of the country; there can be only a redistribution of resources within the country—the consumers losing what the protected producers gain. It is only after the infant industries have reached the stage of maturity that the aggregate national dividend and wealth can be said to have increased; and then alone can it be asserted that the taxable wealth of the nation has grown. Here, and as we shall see later in the whole study of the influence of protection on trade and finance, we have to be careful in distinguishing between immediate and long-period results. Taussig once believed that the period of infancy of an industry under the fostering care of protection was a decade or thereabouts. But he goes on to say: 'An opinion of this sort I should not now support. What has already been said of the tenacity of old habits, and the difficulties of new enterprises justifies the contention that a generation more, or less, may elapse before it is clear whether success has been really attained.' And, if new industries take as much three decades to grow to adolescence in that land of push and hustle, they will surely require a longer time in our country where 'we are conservative to a fault', and where not only powers of industrial organization but the necessary basic as well as subsidiary industries have yet to be created. Something also must be allowed for the constantly growing scale and complexity of industry in general which must necessarily tend to prolong the stage of infancy.

Effect of Protection on the Customs Revenue

If we regard the yield of protectionist import duties by themselves, the revenue-yielding capacity of protectionist finance would appear to be greatly over-rated. The case of Japan has been expressly referred to in the minority note as showing that protective duties are 'a reservoir of national wealth'. But it cannot be said to be a very happy illustration. We can go into the comparison between Indian and Japanese customs revenues in two ways. In the first place, we might consider what proportion of the total national revenue is formed by the customs revenue in the case of each country. Taking the year 1921–22, we find that in India, the customs revenue formed over 21 per cent of the total revenue, that it contributed the largest item of revenue, that its yield was above 50 per cent, larger than that of the income-tax, and was nearly thrice the yield from stamps. In the case of Japan the customs revenue formed 71 million yens out of a total revenue of 1,562 million yens or out of an ordinary revenue of 1,237 millions yens, *i.e.*, about 6 per cent. The customs duties yielded in Japan about one fourth of what the income-tax produced (268 millions yens), and the customs revenue was smaller than the yield from the excise on sugar and textile fabrics. The excise duty on textile fabrics brought in about half the amount of the customs revenue. Again, the customs revenue of Japan was much less than half of what was yielded by the Japanese post, telegraph and telephone services (187 millions yens).

The other way of looking at the matter is to examine the elasticity of the customs revenue in each country and to see how it compares with the rate at which other items of the national revenues have grown.

TABLE 4.1 India

	1904–05 *Rs*	*1921–22* *Rs*
Customs	6.5 crores	34.5 crores
Excise	8 crores	17 crores
Stamps	5.5 crores	11 crores
Income-tax	2 crores	22 crores

TABLE 4.2 Japan[2]

	1904–05	*1921–22*
Customs	23 million Yen	74 million Yen
Excise	14.5 million Yen	75 million Yen
Stamps	17 million Yen	69 million Yen
Income-tax	14.34 million Yen	268 million Yen

The base year 1904–05 has been chosen, because about that time Japan entered upon the paths of protection. The rate of increase of customs revenue in Japan is much smaller than the increase of other items of revenue and is also smaller than the rate of growth of the customs revenue of India.

In the case of Germany, although the yield from import duties is large on the whole, the revenue from the duties on manufactured goods was small. Ashley computed that only about one-fifth of the German customs revenue was obtained from duties on manufactured goods while the duties on food, drink, tobacco and cereals produced nearly one half. The protectionist character of a duty does not in any way improve its capacity and value as an instrument of finance; that capacity depends mainly on the elasticity of demand for the dutiable article on the part of the country levying the duty. Nor is this principle unknown to the high protectionists of Germany. For in 1902 when the duties were raised on both agricultural and manufactured imports no pretence was made of obtaining any additional income from the latter source. The figures for 1913 showed that in the case of Germany the protective duties on foodstuffs contributed 41.2 per cent of the total customs revenue, while the protective duties on manufactures, high though they were, supplied only 15.5 per cent of the net revenue. So also in the case of the United States of America, as regards the yield of revenue the leading items consist of duties on sugar, molasses and tobacco. These three articles contributed about half the customs revenue. Taking the ten leading items contributing about 79 per cent of the revenue we come to find out that duties on manufactures yield about a fourth of the total. France obtains an even smaller proportion of her revenue from duties on manufactured articles, the leading items in the order of relative importance being coffee, cereals, mineral oils, machine and tools, and cocoa.[3]

The Wages Argument

The wages argument for protection has been also perhaps over-emphasised by the Indian Fiscal Commission. As high authorities put it, the direct influence of protection on wages has been exaggerated. Schmoller goes so far as to say that the wages argument for protection is one of the weakest. He urges in support of this view that there are other influences acting upon wages which are of far greater importance than fiscal policy. He advises 'the intelligent labouring class of Germany and its enlightened leaders' to accept protection rather in the general interest of industrial development than in the particular interest of their class. He quotes and agrees with Sir Charles Dilke whose view was that in Canada and Australia protection had neither raised nor lowered general wages.[4] Professor Taussig's opinion on this subject is the same. According to him 'No respectable writer or teacher would say for a moment that high wages are due to the tariff or that the maintenance of a high range of general wages (observe, we speak of general wages) is dependent on the tariff. The main cause of generous wages is at bottom a very simple one: generous productiveness of industry. This makes possible the combination of money wages that are higher than in other countries with prices that are as low as in other countries or lower.'[5]

The above views of the economists depend upon the fact that in the long run, the source of higher wages is higher efficiency of labour, and if high wages are secured by any form of fiscal policy for inefficient labour that can be only at the cost of the consumer. Again, high nominal wages might be secured by the action of fiscal policy to labour, but that does not mean that the real wages are high, since wage-earners will lose as consumers what they gain as producers. Still, one can understand to a certain extent the emphasis laid by some advocates of protection on the wages argument. Because, although an efficient labour force is a condition precedent of sound industrial development, yet on the other hand, industrial development also reacts on the efficiency of labour by placing before it a greater scope for its productive powers and by introducing it to more efficient methods of work carried on with the co-operation of superior machinery. Thus, in the long period, there is some interaction between industrial development on sound lines and the wages of labour. It might also be added that protection can be conceivably so directed and carried out as to cause a substantial increase of real wages, although in practice no country has adopted that form of protection. The labouring class will be favoured directly by a tariff, if it was employed to build up by artificial means those industries in which labour is the principal factor. Such a policy might injure other industries and yet benefit labour on the whole. However, the ingenious devisor of this idea, Professor Carver, admits that as protection has been actually carried out in different countries, its object has been to assist the capitalist class, because the influence of capitalism on politics is much greater than that of labour. Nor is there any prospect that protection will be used in any country to advance the interests of labour at the expense of those of capital.

Protection and National Capital Resources

In India much has been made of the argument that protection will develop the resources of our capitalists and industrialists by increasing the dividends going to them. In other countries the advocates of protection prefer to be reticent as regards this tendency; for, while in one aspect the existence of such a possibility is an argument in favour of protection, in another aspect it is a great admission. The implication is that protection adds to the strength, spirit and resource of capitalism, and that it enables capital to take toll from the consuming class; though, of course, the capitalist would add that he could invest the resources thus transferred to him in a better way. Indeed we are now at the stage where, as some writers put it, the argument for protection to infant industries is extended into an argument for protection to infant capitalism or finance. No one can deny the interdependence between the development of industry and that of finance; at the same time, it is also certain that the increase of capital so far as it is fostered by protection is to a considerable extent at the expense of the domestic consumer. Manufacturing development on protectionist lines admittedly intensifies the inequalities of distribution. As a recent writer on the protectionist side puts it, 'Effective protection to manufactures would act as a force striking the plain of wealth-distribution, and crumpling it up into hills and valleys.' There can be no sort of doubt that protection tends to concentrate wealth at the cost of the consuming public; the saving feature is that 'it will concentrate it in the hands of people who are well-nigh inevitable savers'.

But there is another aspect of the argument, so far as India is concerned, which deserves to be noted here. It seems fairly obvious, that if a protectionist policy can draw out money from the hoards into productive circulation it might render a real service. It so happens, however, that one of the leading economists of India has expressed his disagreement with this view. According to him the money drawn from the hoards will only cause a temporary rise of prices and a resultant increase of imports, and then such money will leave the country. In answer to this chain of reasoning it is submitted here, that in a period of stimulated industrial development the increased imports will very likely consist of machinery and plant for the rising industrial establishments; and so far as the money from the hoards has gone abroad to buy such essentials of industrial development, the result is of a kind permanently beneficial to the country. It is also arguable that a protectionist policy might not only bring forth into active circulation money from the old hoards but might further prevent the formation of new hoards by tempting money which might otherwise have been hoarded into industrial enterprise.

It might then be shown that *if* protection can draw away resources from hoards into industrial enterprise the result would be beneficial. But the more important question remains still to be tackled—whether protection can thus draw on hoarded wealth for industrial development. This question leads us to examine a little more carefully the different kinds of hoards. The hoards once belonging to Rajas and big zemindars are already being utilised in our industrial centres. The hoards belonging to the richer agrarians are not likely to be drawn into industries, there being a competitive demand for them from mortgages and other secure investments in the agricultural field where the rate of interest or of usury to be earned is still very large. Then again, hoarding in general has a social and religious side as has so often been emphasised. The increasing prosperity of certain classes in the country has increased the hoarding for social purposes, by the substitution of the yellow metal for the white in the matter of ornaments, which are in a sense a social necessity. Consequently, it cannot be said that protection will draw from hoards a very material proportion of the resources required for industrial development.

Considering generally the nature of capital resources available for industrial development, we have seen above that something is to be expected from a utilisation of the hoards though not much; another potential item consists of agricultural savings but these are not very large nor are they very likely to be diverted to industries; indeed it is not desirable that they should be so diverted. The third potential source consists of the profits of older industries or of nascent industries which are receiving the benefit of protection. This source of capital is of much larger dimensions than the former two, although the capacity of nascent industries for yielding profits and increasing capital are too often exaggerated; indeed such nascent industries will for many years be requisitioning more and more capital from outside in order to attain a scale commensurate with that of their rivals abroad. We thus see the very great importance of foreign capital for the desired industrial development of India on modern lines.

We have now reviewed the arguments advanced by the Commission in favour of protection. The infant industry argument possesses unquestionable theoretical validity; but at the same time protection to nascent industries has to be used judiciously and with discrimination. The rates of protection should be so determined and the protection should be so graduated to the needs of an industry that no room should be left for the complaint that 'the infant industries argument sooner or later becomes an argument on behalf of the inefficient producer'. It will also be the duty of the Legislature to see that protection on those lines will go to the real infant industries and not to the more influential and powerful but mature industries. As regards the diversified industries argument, we saw that it was in a special measure applicable to Indian conditions. Here again, we have noted that the diversification must be guided by the principle of comparative advantage in national production though that principle need not be interpreted in the usual rigid and static sense. Coming to the wages argument we find that other factors had far more influence on the level of national wages than fiscal policy and that protection could do little in raising that level, although it is not to be denied that in the long period, industrial development reacts on the efficiency of labour and on its remuneration. Both as regards the national wage-level as well as the national revenue any beneficial results of protection are indirect and of a long-period character. Coming to consider the claim that a protectionist policy will improve the revenue resources of the nation, we came to see that in the near future no improvement in revenue position could be expected, unless protectionist duties were kept at a very moderate level so as not to burden the slender resources of the Indian consumer of foreign imports; but if we assume a long period and a successful development of industries due to protection, the taxable wealth of the country might be found to have increased. As regards the potential increase of capital resources to be ascribed to protection, we find that this also is, what the economists would call, a long-period phenomenon.

Notes

1. On this topic the student should refer to Marshall, *Industry and Trade*, pp. 138, 746, and 764; also to the same author's *Money, Credit and Commerce*, p. 218.
2. *Cf. The Fifteenth Financial and Economic Annual of Japan*, pp. 14–15; also *The Japan Year Book, 1921–22*, pp. 400 and 502.
3. Gregory, *Tariffs*, pp. 497–8.
4. Schmoller, *Volkswirtschaftslehre*, vol. II, p. 644.
5. Taussig, *Free Trade, the Tariff and Reciprocity*, p. 141.

L.C. Jain

Source: Iyengar, S.K. (1953), *Economists at Home and Abroad*, Hyderabad.

Biographical information on Lakshmi Chandra Jain is scanty. He was born in 1901. He was lecturer in currency and banking in Allahabad in the 1920s, reader and then professor of economics at Punjab University, Lahore, until Partition, and subsequently professor and head of the department of economics at Sagar University in present-day Madhya Pradesh. Jain had been a Member of the Indian Tariff Board examining the case of the sugar industry in the 1930s and Secretary of the United Provinces Provincial Banking Enquiry, 1929–30. He was elected President of the Indian Economic Association in 1939.

Jain's most important contribution was his Ph.D. thesis from the London School of Economics, published in 1929 as *Indigenous Banking in India*. Other important publications included the *Monetary Problems of India* (1933), *A Reserve Bank for India* (1933), *The Working of the Protective Tariff in India* (1941) and *Indian Economy during the War* (1945).

For his work on indigenous banking, Jain, who was from a commercial caste, set out to find out if indigenous bankers, as opposed to village money-lenders, played a productive economic role. He used a variety of methods and sources including questionnaires, interviews, and personal knowledge.

The result was a classic in its field. It provided a thorough, sympathetic study of a traditional institution and a careful examination of its past and present role. In many ways, Jain was one of the earliest development thinkers in India to seriously examine the possibility of adapting traditional economic institutions to serve new needs and contexts. Like Lokanathan's view of on the managing agency system (see Chapter 11), Jain believed that indigenous bankers could be made to play a useful role in the future.

Many researchers have continued to refer to his work. Vera Anstey in her *Economic Development of India* (1936) described Jain's book as the best account of the problem. Chris Bayly in his *Rulers, Townsmen and Bazaars* (1983), described it as the best account that remained of eighteenth-century banking practices. In some respects, the book anticipated the large body of work which began from around the 1950s, describing the functioning of unorganized money markets and discussing ways of extending monetary policies to impact upon them.

Major Biographical Source: S. Kesava Iyengar, *Indian Economists at Home and Abroad*, Hyderabad, 1953.

I have selected Chapter VIII of *Indigenous Banking in India*, which discusses the future of indigenous banking.*

Before looking into possible future developments, Jain discussed a view, common in some quarters at that time, that indigenous banking and moneylending should be abolished. After a careful examination of the issue, he concluded that given India's size, diversity, and dependence on non-institutional sources of credit, abolition had to be ruled out on practical grounds. Also it was not desirable as a superior alternative could not be put in place that easily or quickly. He proceeded to outline what he regarded as feasible in the future.

First, the 'bazaar', where most credit transactions were taking place, had to be linked to the organized banking system. This was essential if economy-wide credit policies were to be implemented.

Second, while he endorsed the proposal of the Royal Commission on Indian Currency and Finance to set up a Reserve Bank to perform the functions of a central bank, he questioned, on the basis of the South African experience, its ability to control the entire structure of credit.

The key question for Jain was how to link indigenous bankers and money-lenders (i.e. the unorganized sector) to Indian joint-stock banks. India had used *hundis* for centuries and Indian indigenous bankers did not discount their customer's hundis with joint-stock banks, except when demand was great and their resources had run out. Again, joint-stock banks did not buy bills from small traders without the endorsement of indigenous bankers. Finally, agricultural finance and trade in India was done by silver currency and notes, rather than bills. While this might change, it was likely to be a slow process.

Jain believed that the solution lay in the consolidation and reorganization of indigenous bankers and linking them to joint-stock banks. But care had to be taken to ensure that indigenous banks did not get squeezed out. Jain stressed that this would 'involve the loss of a wealth of invaluable knowledge of local conditions, personal contacts, and relationships, extending over centuries, and of ancient banking methods and practices which, if retained and judiciously mixed with modern up-to-date developments would be a source of strength to the Indian banking system'.

Jain's important contribution was to stress that unfettered modernization of institutions could lead to a loss of accumulated knowledge and traditions.

His solution required that in each village or town, indigenous bankers and money-lenders should form themselves into joint-stock companies and perform functions similar to those of existing joint-stock banks, taking deposits, making loans, and discounting bills of exchange. This would help to mobilize dormant capital resources in rural areas

* L.C. Jain (1929): 'The Future Outlook of Indigenous Banking', from L.C. Jain, *Indigenous Banking in India*, London, Macmillan and Co. Ltd, 1929, pp. 229–46.

and lower interest rates on productive loans. Most important, it would create agricultural and rural industrial paper (financial instruments). He dismissed the likely impacts of this on existing operators and institutions in the credit market and hoped that when the proposed Reserve Bank was created, its operations would become more effective due to the open market in indigenous bills created by the new joint-stock banks of erstwhile indigenous bankers and money-lenders.

While one may not necessarily fully agree with Jain's views and the feasibility of implementing his recommendations through private action, the boldness of his approach cannot be denied. Jain's idea of organizing the unorganized has now become very popular, not only for credit management but also for the unorganized or informal commodity-production sector.

5

The Future Outlook of Indigenous Banking

L.C. Jain

An important stage in the inquiry is now reached. An analysis and discussion of the indigenous system of banking, with a view to formulating a policy for the future, have been completed. In the preceding chapter, the remedies both old and new, whether legislative or otherwise, which are being tried to improve indigenous banking, have been subjected to a close examination and made to yield certain suggestions. Such discussion and examination have disclosed beyond doubt the fact that the co-operative movement is full of potential good, if certain conditions are fulfilled. These conditions and circumstances have been outlined and briefly described.

But a question of great importance still awaits an answer. What is the future position which the indigenous bankers are going to occupy in the banking structure of the country? This question is of paramount importance in any scientific study of the subject. The problem has for long agitated the minds of the people and has assumed special significance in the India of to-day, when subjects of banking structure, organization and reform are live problems engaging the attention of both the Government and the public of the country alike.

Need for a Banking Inquiry

In this connection, the External Capital Committee of 1925, which had been appointed 'to consider the question of the flow of capital into India from external sources', made some important recommendations. These are well summarized in paragraph 4 of the summary, in the Committee's Report, which runs as follows:

India possesses a vast store of dormant capital awaiting development, and in order to make this available for investment banking facilities must be increased and extended. The examination of the various technical measures suggested in the replies with this object is outside the scope of the Committee, but we would emphasize the importance of a co-ordinated survey being undertaken at the earliest opportunity of the whole field of banking in India. This should be followed by a detailed examination by an expert committee or committees of the lines along which progress should be effected.[1]

A couple of months after the publication of the report of the External Capital Committee, Sir Basil P. Blackett, the Indian 'Chancellor of the Exchequer', in his memorable speech at the University of Delhi on 'Indian Banking and Monetary Progress', drew pointed attention to the above recommendations of the committee and deplored the fact that 'unfortunately there is very little information available regarding indigenous banks'. He therefore recommended the subject of indigenous banking as one 'on which a special study would be both interesting and instructive'. Soon afterwards he circularised all the Provincial Governments and the Managing Governors of the Imperial Bank of India in regard to the procedure which should be adopted in order to effect a comprehensive survey of the whole field of Indian Banking, with special reference to indigenous banks, such as was recommended by the External Capital Committee. The replies received by the Government of India are to be found published in the Reports of the Indian Legislative Assembly for 31st January 1927.[2]

Recently the Indian public has taken a keen interest in the subject and in 1927 Mr S.N. Haji moved a resolution in the Indian Legislative Assembly in which he asked for the early institution of a Banking Inquiry.[3] Sir Basil Blackett, on behalf of the Government, admitted the desirability of the inquiry into the question of the development of banking facilities in India, which has also been recommended by the last Royal Commission on Indian Currency, but pointed out that the time for its immediate appointment was not opportune, in view of the pending inquiries of the Royal Agricultural Commission, which is considering, *inter alia*, the problems of agricultural banking.

The demand for a Banking Inquiry was reiterated at the fifth annual meeting of the Indian Industrial and Commercial Congress, held at Madras in December 1927. There a resolution was unanimously passed supporting Mr Haji's motion in the Indian Legislative Assembly to which reference has just been made, that an inquiry should be held at an early date with a view to improving and revitalising indigenous banking.[4]

It is evident that there is a keen desire on the part of Indian leaders to have an Indian Banking Inquiry. This is also one of the main recommendations of the External Capital Committee, which has been adopted and on which preliminary action has been taken by the Government in inviting the opinions of the provincial governments and the authorities of the Imperial Bank of India. Whether it will be an all India Committee, or a number of provincial committees, no one, except perhaps the Government, yet knows, but that an inquiry is going to be instituted is only a question of time. When such an inquiry does taken place, one of the most important and complex problems for it will be to determine the future of indigenous banking in India. In the consideration of this problem the committee will be face to face with an entirely new field to investigation, because practically no constructive scheme or suggestion of a detailed character regarding the subject are yet available.

The scheme outlined below in this study lays no claim to the solution of a problem whose urgency is being realized only recently and on which little light has yet been thrown by Indian economists. The proposals in the following pages are made, in all humility, with the object of assisting the process of clarification and presenting something which may provoke discussion and criticism on what is admittedly a thorny problem.

The Nature of the Problem

A Preliminary Question

Now the question as to what part the indigenous bankers should play in the future banking re-construction of the country must be preceded by the question as to whether they should play any part at all. There is in India a school of thought which honestly believes in the complete abolition of the indigenous banker in the immediate or near future. Followers of this school are so disgusted with the atrocities of the money-lending class that, if they were to have their own way, they would do away with the whole lot, root and branch, to-morrow. One has only to look into the official reports of the debates of the legislative councils in the various provinces, especially the Punjab, and of the Legislative Assembly—called the Imperial Legislative Council until the introduction of the Reforms in 1919—for the last quarter of a century to feel convinced not only of the existence but even of the increasing numbers of the votaries of this school. The speeches of several non-official members of these legislative bodies, delivered in connection with the various ameliorative measures in regard to Indian banking which have been discussed already in these pages, if summarized come to nothing more or less than this. The indigenous banker is practically an unmixed evil, he must be done away with entirely and immediately, once and for all. While lending their support to all ameliorative measures, the exponents of this school feel that the measures are insufficient, they want something drastic. They are not content with the progress of co-operative credit societies.

Now one can agree with the view that the ameliorative measures are insufficient and that the progress of co-operative credit societies is not what it should be and yet not be able to subscribe to the main proposition propounded by this school. Two questions must be asked in this connection. Firstly, is it possible or practicable to do away, in the immediate or near future, with all the bankers and money-lenders? Secondly, even if it be practicable, is it desirable to do so? Taking the first question first, it must not be forgotten that it cannot be tackled without taking into consideration the immense area and the peculiar conditions of the country. An idea of the vastness of the problem may be gained by remembering that the population of India exceeds 318 millions, that the bulk of this population is held by the villages, and that village finance of agriculture and cottage industries is almost exclusively in the hands of village money-lenders, inasmuch as there are no joint-stock banks in the villages, that only relatively few villages have co-operative credit societies, and even where a society does exist, it meets usually only a very small part of the credit needs of the villagers. So that to think of the disappearance of all indigenous bankers and money-lenders in the immediate or near future is to imagine an impossibility. But even if such a consummation were practicable, we might very well ask, is it desirable? If to-morrow by state legislation—it is difficult to think how state legislation can bring this about—or in some other miraculous way, all bankers and money-lenders were spirited away or they ceased to function as bankers or money-lenders, would this be desirable? The answer to the question would be in the affirmative, if, at the same time, a better agency to take the place of indigenous banking were, by some miracle, simultaneously provided. Unfortunately in the world in which we live such miracles are of rare occurrence. If, then, it is not possible to build a superior machinery for rural credit in the same short period which it would take for the indigenous bankers, one and all, to be sent to the wall, we are driven to the conclusion that such a step is not desirable. So that it follows that the complete disappearance of the indigenous bankers and money-lenders, in the immediate or near future, is neither practicable nor desirable.

Now if the indigenous bankers and money-lenders are not to disappear wholesale, in the immediate or near future, it is not difficult to see that they must have a place assigned to them in the future of Indian banking. So we return to our original question as to what this place is going to be.

Need of Correlation between the Bazaar and Bank Operations

In this connection, it is important to bear in mind that the organization of the present banking structure of India is not compact. The fact that most of the credit operations of the country, which are in the hands of the indigenous agencies, lie largely outside the influence of organized banking institutions, makes it impossible to pursue any uniform credit policy to which all the credit institutions of the country would readily respond. No answer to the question of the position of indigenous bankers in the future Indian banking system can therefore be regarded as satisfactory which does not make for the correlation of the *bazaar* and bank operations to the mutual strengthening of each other.

Indigenous Bankers and the Proposed Reserve Bank

The necessity of a central institution such as may unify and control the currency and credit mechanism of the country was clearly perceived by the last Royal Commission on Indian Currency. The Commission accordingly recommended the creation of a new 'Reserve Bank of India' entrusted with the powers of note issue and charged with the care of the Government and Banking reserves of the country. This is the approved line along which, from the banking point of view, satisfactory progress has been made by the great trading nations of the west. But whether a Reserve Bank will, by the mere act of its creation, be able to succeed in bringing the entire credit machinery under its influence and effective control, does not appear to us to be free from doubt.

African Experience

The experience of South Africa, where the Reserve Bank established in 1920 has had to deviate from the path which was originally laid down for it, must serve as a warning that, in banking as in other things, what has succeeded in western countries may not be quite suitable to eastern conditions. In Africa the Reserve Bank, after its formation, found itself unable to control the credit policy of the country, by pursuing an open market policy in the discounting of bills, for the simple reason that an open market did not come into being. The volume of trade bills available was insufficient, because, firstly, the existing practices could not be changed very soon, and secondly, the other banks did not make use of the Reserve Bank.

Similar Difficulties in India

It may well be feared that the Reserve Bank of India, when and if it comes into being, will be faced with some of the same kind of difficulties which beset the Reserve Bank of Africa. Unlike Africa, it is true, India has known the use of *hundis* for centuries past, but, like Africa, in India the trade bills are not available to the modern banks in sufficient quantities for purposes of discount or re-discount. This is because, in the first place, the indigenous bankers do not discount their customers' *hundis* with the joint-stock banks except when there is a great demand for accommodation and their own resources run out and, in the second place, because the joint-stock banks do not deem it safe to purchase bills direct from the small traders, without the indigenous bankers' endorsement, because such bills are not accompanied by any titles to or evidence of goods and only carry with them the personal security of the small traders. Above all, a fact which is often not realized, most of the financing of agricultural industry and internal trade in India is done by means of silver currency and notes rather than by bills. It is not easy to see how, by the mere creation of the new Reserve Bank, these conditions will so change as to provide bills in appreciably larger numbers.

The Currency Commission, not unmindful of such difficulties, has specifically recommended the abolition of stamp duties on the bills of exchange, with a view to encouraging their use. The suggestion has been accepted by the Government in regard to cheques, and it may be hoped that this will tend to stimulate their popularity and increase their currency.

If special efforts, like the abolition of present stamp duties on *hundis*, are made, the time-honoured method of financing industrial enterprises by the cash credit may be replaced by bills, but we share with Mr M.M.S. Gubbay, General Manager, P. & O. Banking Corporation Ltd, Ex-Controller of Currency and Financial Secretary of the Government of India, the opinion to which he gave expression in his paper on 'Indian Indigenous Banking', that the change will be slow.

'Even assuming that the change comes about rapidly', Mr Gubbay has well put it, 'we shall still be left with the position that there will be lying beyond the influence and reach of the central authority a very considerable, perhaps a preponderatingly large amount of financial and commercial transactions which, in the hands of bazaar dealers in credit, will be only indirectly responsive to the bank rate policy.[5]

The problem of the future of indigenous banking may now be restated in the following form. How should the indigenous bankers and money-lenders be linked to the Indian joint-stock banks through the development of an indigenous bill market that both may respond to the policy of a Central Bank?

Suggested Solutions

Increasing Contact of Indigenous Bankers with Bank Branches

Now it is suggested by some eminent authorities on Indian and Central Banking, among which mention may be made of Sir Henry Strakosch, that the best way to secure the growth of a co-ordinated credit system in India is to do three things. Firstly, establish the new Reserve Bank, secondly, establish a strong link between the joint-stock banks and the Reserve Bank, and thirdly, establish a close contact between the indigenous bankers and the joint-stock banks by developing the functions of the endorsing *shroff*.[6] It is easy to do the first two; it is with the third that we are most concerned.

In order that the indigenous bankers and money-lenders may be brought into such close touch with the joint-stock banks as to be susceptible to the central bank rates, three things seem to be essential. In the first place, either the joint-stock banks must spread their branches all over the country in order to facilitate contact with the indigenous agencies, or the latter should be so organized as to form an effective link between the village constituents and the joint-stock banks. In the second place, cash must give way to bills in the financial and commercial operations in the country. In the third place, the indigenous bankers and money-lenders must change their existing practice and perform the same functions in the Indian money-market as are rendered by the money and discount broker in the London money-market.

As regards the first requirement, namely, that the joint-stock banks should extend their activities into the interior of the country, it will be remembered that their present position is such as to force on them the necessity of consolidating the existing ground before embarking on any extension. We are, under the circumstances, left with the other alternative of re-organizing the indigenous bankers and money-lenders. To this we shall return presently.

Taking the second point that the bills must replace cash in financial and commercial transactions, this is no easy task and can only be achieved by labour and time and a changed outlook on the part of the indigenous agency.

Coming to the third essential, it presupposes, on the one hand, a new conception of his functions by the indigenous banker and, on the other, a liberal policy on the part of the joint-stock banks and the Reserve Bank.

The present attitude of the indigenous bankers towards re-discounting may well be compared to that of the country bankers in America, before the war.

> In our section of the country we are born and bred with an antipathy to re-discounting. It is the last thing that banks up our way want to do, and we have not done it nor attempted to do it since 1893, not once. We regard it as a signal of weakness, as a flag of distress, and would not resort to it except as a last resort. But of course, under this proposed measure, if it becomes the fashion and is the custom adopted here, I imagine that the banks will fall into it, although it is something that the conservative bank will hesitate a long time about doing—borrowing money and endorsing everybody's note to hire money to lend somebody else.[7]

As Sir Henry Strakosch rightly pointed out in his presidential remarks on Mr Gubbay's paper to which reference has already been made, the change of practice in America came about in a wonderfully short time. This is clearly brought out by the following figures:[8]

TABLE 5.1 Volume During the Month

(Millions)

	September 1915	*September 1916*	*September 1917*
Bills Discounted			
(Bills discounted for Member Banks)	14	14	548
Bills Bought in Open Market			
(Bankers' and trade acceptances)	5	37	109
	19	51	657

From this, however, it does not necessarily follow that progress in India, consequent upon the establishment of the proposed Reserve Bank, will be as rapid as it was in America after the institution of the Federal Reserve system. For one thing, as Sir Henry Strakosch himself remarked, 'America entered the war in 1917, and that might have a good deal to do with the sudden increase of bills discounted, bought in that year'.[9] Besides it must not be forgotten that in 1913 there were in America approximately 30,000[10] independent banking institutions of all kinds, while the corresponding figure for joint-stock banks in India for 1926 is a little over 600 establishments. The indigenous bankers, on our showing, do not stand on the same footing as the pre-war country bankers of America, even though they resemble them in their attitude towards re-discounting of bills.

The weight of all the foregoing considerations forces us to the conclusion that the degree of control of the whole credit fabric by the central bank must depend upon the extent to which the indigenous bankers can be re-organized and linked to the joint-stock banks. In their education consolidation and re-organization must therefore lie the hope of successful banking structure for India and it is with such banking foundation that the prosperity to the country is indissolubly linked. So the problem is one of national importance having far-reaching consequences.

Danger of the Indigenous Bankers being Squeezed Out

We must, however, guard against the possible danger of some of the indigenous bankers and money-lenders being squeezed out, as a result of the growing expansion of such agencies as the co-operative societies and the joint-stock banks. Nothing could demonstrate the truth of this statement more clearly than the banking history of the great trading nations of the world during the last two or three centuries.

The slow but sure disappearance of many indigenous money-lenders will be unfortunate in India, as it will involve the loss of a wealth of invaluable knowledge of local conditions, personal contact and relationships, extending over centuries, and of ancient banking methods and practices which if retained and judicially mixed with modern up-to-date developments should be a source of great strength and solidarity to the Indian banking system.

The belief that the indigenous agency, which had rendered yeoman service in the past, is capable of playing a much more important part in the future and of accelerating the progress in Indian banking which everyone desires has led us to make the following tentative proposals in regard to the manner in which the indigenous bankers and money-lenders may be revitalized and re-organized.

New Indigenous Banks

The scheme of the indigenous bankers' re-organization is quite simple in its theory. All that is necessary is that in every village and small town the indigenous money-lenders and bankers may combine themselves on the joint-stock principles, thus pooling their capital resources and forming themselves into indigenous joint-stock banks. The indigenous money-lenders and bankers, it is expected, will act as the directors and paid employees of the bank, besides earning dividends on their shares and interest on their deposits, if any.

Functions of New Indigenous Banks

A new indigenous bank, as contemplated in the preceding paragraph, will perform the same general functions as belong to a modern joint-stock bank, viz., receiving deposits, making loans and discounting bills of exchange.

It will therefore be a proper banking institution rather than a mere money-lending agency and, in this respect, it will be a distinct advance over the existing indigenous agency from which it will have been evolved. In banking combinations lie strength and economy, and strength and economy inspire confidence and goodwill which is the foundation of the whole fabric of a sound credit edifice.

Hoards as Deposits

It is not idle to expect that with sound working, and through the demonstration of modern banking facilities and their advantages, such a bank should prove a potent factor in tending to create the much-talked-of and much-needed banking habits among the people. The villagers will feel that it is not unsafe to entrust their savings to an institution which they can see with their own eyes, and which they know is composed of their prominent and well-meaning neighbours whom they have known all their lives. And when they once realize that deposits in a bank mean not only safety but also prosperity, it will be the dawn of a new era in which dormant hoards will slowly begin to be synonymous with bank deposits.

The more the bank succeeds in making these hoards available as its working capital, the greater will be the measure of its usefulness in the area of its activities, and the more useful it proves to be, the better will it be able to attract not only more and more of these hoards, but also new savings which it will tend to encourage. One good will thus lead to another and a virtuous circle will take the place of a vicious one.

This mobilization of the dormant capital resources of the country for the development of the rural areas through the proposed indigenous banks will, in itself, be a service of inestimable value. But there are besides other immense possibilities.

Loans

The increasing resources of such an indigenous bank with the consequent expansion of its business will enable it to lend out funds on reasonable terms in place of the present extortionate rates of interest. Some business of an unproductive nature it will find itself unable to undertake, consistent with prudence, but, for that very reason, it will discriminate between productive loans, on the one hand, and unproductive, on the other, between provident people, on the one hand, and the spendthrift, on the other. Such a discrimination will naturally place a premium on the habits of thrift, self-help and labour, and give a great impetus to their cultivation. This will of course be an asset of considerable value in the economic reconstruction of rural India.

Creation of Indigenous Paper

The most important of all the probable developments in consequence of the formation of the new indigenous banks will, however, be the creation of small indigenous paper which they will readily discount. As is the general practice of joint-stock banks in rural areas in Canada and elsewhere, the new indigenous banks in India will soon find it best to invest their funds in agricultural or commercial paper drawn against commodities, either in process of production, or in the course of transfer from the producer to the consumer. The indigenous banks will therefore take steps to encourage the creation of agricultural paper for the purpose of financing the agricultural crops as well as for the purpose of moving them. Similarly they will finance the cottage industries by discounting *hundis* drawn against the commodities under production, rather than by granting cash credits. With such agricultural and commercial paper the new indigenous banks will be best qualified to deal, in view of their special knowledge of the local conditions and the financial standing of their constituents.

Technical Objection

A technical objection which may be raised against the formation of the new indigenous banks may now be anticipated. It may probably be urged that they will enter into competition with the existing banking agencies and thereby adversely affect the growth of banking in India. If this should happen, the scheme, whatever attractions it might otherwise possess, cannot commend itself for a moment.

In order to examine the validity of the above objection, let us first enumerate the existing banking agencies. They are the indigenous bankers and money-lenders, the co-operative credit societies, the joint-stock banks and the Imperial Bank of India. Let us now take these one by one and see how the new indigenous banks will affect them and what will be the net effect on the progress of banking in India.

New Indigenous Banks and the Surviving Bankers

In so far as the effect of the new indigenous banks on the surviving indigenous bankers and money-lenders is concerned, two things might happen. In the first place, some of the remaining indigenous bankers and money-lenders may be led to amalgamate their business with the new institutions either because of better prospects, or through inability to stand the force of competition, or as a result of both these causes. In the second place, some of the indigenous bankers and money-lenders may be driven to the necessity of confining themselves largely to business which the new banks would not attempt to touch, viz., to advance funds to the spendthrift for unproductive purposes. In so far as the remaining indigenous bankers and money-lenders amalgamate with the new institutions, they will strengthen the new banks by bringing to them more resources and more business and will help their provident constituents by enabling them to get better service on favourable terms. Some of their improvident customers will therefore be forced either to improve their lot or to seek accommodation from the surviving money-lenders. In so far as the new indigenous banks cause the remaining indigenous bankers and money-lenders to restrict their business to that of a mere money-lender or pawn-broker, no remedy can be suggested, nor does it much matter. In no country is the tribe of money-lenders extinct, but their dubious business is certain to become less and less with the increasing prosperity of the people which the indigenous banks will bring in their wake. The new indigenous banks cannot therefore be condemned because of their probable effect on the surviving indigenous bankers and money-lenders.

New Indigenous Banks and Co-operative Credit Societies

Next we must consider the effect of the new indigenous banks on the co-operative credit societies. Now it has been already pointed out in the last chapter that there is a wide field of credit activities in rural India, that this field is increasing and must increase at an accelerated pace and that the co-operative credit societies, in spite of their progress, do not yet cover even half of this field. There is therefore ample scope for other credit agencies to function, provided their interests do not clash.

In fact, the proposed indigenous banks, formed as they will be by the amalgamation of some of the indigenous bankers and money-lenders, will take the place of an existing agency whose existence, at present, is a hindrance to the progress of the co-operative societies. For the indigenous banks, it will be to their interest to derive advantage from the existence and progress of the co-operative credit societies by discounting indigenous paper which the latter might endorse. Such paper will naturally be welcomed by the indigenous joint-stock banks, as it will give greater security to their business; while the co-operative credit societies, in their turn, will have a ready market at hand in which to turn into liquid resources the thrift and honesty of their members. So the two will be a source of strength rather than of weakness to one another.

New Indigenous Banks and Indian Joint-stock Banks

Now we come to consider how the proposed indigenous banks will affect the existing Indian joint-stock banks. The proposal that the new indigenous banks should be first started in villages and small towns where Indian joint-stock banks do not exist at present must remove all misapprehension in regard to the possibility of any hurtful competition arising between the two. In fact, the new institutions will come into being in rural areas, which, as our analysis has disclosed, do not offer fertile soil for the latter to plant their branches under the present economic conditions. We might repeat that the immediate question before the Indian joint-stock banks is the consolidation of their present position rather than the extension of their business into new areas. To this end, the new indigenous banks will be a help, in so far as they succeed in drawing the capital resources of the country into the domain of banking and in creating in the people the desire to deposit in place of their eagerness to borrow.

The new indigenous banks will thus be able to render useful service in the expansion of sound banking in the rural areas for which the present Indian joint-stock banks are not competent and are not likely to be for some time to come. To the extent that the new banks are formed, they will add to the number and resources of the joint-stock banks in the country and remove the reproach which, at present, attaches to them in India.

But perhaps the greatest service of the new indigenous banks to the Indian joint-stock banks will lie in the creation of an increasing quantity of indigenous paper which the former will readily discount and the latter will re-discount. So that, on the one hand, the indigenous banks will always be able to turn their bills into liquid resources for meeting any demands of their customers on them, and on the other hand, the joint-stock banks will have the proper means available for investing their funds in conformity with modern banking principles and practice.

New Indigenous Banks and Imperial Bank of India

This brings us to the question of the relationship of the new indigenous banks to the Imperial Bank of India. The latter, it will be remembered, occupies at present a strange position in the Indian money-market. It is neither a central bank of the orthodox type, nor an ordinary joint-stock bank. According to the recommendations of the Hilton Young Commission, a new Reserve Bank is proposed to be established and the Imperial Bank will then be free to function as a commercial bank. The proposed indigenous banks can be an instrument of great value in making central banking policy effective by providing an open market in indigenous bills for the central bank to operate upon. The central bank, in its turn, will thus be able to function as the bankers' bank and assist the indigenous banks by giving to them confidence that their endorsed paper can be turned into ready cash in unlimited quantities. If this happens, the indigenous banks will have provided the most important missing link between the modern money-market and the indigenous money-market through the development of an open discount market. And this is the goal towards which we are all striving.

Practical Objection

The technical objection to the formation of new indigenous banks, therefore, seems to be untenable. But we have yet to meet a formidable objection from the practical point of view. It may be urged against the scheme that although sound in theory, it is a fiasco in practice. To begin with, who is to take the initiative in the promotion of the proposed banks? The Government or the public?

The answer is that the initiative must undoubtedly come from the public, and certainly not from the Government. There is perhaps no industry in the case of which nationalization seems more inappropriate than that of banking. One of the main causes why the co-operative societies have not made such good progress in India as they have done in other countries seems to be the large part which the Government have played in originating and running the movement in India. Of course, in the existing economic conditions of the country, this was inevitable. But in the building-up of joint-stock banking in rural India, the initiative and support must, in the first instance, come from the public.

How are the public to respond to such a proposal, when there is only 13 per cent male literacy in the country? This is another consideration which might will occur to a critic. The answer is that this illiteracy must be fought, as was suggested in the last chapter. But even at present, the people who are asked to form the new indigenous banks are the indigenous bankers and the money-lenders. Few of them have received English education, but it is known that they are far from illiterate. They are well versed in the old banking methods and are shrewd enough to be able to learn new methods.

Indigenous Bankers not Conservative

But it may be said that the indigenous bankers are so conservative in their outlook that they will simply not look at the suggestion. This kind of criticism does not do full justice to the indigenous bankers, who have often given evidence of their adaptability to new methods or conditions, if only they can be made to realize that that way lies their self-interest. For instance, we saw, in the sixth chapter, how in the nineteenth century, when some new joint-stock banks offered cheap facilities for transferring funds from one trade centre to another, the indigenous bankers were not slow to take advantage of them. In the same chapter, we saw also how more recently, in our own times, both the traders and the indigenous bankers and the money-lenders have been taking increasing advantage of the remittance facilities afforded by the Government through the Currency and by the Imperial Bank since its inauguration in 1921. There is nothing more respected in India than a religious injunction, but, as we have noticed in the case of the

Punjab Mahomedans, in spite of the acceptance of interest being forbidden to them by their religion, they are now taking to the business of money-lending, being driven to it by purely economic forces. Admitting that it is possible to persuade the indigenous bankers to combine in order to save themselves, who must do the persuading? The answer is that the banking experts, and the captains of industry, on the one hand, and the increasing number of under-graduates and graduates, on the other.

If the proposals are accepted in the original or a modified form by the banking experts of the country, it will be their duty to give the right lead by earnest propaganda through the vernacular press and in the villages.

The new indigenous banks will also provide a new opening to the many graduates and under-graduates who are being produced every year by the Indian universities, and will thus go some way in solving the problem of unemployment among the educated. This might open a career of usefulness also to some of the Indian young men who come abroad for higher studies and who return home only to find that the Government posts are limited.

Thus the indigenous bankers in the new indigenous banks are assured of playing a most important role in the national life of the country. If progress is made along the lines indicated, we may look forward to the day when not only every town, but every village in India will have its own joint-stock bank, which would perhaps be a branch of the bigger joint-stock bank in a principal town. The big joint-stock banks may not be many in number, but their total resources would compare with those of the principal banks of any other country and they would be working under the aegis of a central bank. The central bank will not be an isolated institution of the country, but will be working in unison with the central banks of other countries for the common weal and welfare of the whole world.

This inquiry may well be concluded with a warning and a hope. It is true that the indigenous banking of India has its roots in the ancient past, the good old days of which we are all truly proud. Let us, however, not be obsessed by the remembrance of our past greatness. Dreams of the past golden age are beautiful, but of no avail except in so far as they inspire us to action. We cannot live in the past. There is the present and the future. What is required is sound constructive work keeping pace with the march of progress. With the increasing earnestness of the public workers, the growing spread of education—using the word in its broadest sense—and of intelligence amongst the masses of the people in Indian villages, the growing network of modern credit institutions and credit facilities and the growing share of the indigenous banks in the movement, will widen the scope of co-operation, leading to the establishment of a sound banking system such as will bring prosperity and wealth to the peoples of India.

Notes

1. *Report of the External Capital Committee*, 1925, p. 15.
2. See *Legislative Assembly Debates* (Official Report), vol. i, pp. 223–76.
3. See *Legislative Assembly Debates* (Official Report), vol. i, p. 674 (10 February, 1927).
4. This information is based on a short account of the proceedings of the Congress which appeared in the *Pioneer Mail* of 6 January, 1928, p. 10.
5. See Mr Gubbay's paper published in the *Journal of the Royal Society of Arts*, 2 December 1927, p. 64.
6. See Sir Henry's presidential remarks on Mr Gubbay's paper, *Journal of the Royal Society of Arts*, 2 December 1927, pp. 70–4.
7. Statement of N.F. Bonfield, Vice-President, First National Bank, Austin, Minn., Hearings before the *Committee on Banking and Currency*, United States Senate, 63rd Congress, 1st Session, Senate Document, 1913, No. 232, vol. ii, p. 2462.
8. *Journal of the Royal Society of Arts*, 2nd December, 1927, p. 72.
9. Ibid., p. 73.
10. *The ABC of the Federal Reserve System*, by E.W. Kemmerer, Princeton, 1926, p. 3.

APPENDIX 5.1

Statistics

Number of Bankers, Money-Lenders, and their Employees in 1921

	Total workers and dependants	*Actual workers*		*Population*	*Actual workers per 10,000 of total population*
		Males	*Females*		
India	993,492	289,665	54,470	318,942,480	11
Provinces	699,009	208,174	37,499	247,003,293	10
Ajmer Marwara	5,949	1,920	122	495,271	4
Assam	4,717	1,573	342	7,606,230	2
Baluchistan	908	224	–	420,648	5
Bengal	153,044	46,110	4,010	46,695,536	11
Behar and Orissa	39,235	12,762	2,345	34,002,189	4
Bombay	72,709	23,523	2,847	19,348,219	14
Burma	22,210	8,706	2,909	13,212,192	9
Central Provinces and Berar	35,623	11,243	3,346	13,912,760	10
Coorg	204	96	16	163,838	7
Delhi	5,474	1,197	108	488,188	26
Madras	103,924	30,101	9,962	42,318,985	10
North-West Frontier Province	4,309	1,698	4	2,251,340	7
Punjab	138,015	35,043	3,089	20,685,024	18
United Provinces	112,686	33,987	8,399	45,375,787	9

C.N. Vakil (1895–1979)

Source: Ms Leena Vakil.

Chandulal Nagindas Vakil was born in 1895 in Hanskot in present-day Gujarat. He graduated from Wilson College, Bombay in 1916 and obtained his MA in economics from Bombay University in 1918. From 1919 to 1921 he was at the London School of Economics working with Edwin Canaan. He was awarded an M.Sc. degree in economics in 1921.

On his return to India he joined the newly started department of economics at Bombay University as Assistant Professor, became Professor in 1927 and Director of the School of Economics and Sociology in 1930. He continued as a Professor until 1956. He was later Director of the UNESCO Research Centre in Calcutta, Director of the Reserve Bank of India, and Vice-Chancellor of South Gujarat University. He died in Bombay in 1979.

Vakil was a prolific writer who did not shun controversy either before or after Independence. Among his early writings was *Our Fiscal Policy* (1923), which propagated a strong protectionist approach. His *Financial Developments in Modern India* (1924) based on his research work at the London School of Economics, was a thorough analysis of developments between 1860 and 1924. He published several more volumes before Independence covering issues relating to currency and prices and industrial development. After Independence, Vakil was one of those who opposed the Mahalanobis model for the Second Plan and, along with P.R. Brahmananda, produced a widely regarded alternative approach, *Planning for an Expanding Economy*, in 1956.

As a teacher of economics, Vakil trained successive generations of economists and produced many Ph.Ds. His most illustrious students include V.K.R.V. Rao, M.L. Dantwala, D.T. Lakdawala, R.K. Hazari and P.R. Brahmananda. He was elected President of the Indian Economic Association for the Patna session in 1934. Vakil had a very strong personality and his relations with some of his colleagues, notable G.S. Ghurye, the sociologist, and K.T. Shah, the first professor of economics in Bombay University, were marked by conflict and some bitterness. He was, however, very attached to his students and is known to have helped B.T. Ranadive and M.L. Dantwala, when they were in jail during the freedom struggle.

Vakil wrote several articles which were published in the journal *Young India*, edited by Mahatma Gandhi. Particularly interesting were articles he wrote, at Gandhi's request, on remedies for India's poverty, where he outlined what he saw as India's major economic problems and their solutions.

Along with Professor K.T. Shah, his Bombay colleague and another strong critic of British rule, Vakil was regarded by the British as an economist who voiced the views of the Bombay industrialists, seeking blanket protection for all industries and the repeal of the cotton excise duties. While he was probably not an industry lobbyist, there is little doubt that Vakil was a strong critic of British rule.

Major Biographical Sources: Subodh Sinha, *Contribution of C N Vakil to Indian Economic Planning*, Delhi, Deep and Deep Publications, 1994; G.S. Ghurye, *I and Other Explorations*, Bombay, Popular Prakashan, 1973; and P.R. Brahmananda, 'Professor Vakil: A Crusader Against Inflation', *Commerce*, 10 November, 1979.

It was not easy to select from Vakil's numerous writings. I feel that this piece* has great relevance today when questions of reservation and reverse discrimination are being actively debated and where communal issues are also being debated fiercely. It is particularly fitting that this lecture was delivered in December 1930 at Elphinstone College, Bombay under the chairmanship of M.A. Jinnah, who was to become the founder of Pakistan.

Vakil argued that the religious aspect of communal tensions was overemphasized at the cost of the underlying economic issues. He stressed the frustrations of Indian graduates who were unable to find work in industry and trade and who would not contemplate taking up agriculture. The only option for the Indian graduate who did not have technical skills was to seek government employment, typically at the lower levels.

After the First World War, higher positions in government were being opened up to Indians, and there was some growth in industry and trade. However, this did not lead to many jobs being created and many job-seekers did not have the requisite skills. Education had raised expectations among young men, but the available jobs were few. This led to growing discontent.

In the 1920s communal representation in membership of the legislatures was introduced. This in turn led to demands by legislators for job reservation on the basis of community. Mohammedans and the so-called 'depressed classes' were treated as 'backward classes' and some appointments were reserved for them at all levels in government. As a result the principle of efficiency was replaced by recruitment on the basis of community. If efficiency was the criterion, Vakil felt that most of the new jobs would have gone to Hindus who had the lead in higher education.

It hit the advanced and better-educated classes, according to Vakil; they had educated themselves at great cost in the hope of benefiting from Indianization, only to find that when Indianization came they were rejected for being advanced. This, Vakil believed, was the root cause of communal tension; 'it is the natural consequence of creating two opposite camps of educated classes, each of which looks on the other from the point of view of bread and butter'. Also the beneficiaries of this reservation allied with the foreign ruler against the Hindu community and the national cause.

* C.N. Vakil (1930): 'The Economic Basis of the Communal Tension in India', from C.N. Vakil: *Poverty and Planning*, Bombay, Allied Publishers, 1963, pp. 283–95.

The solution to the problem, according to Vakil, lay in rapid economic development. He noted that it was educated unemployment, not general unemployment, which needed to be tackled if communal tension was to be reduced. The will and the organization to tackle the problem of all-round development were needed. If adequate job opportunities were created, 'there would be no need for such dangerous palliatives like communal representation or communal preference in the struggle for jobs'.

Like many contemporary analysts of armed conflict, Vakil believed that lack of access to employment was a root cause of tensions and conflict. He saw rapid economic development without reverse discrimination as the path to a final reduction in communal tensions. In his words:

> If this is realized by the leaders of both the communities and the Government, that the problem is essentially economic and that by an active and comprehensive organisation the restless energies now in existence and likely to be created in the near future, can be diverted to useful channels—then instead of finding excuses for communal riots, people will settle down to useful work.

Many readers today may not agree with Vakil; his views perhaps reflect upper caste Hindu thinking in the early 1930s. A record of the discussion that followed Vakil's lecture and particularly the comments of the chairman would have made very interesting reading. Unfortunately, they are not available.

6

The Economic Basis of the Communal Tension in India*

C.N. Vakil

Introduction

One of the most prominent, yet unfortunate questions which is before the public at present is the communal tension between the two great communities of this country. The tension is gradually assuming such proportions that the life of the country may be dominated by this issue to the sacrifice of more vital things.

This unfortunate problem has been given a religious aspect; each community is supposed to look at it from the point of view of the religion it professes. It is also given a political colour of great importance in view of the impending constitutional changes. The deeper causes of the trouble are however economic, which are forgotten due to religious fanaticism on the one hand and political excitement on the other.

The Problem

The outward form which the tension has taken is that of cow killing and music before mosques. If these questions were of a fundamental nature, why were they not raised all these years? I come from a village in which the population is almost equally divided half Hindus, half Mohammedans. But they have lived peacefully all these years and respected the feelings of one another. The Hindus invariably stop music if they are going in a procession accompanied by music as soon as they come near a mosque; the

* Lecture by the author at Elphinstone College, Bombay, with Mr M.A. Jinnah in the chair, December 1930.

Mohammedans have not thought of killing a cow in a Hindu locality or of passing through a Hindu locality with a killed cow.

To a complete stranger not familiar with Indian conditions, it would be an inexplicable mystery if he were told that people fly at one another's throat on the questions of asserting their so called rights regarding cow killing or music before mosques. To me it appears that the real causes of the present tension are deeper and of a different nature; that these causes are responsible for a certain amount of heart-burning among these two communities; cow killing or music before mosques have become the excuses for manifesting this heart-burning; and when once let loose, the excuse has become a dangerous weapon in the hands of fanatics.

If we think over the problem calmly and dispassionately the real reason is not far to seek; and if this reason is appreciated or is brought home to people, the remedy is also within our reach.

I submit that the real reason of this unrest is economic. It is due to the general poverty and the low standard of life not only of the masses, but also of the increasing number of the educated middle class, which must be the backbone of any society, and which find nothing but disappointment in its efforts to have a better standard of life and comfort.

The Indian Graduate

In every country some of the best youths look forward with ambition to a career of public service either as high administrative officers or as ministers of state. Such careers are sought not only because of the pecuniary value attached to them, but also because of the public esteem in which they are held, and above all because of the patronage which they bring to the successful few, patronage which they usually bestow upon their circle of friends and sympathizers or admirers. The tactful distribution of this patronage enables them in turn to continue or rise in power and position and therefore in public esteem.

In countries like England and America, the rising generation has splendid opportunities in trade and industry including agriculture. In spite of the great avenues open to the young men of such countries in such other walks of life, the attraction for public service of the kind mentioned above has not diminished.

Now let us consider the position of India in 1914, or during the period immediately preceding the War. The Indian Universities were fast turning out a large and increasing number of graduates every year. But the ambitious designs of most young graduates could not be realized; to their utter disappointment they found that their market value was very low after graduation. They considered themselves above others, in fact, their education made them unfit for the greatest industry of the country, namely, agriculture. The trade and industry of the country could offer a few small openings to only some of them. There are several reasons for this. In the first place the trade and industry of the country have not yet developed to such an extent as to be able to absorb such large numbers of men, who could only do general work of a clerical nature, and were unfit for technical work, for which foreigners had to be imported. Besides, some of our biggest concerns are in the hands of non-Indians, who prefer men of their own nationality for important work. In the case of those concerns which are in the hands of Indians, the opportunities have also been curtailed because of two reasons. First, the Indian capitalist is expected to and usually does find employment for young relatives, who left on their own would fare much worse. Second a good deal of our business is in the hands of uneducated people, who are not able to appreciate the value of educated men in their concerns, except in a very subordinate position. On account of the combination of these causes the Indian graduate found that he had very limited opportunities for a career in trade and industry.

In many cases he therefore turned to the only other career, namely, Government service. Here too the highest ranks were shut against him; he was expected to begin at the lowest stage, in many cases with a clerkship of Rs 40 per month, and his maximum rise was upto the position of a subordinate officer, of the rank of say a Mamlatdar. Only a fortunate few could penetrate the bureaucratic preserve by passing at great sacrifice the ICS examination, then held in England.

In brief, we had a steady stream of educated young men coming out of the Universities, who learnt in their college days modern ways of life, and were taught among other things that the low standard of life in India was a curse, and felt in them the ambition and power to raise their own standard of life with the help of their education. Whether this utilitarian view of education is correct or not is another question; that it has been in existence is a fact that cannot be denied.

On the other hand as we have seen above, the openings for these young men were comparatively few, and therefore disappointment was naturally in store for most of them. A growing discontent with things around them was the inevitable consequence; and a conscious desire to get out of this predicament somehow was bound to be created. Unlike the masses of our people, who are not vocal, these increasing number of educated men could understand and voice their difficulties with growing intensity. But with the existing political and economic organisation of the country, they found that their aspirations were controlled and even chained on all hands.

Indianisation

There was however one ray of hope. It was this very state of affairs which had made the demand for Indianisation of the public services louder and louder, and the authorities were slowly preceiving the necessity of yielding to it, lest it may lead to undesirable consequences. And the same demand for Indianisation of private services in trade and industry was also being increasingly felt.

It was at such a time that the appointment of an eminent Indian like Lord Sinha (then Sir P.P. Sinha) to the high post of the Viceroy's Council was hailed with joy by educated India. For in such an appointment, irrespective of the man's community, both Hindus and Mohammedans, had a common feeling that here was a beginning of a process by which positions both high and small would be available to them in increasing numbers. And by this time the successful working of the highest industrial venture in the country, namely, the Tata Steel Works, also led to similar hopes of an early day when Indian industrial and commercial magnates would be able to provide increasing opportunities to the young educated men of the country.

War Period

Like many other things, the effective realization of these hopes had to be postponed during the War period. But the War itself provided an opportunity hitherto not available to Indians. Both in private and public work of importance, which had grown on account of the war, large numbers of educated men were wanted to fill the places of Europeans who had been called away to serve in the war, or who could not be imported because of the same reason.

The Reforms

But what was an inevitable experiment during the War period had to be made a matter of policy in the immediate future, with the introduction of the Reforms in 1921. Indianisation in the various services to a certain extent was definitely laid down, and Indian ministers and elected legislatures came into existence to see that these pledges were carried out. The long delayed hopes of educated India were at last to be realized, if not wholly, at least partially. And the same effect is found in trade and industry. For, with the Reforms has come the policy of Discriminating Protection, by which an industry receiving protection is bound to carry out Indianisation of its services as far as possible. And the effect of this in unprotected industries or in business in general is bound to be felt.

But the prizes thus thrown open to Indians by a partial policy of Indianisation are yet comparatively speaking few. For to the already patiently waiting numbers of disappointed educated Indians the Universities were adding large number of graduates every year. Besides, the number of Universities was also increasing, and they, with some honourable exceptions, continued to commit the mistake of providing only general education to the neglect of scientific and technical or vocational education, which may enable young men to take to other fields of work.

This naturally resulted in a struggle among the educated classes to capture the few prizes thus available in Government or private service. But this struggle was now on a large scale than ever, because the prizes available were also larger in number and greater in value, though compared with the number of the educated they were still few.

Communal Preference

In the midst of this struggle, was introduced another element pregnant with dangerous issues. The only real test of the success of any piece of work, Government or private, is efficiency. On the grounds of efficiency only those who were by their education or experience qualified for these new careers were likely to obtain them. If this had taken place, the great majority of these careers would have gone to Hindus among whom were to be found men in large numbers with superior qualifications.

The Mohammedans had not taken sufficient advantage of the educational facilities available to all alike in the different Universities. And as a community they found themselves unprepared to capture with success that share of these new careers which they thought was due to them in proportion to their population. And this feeling was accentuated by the fact of communal representation in the Reformed Legislature. It is not suggested that those eminent Mohammedans who now sit in the Indian

Legislatures would not have been there in the absence of communal representation. They would indeed have been there in the same strength, but they would then have felt their responsibilities as Indians first, and Mohammedans next. But when once this communal feeling was developed in members belonging to one community, it was natural that the same should be the case with others. Instead of developing a truly national spirit, the fact of their being in the legislatures as representing their community makes the legislators think more in terms of the community than in terms of the nation as a whole.

This being the case, the Mohammedan legislators felt it their duty to find a way out of their difficulty mentioned above, namely, the possibilities or otherwise of obtaining a suitable number of the new careers for members of their own community. And in this effort they found useful allies in the so-called Depressed classes of the Hindus, in some provinces known as non-Brahmins. All this has led to the distinction between the so-called 'advanced' and 'backward' classes for the purposes of Government appointments—high or low. A certain number of such appointments came to be reserved for members of the 'backward' classes, among whom were put Mohammedans and the 'Depressed classes'. The distinction was applied not in small appointments only; it was carried in the hitherto most highly prized service, namely, the ICS. A certain number of candidates who have not been successful at the competitive examination are nevertheless taken in the ICS on the ground of making up for communal inequalities, as can be seen from the Government communiqués issued every year in connection with the ICS examination.

The Efficiency Test

Lest we may be led away by personal bias, let us look at the question from a detached point of view. When we were asking for the Indianisation of the services, even as we do now, our demand amounted to and amounts to this: that so long as an Indian of the necessary qualification is available, an Englishman should not be appointed. We do not say, we dare not say, that an unqualified Indian shall be appointed to a post simply because he is an Indian. We may say with justice that if qualified Indians are not available for particular kinds of work, steps should be taken by a system of foreign scholarships or practical apprenticeship to train Indians. We all know that though Indianisation has been accepted in principle, in certain cases Indians are not yet appointed on the ground that an Indian of the requisite qualification is not available. In short, the progress of Indianisation is limited by the qualifications of the Indian candidates available. In other words efficiency is the test in putting the principle in practice.

But within the limits of Indianised Services, the test of efficiency has been given up in preference to the pressure of communal claims. Within these limits an Indian of the backward classes may be appointed, and is certainly appointed even though he may be inferior in qualifications to other candidates who are brushed aside because they belong to the advanced classes, who find that out of the new careers created by the Reforms, a very great percentage is reserved for the backward classes.

Super Castes

The advanced classes or the more educated classes are doubly hit; they have equipped themselves at a great sacrifice with certain qualifications; their claims have been hitherto denied because Indianisation did not exist. When Indianisation does come their claims are restricted by being told that they are advanced. The fact of their being advanced is now put at a discount, and they are made to scratch their heads to find a solution out of the dilemma. 'Down with the caste-system' is the slogan of our Social Reformers and of our English rulers. We are taught to do so many things in a broad catholic spirit 'irrespective of caste, colour or creed'. And here is a policy of the Government which leads to the creation of two hostile castes or super-castes of backward and advanced classes, based on the fact of their education, and sustained by the distribution of Government favours on grounds other than those of efficiency.

The Root Cause

I submit that this policy has created and is creating a deep seated feelings of discontent and resentment among the educated classes, and the smouldering smokes of this feeling are really responsible for the communal tension.

Let me put the matter in the form of an illustration. Suppose that the head of a family, has a son or brother, or another dependent for whom he wishes to get some suitable employment. The party has obtained certain qualifications, say a good University education. He applies for an appointment which is quite within his abilities. He is told that he belongs to the advanced class, and therefore has no chance; that a member of the backward class, even though of inferior qualifications has been appointed, and that this is done under the orders of the Government. As a human being, both the candidate, and the head of the family anxious for his welfare, are bound to have a burning feeling at this undeserved rebuff, a feeling of injustice and wrong done by the state as a matter of policy. In the circle of their friends and sympathizers this episode with all its communal significance will filter down, and a conviction will be created that the Government is unduly favouring the Mohammedans or the non-Brahmins as the case may be against the advanced classes or the educated Hindus.

Its Effects

A feeling of hatred between the communities is the inevitable consequence when such events take place in large numbers, in cases small or big. The 'backward' community tries to be aggressive and therefore offensive at each step of its forward march; if there is any delay in its progress it kicks up a row and looks upon the other community with jealousy and anger; the 'advanced' community feels it is losing ground at each stage and finds itself in a terrible dilemma at an order of things which it explains by the belief that the Government has adopted the policy of Divide and Rule between the different communities of this country. We are sometimes told that behind the communal riots which occur now and then in the country, there is some intelligence; if there is any truth in this, the reason why intelligence should be so misused is obvious; it is the natural consequence of creating two opposite camps of educated classes, each of which looks on the other from the point of view of bread and butter.

While this is the obvious effect, there are others, which may lead to a continuation of the tension, and retard the national progress of the country. They may be briefly stated as (a) demoralisation of the public services, and (b) of political life in the country.

When the test of efficiency is suspended in appointments to public services, high and low, we are bound to have in them people who instead of proving the capacity of Indians for administration and organisation, may give illustrations of weakness and inefficiency to the enemies of Indian progress. At a time when we require the best available men to join the higher services and prove the administrative capacity of Indians in comparison with the most efficient European in any department, we have a situation by which quite the opposite results may ensue.

The political life of the country is demoralised because the minority and so called backward communities are thus taught to believe that the existing foreign Government is their real benefactor, and the advanced Hindu Community is their great enemy. Legislators and ministers who happen to be Mahommedans or members of the backward classes find that they can get Government appointments for members of their community, if they keep well with the Executive Government; and the Executive Government finds on the other hand that in exchange for the distribution of Government patronage in this way, they can rely on the votes of the legislators belonging to these communities; the result is that the officials in each legislature—provincial or central—who are in a minority, and who represent no section of the people, plus the members of the minority communities, form a majority as against the representatives of the majority community in the country. We have therefore a situation by which the English Government can pass an important piece of legislation or other measure, which is against the wishes of the majority of the elected members, because of this unholy alliance. The actions of the legislatures may not therefore be national in spirit and outlook; and the limited measure of self-government that we have got under the present system is nullified.

The same demoralisation of political life is likely to affect the future as is evident from the attitude of different political parties and groups towards the Simon Commission and its work.

I do not hold a brief for the advanced classes. I have every sympathy with the aspirations of the backward classes. I am trying to analyse and understand the effects of the situation created by this policy. I do not attribute motives in the adoption of it either. But granting that this has been done with the best of intentions, the consequences as briefly outlined above, cannot be denied. I would not have cared to pen this picture of the communal tension, unless I was convinced that this apparently religious and political struggle is really due to economic causes, briefly mentioned by me and therefore the real solution is also of an economic nature. We have drifted along wrong lines; we must cry halt and put the progress of the country on sound lines, based on sound economic foundations. No amount of Unity Conferences and Unity resolutions or anti-Goonda legislation will be of any avail so long as these fundamental causes are in operation. The real unifying force among the communities must be economic—a consciousness that there is enough in this country to occupy the energies of the members of all communities, educated or not—a consciousness followed by an early practical realization that the work available to all is fruitful and is worthy of an ambition created by modern education.

Remedy

If this analysis of the situation is correct, the remedy is obvious. What we want is rapid economic development of an all round character which will provide wider and greater opportunities to all classes of people—advanced or backward; high or low; Hindus or Mahommedans. In other words it is a question of finding suitable employment for the unemployed, or the under-employed or the ill-employed of different classes.

Unemployment

We have heard of unemployment in England and other countries after the war and the steps taken in that connection. These countries have been wiser; their statesmen realized in time the evil effects on society of large numbers of the unemployed. Unemployment in a general sense is much greater in our country than in Europe. The difference is that European countries have statistics of the unemployed which speak; they take definite measures to remove the evil and these are reported. The unemployment in our country is so chronic, that it has become natural or normal, and is therefore not noticed; and it is so great and frightening in volume that our leaders, Government or national, even when they realize it are afraid of referring to it. But the unemployment of the agriculturists for several months in the year to which I refer, did not create that restlessness which has arisen by the unemployment of large numbers of educated young men in the country.

And let me here pay a tribute to that much misunderstood, but universally respected person, Mahatma Gandhi. He has above all others appreciated the fact of this chronic unemployment of the people of this country, and his economic weapon, the charkha, however feeble and insignificant against modern machinery, is a standing reminder of this great unemployment, and is under our present conditions, the only possible first step towards the removal of the great unemployment which we witness in this country.

But the charkha does not appeal to the educated Indian in his disappointment. His dreams have gone much further. Just as an Englishman may legitimately aspire to be the Prime Minister or an American to be the President of the Republic, the educated Indian delights in the splendid dream of being a Minister under the Reformed Government. But when in his efforts to advance in life, he finds himself kicked off the ground on communal considerations, he wants something more powerful, something more active than the charkha. Unless the restless energies of such disappointed people find congenial work, the danger of their being led to acts of violence or leading others to them must remain.

The Need for Prompt Action and Comprehensive Organization

When I say that we want rapid economic development of an all round character what I mean is something like what Mussolini does at present for Italy. The difference between the work of Mussolini and that done in India is that whereas the former acts, we are still in the inquiry stage. We have had in recent years various committees and commissions of enquiry of an economic nature. They are all good in their own way. But it is indeed unfortunate that when other countries like Japan could seize the opportunities created by the War, we were still busy with such enquiries instead of prompt action. By now we have had plenty of such inquiries, and we may add to our information in a similar way in future, whenever necessary. But what we want more urgently is the will and the machinery to take consistent and systematic action to bring about the development of the country in all directions as rapidly as possible. What we lack is an efficient organisation which will take stock of the position from time to time and coordinate the activities of an economic nature, either Government or private, on the one hand, and initiate new activities under a comprehensive plan on the other. If England has a Minister of Unemployment to-day, we need ministers of unemployment in every province.

If by such comprehensive organisation we are able to create careers for our educated young men, and work for the masses, in which men of different capacities will find ample scope and opportunities of a varied character, the need for such dangerous palliatives like communal representation or communal preference in the struggle for jobs will no longer remain. If this is realized by the leaders of both the communities and by the Government, that the problem is essentially economic and that by an active and comprehensive organisation the restless energies now in existence and likely to be created in the near future, can be diverted to useful channels—then instead of finding excuses for communal riots, people will settle down to useful work. We have such an enormous amount of work at our very doors, that if we are all properly employed in carrying it out, we shall be doing good to ourselves individually and advancing the country as whole—and incidentally there will neither be time nor leisure of that mischievous character which finds expression in communal riots.

If out of present chaos, we are to take steps that will lead us on to this very desirable state of affairs, we should all be in earnest, and actively cooperate in devising and working out a comprehensive organisation, which alone can help us to realize the goal. And though private efforts must also be organised and brought in line with public efforts, the initiative must lie with the Government in view of the magnitude of the problem. It is comparatively more easy to work out such a scheme than to work out temporary pacts to patch up the communal tension. It would be a more fruitful, more effective and permanent remedy than the occasional compromises which are flung at us from different quarters. I am not attempting to give such a scheme here, because that would be beyond my scope; my purpose has been to establish the real causes of the communal tension and to indicate that the remedy must also be economic. The general nature of the remedy I have explained; details may be left to experts.

The European Community

But let me give one warning. In any systematic effort of a comprehensive character to remove unemployment in this country and to provide adequate work for all classes of people, we shall be faced with a communal problem of another character. The vested interests of the European community in India, in trade and industry, as well as in Government service will have to be overcome before we can hope to achieve the goal. That more than ourselves, the European community is alive to this possible conflict is seen in their demand before the Simon Commission that though a definite advance towards self-government in India be made, the future legislatures of India should not have the power to legislate in economic matters, which may endanger their position in any way.

Rajani Kanta Das

< *Source*: ILO Archives.

Rajani Kanta Das, one of the earliest professional Indian economists, is little known in India today. He was born in Bengal in 1881. After studying at Calcutta University for four years, he went to the US and studied at Ohio State University, University of Missouri, and University of Chicago to obtain a B.Sc. and M.Sc. in agriculture and an MA in biology. Probably the first Indian in the US to be awarded a doctoral degree in economics, he obtained his Ph.D. in economics from the University of Wisconsin in 1917. His supervisor was Professor John Commons, famous for his work on labour economics and institutional economics.

Das taught at De Paul University and Northwestern University in Chicago during 1919–20. From 1920 to 1922 he was lecturer in economics at the College of the City of New York and New York University. He worked as Special Agent for the Bureau of Labour Statistics of the US government producing a report on Indian migrants on the Pacific Coast. On his return to India he was associated with Visva-Bharati University during 1924–25. From 1925 to 1940, Das was a senior official of the International Labour Office in Geneva. Subsequently, he worked for the US government in China and South Korea. It appears that he spent the rest of his life in the US but I do not have information on his activities after about 1960.

Das's first major publication was *Hindustani Workers on the Pacific Coast* (1923), based upon a study he did for the US Department of Labour. It was a pioneering work which objectively analysed the problems of Indian migrants on the west coast of the US. His other books on factory legislation, industrial efficiency and other such topics made him the foremost authority on Indian labour economics.

As a staff member of the International Labour Organisation (ILO) he contributed reports and other material which were used by the Royal Commission on Labour in 1931. Several major papers, including the one selected for this volume, first appeared in the *International Labour Review*, the official journal of the ILO. These articles provided analyses of major Indian labour problems relating to factory labour and legislation, child labour, and women workers. These were, in many respects, far ahead of their time. For example, his work on child labour is probably one the earliest in the field and is remarkable for its emphasis on education as a solution to the problem. He also published several short pieces on a variety of topics in Indian periodicals.

Major Biographical Sources: The archives of the International Labour Office, Geneva; the archives of the University of Wisconsin, in Madison.

This is certainly one of the earliest works on women workers in India and predates the huge volume of work on this subject in the 1960s and thereafter.* Das examined the increases in the numbers of women employed in plantations, mines, and factories and looked at conditions of employment, health and safety, hours of work, efficiency, wages and incomes, standard of living, welfare, and social conditions. (The section on health and safety has not been reproduced.) Das broke new ground and presented the best evidence available on each of these issues. We may selectively examine his analysis.

The low participation of women in factory employment was explained by Das in terms of four factors: first, social custom, which militated against women working outside the household unless accompanied by their husbands; second, their preoccupation with household industry; third, factory legislation which provided for different working hours and rest periods for men and women and led to the displacement of women, and last, general illiteracy and lack of skills which made them less attractive to employers.

Das regarded women's employment in organized industry as a boon to them. It provided them with new income sources, increased economic independence and self-expression, and provided wider social contact and exposure to new ideas. It also awakened class consciousness and class solidarity among women. However, there were drawbacks. These included poor working conditions relating to age of employment, recruitment, sanitation, safety, hours of work, wages, and insurance. He believed that poor housing was a major problem leading, among other things, to high infant mortality, low female population in industrial centres, and immorality and drunkenness. The special housing needs of single and young women are also stressed by Das.

In perhaps the most important and interesting part of the paper Das clearly set out his views on social policy.

> In spite of biological distinctions between the sexes, indicating functional differences in certain life processes, and in spite of the existing inferior position of women in most communities, which is more or less historical and accidental, men and women are equal partners in Society, and social progress depends largely upon the fullest expression of both in all social, political and industrial spheres of life.

In his view, if women enjoyed the rights and privileges as well as the duties and responsibilities of society, they as well as their communities would gain. Hence he believed that India should adopt policies to equalize social, political, and economic opportunities for men and women alike. To this end he proposed free and compulsory general and technical education for girls, the creation of new industrial opportunities by regulating working conditions to meet their requirements, the abolition of child marriage, the purdah system and the caste system, and the political enfranchisement of women.

* Rajani Kanta Das (1931): 'Woman Labour in India', from *International Labour Review*, vol. 24, 1931, pp. 376–97 and 566–72.

While he may have been influenced by thinking within the ILO, Das was probably expressing his own strong beliefs about what India had to do. As in the case of the other papers in this volume, this paper is refreshingly modern in its approach and views. It moves beyond a concern for greater female participation in work and improving women's welfare at the workplace towards an approach to empower women and make them 'equal partners in Society'.

It is important to note that this paper was written before the publication of the Report of the Royal Commission on Labour, which appeared in 1931. The author made only 'a few changes' in the final version of his paper. (see note 1 of his paper.)

7

Woman Labour in India[1]

Rajani Kanta Das

In accordance with a resolution of the International Labour Conference, the International Labour Office has for some time been engaged on a documentary enquiry into working conditions in certain Asiatic countries. Some of the material collected in the course of this enquiry has been used by Dr Das in the following study of a question on which little information has hitherto been available in an accessible form. After describing the increase in the number of women employed in the main branches of industry (plantations, factories, and mines) since the middle of the last century, he outlines the development of labour legislation over the same period, and then discusses—for each of these branches of industry in turn, and with special reference to women—conditions of employment, health and safety, hours of labour, efficiency of labour, wages and income, standard of living, welfare work, and social conditions. He concludes by indicating some directions in which reform is needed, and suggests a number of measures for the elevation of the political, social, and industrial status of women.

In spite of the fact that women in India are deprived of many social and political privileges, they play an important role in the production of national wealth. According to the census of 1921, which is still the latest source of information on this subject, out of a total of 146 million actual workers or persons engaged in gainful occupations, 46 millions are women.[2] In comparison with some European countries, a very fair proportion of Indian women, therefore, is employed in the industrial activities of the country. Of the total number of persons gainfully occupied, for instance, the percentage of women is 31in India, as compared with 29 in Italy, 30 in England and Wales, and 35 in Germany.[3]

The proportion of women in comparison with men is, however, much larger among the wage earners. Thus, out of 29 million wage earners in 1921, for whom definite information is available,[4] 13 million, or 44 per cent, were women, as shown in Table 7.1.

TABLE 7.1 Classification by Industry of Wage Earners in India, 1921

Category	*Men*	*Women*	*Total*
Field labourers	9,490,210	8,865,284	18,355,494
Farm servants	2,252,860	1,067,753	3,320,613
Domestic servants	1,710,157	821,709	2,531,866
Unspecified workers	2,894,236	2,257,164	5,151,400
Total	16,347,463	13,011,910	29,359,373

Source: *Census Report of India*, 1921, vol. I, pp. 272–3.

The table also shows that the majority of women workers were employed as field labourers and farm servants, forming together 9.9 millions out of a total of 13 millions, or 74 per cent. The preponderance of agricultural workers over other classes is due to the fact that about 73 per cent of the people depend upon agriculture as a means of livelihood.[5] The distinction between field labourers and farm servants is not clearly defined, but in all probability the former are more or less free in the choice of their work, while the latter are attached to the land by custom, if not actually by law. In the unspecified group must be included a large number of casual workers.

The number of women employed in organised industries, such as plantations, factories, and mines, is, however, very small. In 1921, the total number of workers in large-scale industries or in industrial establishments employing 20 persons or more amounted to 2,681,125 of whom only 686,811 persons, or 26 per cent, were women.[6] There are two main reasons why so few women are employed in organised industries. First, in comparison with other countries, the proportion of modern industries is very small in India. The number of persons supported by industry, commerce, and transport, for instance, is only 18 per cent in India, as compared with 65 per cent in Great Britain, 62 per cent in Germany, 50 per cent in the United States, and 47 per cent in France.[7] Secondly, social customs, such as early marriage, the joint family system, and the purdah (seclusion) system, prevent women from taking advantage of economic opportunities outside the household or the immediate neighbourhood.

Nothing is definitely known about the conditions of work and life of the labourers in unorganised industries, such as agriculture and domestic service, nor even in those organised industries which are still outside the scope of Government control. The employment of labour in large-scale industries, such as plantations, factories, and mines, is, however, regulated by labour legislation, and the present study is confined to the conditions of the work and life of women employed in these industries.

The Rise of Women Workers

Women on Plantations

By far the largest number of women workers are employed on plantations, which form one of the most important classes of organised industries in India, especially those for the production of tea, coffee, and rubber. The importance of these industries is best indicated by the fact that in 1928–29 the paid-up capital of the joint-stock companies amounted to Rs 51.59 crores,[8] the value of their products exported to Rs 30 crores,[9] or about 9 per cent of the value of the total export trade of the country, and the total number of tea, coffee, and rubber plantations to 10,867.[10]

According to the census of 1921, out of 1,003,456 on workers on tea, coffee, rubber, cinchona, and indigo plantations, 474,626, or 47 per cent were women.[11] The present number of workers on all kinds of plantations is not known, but the average daily number of workers in 1929 was 930,472 on tea gardens, 92,504 on coffee estates, and 48, 704 on rubber estates, that is, a total of 1,071,680.[12] The number of women on the same basis may be estimated at 503,689. The proportion of women workers on plantations is not only large, but compares very favourably with that of men workers.

There are several reasons why a proportionately large number of women workers is found on plantations. First, plantation work is only a special kind of agricultural industry, and is therefore more congenial to the majority of Indian women who are drawn from the rural districts. Secondly, the very fact that men workers have to live on, or in the vicinity of, the plantations gives their wives and daughters a chance to work with them. Thirdly, the system of labour contract based on the principle of utilising every able-bodied person in the family for labour, and of fixing the wage rates accordingly, compels many women to seek employment in order to balance the family budget. The contract system has been abolished, but the wage rates and the custom of woman labour still remain.

Most of the plantation industries are located in two areas, namely, the North, including Assam and Bengal, which employ an average daily number of 557,484 and 196,899 workers respectively, and the South, including Madras and Coorg, which employ 102,826 and 23,001 workers respectively.

The most important areas in Assam are the Brahmaputra or Assam Valley and the Surma Valley, employing 400,995 and 156,489 workers respectively; in Bengal, Jalpaiguri (the Doors) and Darjeeling (including the Terai), employing 125,632 and 65,522 workers respectively; and in Madras, the Nilgiris, Coimbatore (the Anamalais), and Malabar, employing 43,560, 30,222, and 19,768 workers respectively.[13]

Tea cultivation is by far the most important plantation industry in India. As noted before, out of 1,071,680 workers, 930,472, or 87 per cent, were employed on tea plantations in 1929. Although the tea gardens are scattered all over India, by far the majority of them are located in Assam. Thus, out of a total of 930,427 workers employed in all tea gardens in 1929, 557,484, or about 60 per cent, were in Assam.[14] Assam not only employs the largest number of tea-garden workers, but it is also one of the oldest centres in which plantation labour began to appear, and for which plantation legislation first began to be enacted. The condition of women workers on plantations may therefore be best studied in connection with those in Assam tea gardens.

The first available records on labour in Assam gardens are for 1877, when there were 59,923 men, 50,752 women, and 46,544 children living on the plantations; in 1929–1930 these figures stood respectively at 341,580, 283,730, and 463,652, as shown in Table 7.2, indicating an increase of over five times in the case of both men and women and of about nine times in the case of children. The table also shows that the largest increase in the number of all these groups took place in 1919–20. This was partly due to the industrial boom at the end of the war, and partly to the sudden increase in the number of immigrants as a result of the previous year's famine in a larger number of recruiting districts.

TABLE 7.2 Labour Population on Assam Tea Gardens in Specified Years*

Year	*Men*	*Women*	*Children*	*Total*
1877	59,923	50,752	46,544	157,219
1900	204,492	205,603	252,376	662,471
1919–20	323,781	305,850	480,733	1,110,364
1929–30	341,580	283,730	463,652	1,088,962

Note: * Average annual strength, except for 1929–30, the figure for which represents the number remaining at the end of the year. Adapted from the *Reports on Immigrant Labour in the Province of Assam* for the years indicated.

The number of women who are actually employed is, however, much smaller than the number living on plantations. Thus, out of 283,730 women living on tea gardens in Assam in 1929–30, only 231,715, or 81 per cent, were workers.[15]

Until recently, a considerable number of plantation labourers were employed under the penal contract and the indenture system, which were introduced by the Assam Labour and Immigration Act of 1863, the Madras Planters' Act of 1903, and the Workmen's Breach of Contract Act of 1859. In Assam tea gardens, for instance, out of 110,675 labourers in 1877, 46,765 or 41 per cent were indentured labourers, and of the latter 21,656 were women. Between that year and 1915–16, when the indenture system was abolished, there was great variation in the number of indentured women. It will be seen that the number of indentured women rose as high as 69,056 in 1897 and declined to 2,152 in 1915–16.

Table 7.3 Number of Indentured Workers on Assam Tea Gardens in Specified Years*

Year	*Men*	*Women*	*Total*
1877	25,109	21,656	46,765
1897#	79,136	69,056	148,192
1915–16	2,910	2,152	5,062

Notes: * Compiled from the *Reports on Immigrant Labour in the Province of Assam*, for the years indicated.

In 1897, the number of indentured workers was the largest.

As might be expected, the number of indentured workers as compared with free workers was highest in the early years, but gradually declined with the growth of settlements on tea gardens and with increasing facilities in transportation. Moreover, with increasing restrictions on the indenture system, planters found it more profitable to employ their workers under the Workmen's Breach of Contract Act. The actual number of women employed under this Act is not known, but the total number of workers, both men and women, amounted to 278,242 in 1921–22.[16] The Act was repealed on 1 April 1926, but 17,978 workers were still under contract in Assam Valley up to 3 March of that year. At present there is no worker under the penal contract or the indenture system, except in Coorg, where it will terminate by the end of 1931.[17]

Women in Factories

The most important class of organised industries, however, is factories, especially cotton and jute mills, which were started near Bombay and Calcutta in 1851 and 1854 respectively and have since then become India's premier industries.[18] The importance of these industries may be seen from the fact that in 1928–29 the paid-up capital of the joint stock companies was Rs 37.9 crores in the cotton mills and Rs 25.9 crores in the jute mills, and the total number of looms and spindles amounted to 148,847 and 7,653,033 respectively in the former, and 52,847 and 1,108,147 respectively in the latter.[19] The number of cotton and jute mills rose also from 58 and 22 respectively in 1879–1880 to 293 and 93 in 1928.[20] In the meantime, the factory industry as a whole has also made immense progress, the number of all classes of factories rising from 656 in 1892 to 7,863 in 1928.[21]

The earliest available records for workers in all classes of factories are for 1892, when the total number of workers was 316,816, consisting of 254,336 men, 43,592 women, and 18,888 children. In 1928 the total number of factory workers amounted to 1,520,315, consisting of 1,216,471 men, 252,933 women, and 50,911 children, showing an increase of 480 per cent for women as compared with 378 per cent for men and 170 per cent for children.

TABLE 7.4 Average Daily Number of Factory Workers in Specified Years*

Year#	*Factories*	*Men*	*Women*	*Children*	*Total*
1892	656	254,336	43,592	18,888	316,816
1912	2,654	685,822	130,025	53,796	869,643
1922	5,144	1,086,457	206,887	67,658	1,361,002
1928	7,863	1,216,471	252,933	50,911	1,520,315

Notes: * *Statistical Abstract for British India*, 1900–01, p. 265; 1923, p. 654; *Statistics of Factories subject to the Indian Factories Act*, 1922 and 1928.

The years chosen to indicate the number of workers are those when a new or amended Act came into force.

The real increase in the number of women is, however, still greater than that indicated above. Since 1892 there has been an increase in the minimum and maximum ages of girls, and many girls between the ages of 12 and 15, who were included among women before 1922, have been excluded from them since then.

There are several reasons for the proportionately larger increase in the number of factory women. First, increasing transport facilities have opened up greater opportunities to women in factories. Secondly, the gradual amelioration of working conditions has also attracted more women to factories. Thirdly, the stricter regulation of the employment of children has decreased their number and increased that of women.

Table 7.4 also shows that in proportion to men, the number of women is very small in factories in India. Thus, out of 1,520,315 workers in 1928, 1,216,417 or 80 per cent were men, 252,933 or 16 per cent were women, and 50,911 or 4 per cent were children. Including girls, the total number of women was 260,848 or 17 per cent, as compared with 51 per cent in Japan.[22] What is still more surprising is the fact that even in textile mills, in which by far the majority of the workers are women in other countries, the number of women is rather insignificant. Out of 657,433 workers in cotton and jute mills in 1928, only 113,546 were women and 3,150 girls, these forming together only 18 per cent of the total number of workers, as compared with 81 per cent in the textile factories of Japan.[23]

There are various reasons for so small a proportion of women workers in factories. In the first place, social custom, to which reference has already been made, acts as a great obstacle to the occupation of women outside their immediate household, unless they are accompanied by their husbands and relatives, as in the case of plantations. In the second place, both spinning and weaving, especially the latter, are still carried on in the household with the help of women. According to the census of 1921, there were about two million hand looms in seven out of the ten provinces of India.[24] In the third place, the provisions of factory legislation fixing different working hours and rest periods for men and women were also responsible for the tardy growth of the number of women workers in textile industries. After the enactment of the Factories Act of 1891, for instance, 259 women were discharged from the Ahmedabad mills, where they were doing the same kind of work as men.[25] Finally, general illiteracy and lack of skill have made women as workers less profitable to employers in India.

Since women workers are mostly employed in textile mills, the majority of them live in Bombay and Bengal. In 1928, for instance, out of 252,933 women workers, 75,498 or over 30 per cent were in Bengal and 75,092 or over 29 per cent in Bombay. These were followed by Madras, with 32,095 or 12 per cent, and the Central Provinces and Berar, with 24,591 or

9 per cent. The remaining 18 per cent were distributed chiefly among Assam and Burma.

TABLE 7.5 Distribution by Provinces of Women Factory Workers in India in 1928*

Province	*Number*	*Per cent of total*
Bengal	75,498	30
Bombay	75,092	30
Madras	32,095	13
Central Provinces and Berar	24,591	10
Others	45,657	18
Total	252,933	100

Note: * Adapted from *Statistics of Factories subject to the India Factories Act*, 1928, p. 26.

Women in Mines

Another organised industry which employs a considerable number of women is mining. Mining is an important industry in which the investments of joint-stock companies amounted to Rs 146 crores[26] and the value of the products to Rs 29 crores in the year 1928–29.[27] Of the various mining industries, such as coal, manganese, mica, iron, and lead, the most important is coal. In 1929, the total production of coal was 23 million tons,[28] and of 1,732 mines working under the Indian Mining Act, 584 were collieries.[29]

The earliest year for which records of mining labour are available is 1901, when, out of 104,660 workers, 69,025 were men, 30,488 women, and 5,147 children. As a result of the Act of 1923, the employment of children under the age of 13 came to an end in 1926. In 1929, the number of men was 199,045 and of women 70,656, as shown in Table 7.6, thus indicating increases of 174 and 160 per cent respectively.

By far the largest number of mining workers are employed in coal mines. In 1929, for instance, out of a total of 269,701 workers, 165,658, or 61 per cent, were in coal mines, and of the latter 42,477, or 25 per cent, were women. Most of these women were employed in the coalfields of Jharia in Bihar and Orissa and of Raniganj in Bengal, employing 18,086 or about 43 per cent and 12,667 or 30 per cent of the women respectively. Of the other mines, manganese mines employed 27,233 persons, of whom 11,784 were women, and mica mines employed 16,555 persons, of whom 3,442 were women.[30]

TABLE 7.6 Number of Mining Workers in Specified Years*

Year#	*Men*	*Women*	*Children*@	*Total*
1901	69,025	30,488	5,147	104,660
1924	164,402	87,434	6,381	258,217
1929	199,045	70,656	–	269,701

Notes: * Compiled from the *Annual Report of the Chief Inspector of Mines in India*, for the respective years.

The years chosen to indicate the number of workers are those when a new or amended Act came into force.

@ Children under 12 years of age; cf. *Annual Report of the Chief Inspector of Mines in India*, 1924, p. 2.

A large number of women are employed underground. In 1901, out of 30,481 women, 19,247 or 63 per cent were employed underground, and in 1929, out of 70,656 women, 24,089 or 34 per cent were employed underground and at the same time 28,728 or 40 per cent were employed in open workings—a classification which has been adopted since 1926. A considerable number of women who were formerly included among the workers employed underground are now classified as in open workings.

TABLE 7.7 Number of Women Employed in Mines in Specified Years*

Year	*Total*	*Employed in open workings*	*Employed underground*	
			Number	*Per cent*
1901	30,481	–	19,247	63
1924	87,434	–	60,375	69
1929	70,656	28,728	24,089	34

Note: * Compiled from the *Annual Report of the Chief Inspector of Mines in India*, for the years indicated.

The women employed underground are found mostly in coal mines. Thus, out of 24,089 women employed underground in 1929, 21,880 or 90 per cent were in coal mines; of the remainder, 1,483 were in mica mines and 726 in other mines.[31]

Labour Legislation[32]

The rise and growth of these industries, in which an increasing number of workers, and especially of women and children, were employed, made it necessary for the Government to bring them under control by legislative measures. This legislation has been enacted according to the needs of each industry, and even of each province, and there is therefore no uniform legislation for all classes of workers throughout the whole country.

The first organised industry to come under legislative regulation was plantations. Plantation legislation in India dates back to 1863, when, for the control of the abuses arising from the recruitment of labour by contractors, an Act was passed requiring recruiters to be licensed and emigrants to be registered. The Act was amended in 1865, fixing the scale of wages, making desertion and indolence on the part of labourers under contract punishable by law, and granting planters the power to arrest absconders without warrant. Thus the indenture system was established, under which men and women were employed on tea gardens in Assam.

From 1870 to 1915 the Act was amended several times, introducing such changes as free recruitment subject to civil contract, recognition of local contract, stricter restriction of recruitment, and better arrangement for sanitation. But by the Act of 1915 the indenture system was abolished, recruitment by contractors was prohibited, and provision was made for the creation of a Labour Board for the supervision of recruitment for Assam by local agents and garden *sardars*.

Reference has already been made to the application by planters of the Workmen's Breach of Contract Act of 1859. This Act was passed for the benefit of employers in general and was taken advantage of by planters. It gave them a hold over the workers and at the same time saved them the expense of importing labour from abroad. In 1920 the terms of the Act were somewhat modified, and in 1925 the Act was repealed, as well as the two sections of the Indian Penal Code under which workmen could be punished for neglect of duty. The new Act came into force on 1 April 1926. In 1927 the Government of Madras also repealed the Planters' Labour Act of 1903 which provided criminal penalties for breaches of contract, the new Act coming into force in the beginning of 1929. In the meantime the Coorg Assembly passed an Act in 1926 retaining criminal penalties for such employment until the end of 1931. Thus, except in Coorg, both the penal sanction and the indenture system under which women could be employed have been abolished all over British India.

The origin of factory legislation also dates back to the seventies, when attention was drawn to the necessity of regulating labour in the rising cotton mill-industry, which employed a large number of women and children and which at the same time aroused the spirit of rivalry among the Lancashire manufacturers. The first Factories Act of 1881,which failed to give any protection to women, was amended in 1891, and the hours of labour for women were restricted to 11 a day. A new Act was passed in 1911, but it did not affect the conditions of work in factories as far as women were concerned.

The war was followed by the inauguration of the International Labour Organisation by the Treaty of Versailles in 1919. In the same year the International Labour Conference adopted several Draft Conventions and Recommendations, of which the most important, from the point of view of women, are the Draft Conventions on hours, minimum age of employment for children, and the employment of women at night, and the Recommendations for the prevention of anthrax, the protection of women and children against lead poisoning, and the prohibition of the use of white phosphorus in the manufactures of matches. Although the general principle of the Hours Convention was 48 hours a week, a concession was made to India and the weekly hours of work were fixed at 60. The minimum age of employment for children was also fixed at 12 for India, instead of 14 as in other countries. Some of these Draft Conventions and Recommendations were given effect to by the amendment of the Factory Act in 1922. The Factory Act was further amended in 1923, 1926, and 1931, bringing about minor changes, especially regarding the employment of children and the provision of better safety devices.

One of the most important effects of these successive amendments is the extension of the scope of the Act to smaller industrial establishments employing from 100 to 20 persons, and even 10 persons in special cases at the option of local Governments. Many small establishments, such as cotton ginning and jute pressing mills, in which a large number of women are employed, have thus been brought under factory legislation.

The next important class of labour legislation relates to mines, which, although established about the middle of the last century, did not come under legislative control until 1901, when the first Mines Act was passed. This Act only defined a mine and provided for the appointment of the chief inspector of mines, who was empowered to stop the employment of children under twelve and of women in a mine where conditions, in his opinion, were dangerous to their health and safety. After the adoption by the International Labour Conference in 1919 of the Hours Convention, which applies to mining industries, and the ratification of this Convention by the Government of India in 1921, it became necessary to amend the existing mining law, and a new Mines Act was passed in 1923. By this Act, the hours were limited to 54 a week for underground work and 60 for surface work, and the days of work were limited to six a week; and at the same time the employment of children under 13 years of age was prohibited. The Act was again amended in 1928, limiting the daily hours of work to 12 in 24 hours. But mines can work two shifts of 12 hours each if the shifts do not overlap.

Transportation is another class of organised industry which has been brought under legislative control as far as the employment of labour is concerned. But there are very few women employed in transport industries. Among the other classes of legislation which concern the employment of women must be included the Acts relating to social insurance, trade unionism, industrial disputes, and especially maternity benefits, some of which will be discussed later on.

The most important question of labour legislation, however, is administration, which differs for different industries in India. The enactment of plantation legislation lies within the power of provincial governments, subject to the approval of the Central Government. When the indenture system existed, plantation legislation made specific provision for the forwarding of the recruits from the place of residence to the place of work, and also for health and sanitation on the plantations themselves. With the abolition of the indenture system, administration has been greatly simplified. The enforcement of the law is left mostly to the *ex-officio* inspectors, consisting of deputy commissioners, assistant commissioners, civil servants and other agents.[33] Mining legislation is within the competence of the Central Government, and inspection is carried on under the supervision of the Chief Inspector of Mines all over British India, which, for convenience, is divided into two circuits. The staff consists of a Chief Inspector, three inspectors, and four junior inspectors. The administration of factory legislation is different from both kinds of legislation mentioned above. While the enactment of the legislation is the concern of the Central Government, its administration is left to provincial governments, which make special rules, subject to the approval of the Central Government, to give effect to the law. The inspecting staff differs in different provinces, the largest being eleven in Bombay, one of whom is a woman.[34]

Some idea of the efficiency of the inspection may be had from the proportion of industrial establishments annually inspected as compared with their total number. As far as the inspection of the Assam tea gardens is concerned, it must be mentioned that under the Act of 1882 as modified in 1904–05 and 1915, tea gardens employing 50 persons or more are liable to inspection only every two years. A few gardens are also specially selected for inspection in a particular year because of their health conditions in previous years. According to these rules, out of 868 Assam tea gardens, employing 50 persons or more, in 1929–30 only 434 were liable to inspection, consisting of 411 which were not inspected in the preceding year and 23 which were specially selected for annual inspection. Out of this number, 421 were inspected.[35] In other words, over 52 per cent of the larger tea gardens were left uninspected during the year. Similarly, out of 1,732 mines in 1929, only 1,016, or 59 per cent, were inspected, although some of them were inspected more than once.[36] The system of factory inspection, however, is much more satisfactory. Out of 7,863 factories in 1928, 7093, or 90 per cent, were inspected during the year.[37] As a rule, permanent factories are inspected once a year and even more. It is only some of the seasonal factories and out-of-the-way factories that escape annual inspection.

Another important question in connection with the administration of the law is enforcement. This involves prosecution and conviction for contraventions of the law, and the infliction of penalties. The number of persons convicted increased from 72 in 1924 to 99 in 1929 in the mines, and from 223 in 1923 to 419 in 1928 in the factories.[38] This increase in the number of convictions is mostly due to the strict enforcement of the law.

Employment of Labour

Supply of Labour

The rise of organised industries in different parts of the country has created a new demand for labour, but in spite of immense potentialities there was until recently a shortage of labour in factories and there still is on plantations and in mines. The movement of labour from the sources of supply to the centres of industry is difficult in India for several reasons, of which the most important are ignorance of industrial opportunities outside the immediate neighbourhood, the caste and joint family systems, lack of transport facilities, and the extreme poverty of the masses. Some of the industrial centres are not attractive to labourers because of their unhealthiness, low wages, and bad housing. Moreover, women have some additional difficulties inasmuch as they are prevented by social custom from free movement, and can go to look for work only with their men folk.

Different industrial centres draw their labour supply from different sources. Plantations in the South are mostly located in the sources of labour supply and recruit their labourers from the surrounding districts. The tea gardens of Bengal depend upon Nepal, Sikkim, Chota Nagpur, and the Santhal Parganas for their labour supply. The Assam tea gardens draw their labour force from a much wider region, namely, Bengal, Bihar, the United Provinces, Chota Nagpur, the Santhal Parganas, and the northern part of Madras, only about one-tenth of the labour supply being recruited from the locality.[39] A considerable number of these workers belong to aboriginal races.

The workers in mines may be classified in three groups, namely, (1) those who belong to the locality, (2) those who have come there and settled permanently, and (3) those who are recruited from outside. The last group, however, is the largest. In the coalfields of Jharia and Raniganj, for instance, about 75 per cent and 50 per cent respectively of the workers are recruited from the Santhal Parganas, Birbhum, Hazaribagh, Munghyr, and Bilaspur.[40] The majority of the mining workers also belong to aboriginal races. As far as the women workers are concerned, about 75 per cent are recruited in the locality.[41]

Factories are scattered all over the country and the sources of labour supply also vary in different industrial centres. Bombay draws its labour supply from surrounding districts, provinces, and even Indian States, although the bulk of its workers come from the nearby districts, such as Ratnagiri.[42] Calcutta depends for its labour upon Northern Madras, Orissa, Bihar, the Central Provinces, and the United Provinces. In the early years, the Bengalis supplied labour to the jute mills, but they have been gradually replaced by the hardier and cheaper labour from outside.[43] Jamshedpur gets its skilled labourers from all parts of India and its unskilled labourers mostly from aboriginal races in the neighbourhood.[44] Madras, Ahmedabad, Cawnpore, and Nagpur also depend on outside labour, although they draw it mostly from the areas closer at hand.[45]

Most of the workers, however, are still attached to their native villages. A large number of workers in Bombay city, for instance, live there as boarders, although they are married, and keep their dependants in their village. Even those who live with their family in industrial centres have some of its members living in the village. The average working-class family, for instance, consists in Bombay of 4.8 persons and in Ahmedabad of 4 persons, of whom 0.6 and 0.13 persons respectively live in the country.[47] The workers visit their homes regularly, either in the planting or harvesting seasons, or at some other convenient time, depending upon the seasonal fluctuations in industry or on climatic conditions in the industrial centres.

A permanent class of workers who are solely dependent upon wages as a means of livelihood and are wholly detached from the land is, however, rapidly growing in most of the industrial centres, such as Bombay, Ahmedabad, Cawnpore, Jharia, and Raniganj. Every year a number of people are driven from the country to the city by a diversity of causes, such as the scarcity of cultivable land, lack of suitable secondary industries, extreme poverty and heavy indebtedness, and the growing sense of inequity to which some of them are subject because of the caste system and untouchability. The amenities of town life are also attractive to some workers. With the increasing pressure on land and the industrialisation of the country, there is no doubt that the number of industrial workers will grow in the near future.[47]

A comparatively large number of women are found on plantations where workers live in families. This is due to the fact that plantations offer work to all the members of the family. Even the children from the age of the five are found working there. This used to be more or less true also in the case of mines, where the employment of children under 13 was permissible until 1926. The gradual elimination of women from underground employment is also likely to affect the number of families that may be willing to live in mining centres. The number of families living in the factory towns is, however, very small. Single women are also few in number among workers. Women of high caste scarcely ever go to work in factories unless they offend family traditions in some way or other and are thrown out of the caste or the family circle,[48] and those of lower caste are too ignorant to avail themselves of industrial opportunities in a town unless they happen to be in the close vicinity. Almost all the girls are married before they become eligible for work in factories and mines.

Systems of Recruitment

The scarcity of labour supply, as shown above, has led employers to devise different systems of recruitment, which may be classed under two headings, the direct and the indirect. The former means recruitment by employers themselves or by their paid and accredited officers, and the latter recruitment through intermediaries. In some cases the two systems may be modified or combined.

Almost all the labourers on plantations in the South are recruited through contractors called *kanganis* or *maistries*, who receive from planters loans free of interest from which they advance the money to individual labourers or families wishing to go to plantations.[49] The Bengal tea gardens recruit their labourers through *sardars* or agents. By far the majority of the workers are now settled on or near the gardens. The Assam tea gardens, however, have experienced great difficulties in recruiting their labour force. After long experiment with the contractor system, they have now adopted what is called the *sardari* system. The sardars are common workers who are sent out to their native villages for recruitment. They work under the supervision of local agents and the Assam Labour Board referred to above. In 1929–30, for instance, there were 42,829 *sardars*, including both men and women, who recruited 58,150 persons, that is, an average of 1.35 per sardar.[50] The essential feature of this system is the recruitment of families rather than individuals.

There are several systems of recruiting labour for mines. First, some of the mines recruit their workers through contractors, but employ them under direct management. Most of the mines, however, engage raising contractors for mining coal and loading wagons for a fixed rate of payment. About 70 per cent of the output at Jharia and 40 per cent at Raniganj is mined by raising contractors.[51] In this case, the workers are recruited and employed by the contractors themselves. Secondly, some of the *sardars* bring workers to the mines and employ them in gangs, undertaking the responsibility for their work. Thirdly, most of the mines send some members of their staff to visit villages and make advances to prospective workers.

The system of labour recruitment for factories also varies in different centres. A number of migratory and local workers, specially of the unskilled type, present themselves at industrial establishments and are appointed on the spot, while others are recruited in their native villages by employers' agents.[52] The most common system of recruiting labourers is, however, through supervisors or foremen, both men and women, who are variously called jobbers, *sardars*, *mukkadems*, or *maistries*. The workers often belong to the same village or the same caste as the foreman.[53] The essential feature of this system is that the workers recruited by a foreman are employed directly under him, so that the foreman's control over the workers remains as long as the latter retain their jobs.

The *sardari* system of recruitment is objectionable on several grounds. First, it is liable to abuses. In the earlier days contractors and *arcattis* (professional recruiters) were accused of fraud, deception, and misrepresentation. Even to-day, garden *sardars* are not altogether above reproach, especially as they expect a commission of Rs 10 in the Surma Valley and Rs 20 in the Assam Valley for each recruit. Women are specially liable to become their victims. Secondly, it is wasteful. It has been estimated that every year the Assam tea gardens send out as *sardars* an average of 7 per cent of their adult labourers to recruiting districts, of whom about one-half are unsuccessful and about one-third never return to the gardens. Thirdly, it is very costly. The cost of recruitment for mining industries, for instance, is estimated to be an average of 3 or 4 annas per ton of coal raised.[54] On the basis of the average *per capita* production of 135 tons in 1929,[55] the total cost would amount to from Rs 25 to Rs 34 per person per annum. The advances made to recruiters by plantations in the South would average about Rs 15 for each labourer.[56] The cost is, however, highest for Assam tea-garden labourers, for whom the average cost has been estimated to be Rs 150 each. That the cost of recruitment for factories is also very high may easily be imagined. It must be remembered that the expense of recruitment ultimately comes from the wage budget.

The *jobber* system of recruitment as existing in factories is liable to more serious abuses. First, it leads to graft, which is prevalent in Bombay and other places. 'That the system leads to intensive "graft"', writes the Government of Bombay in its *Memorandum to the Royal Commission on Labour*, 'is indisputable, and both the jobbers and their female counterparts, the *naikins*, levy contributions from the workers.'[57] Secondly, it has been reported that besides paying fees for a job, the workers have to continue to pay a part of their wages during the continuance of their service.[58] Thirdly, it is responsible for inefficiency, owing to the fact that it is not the best workers who are chosen by the jobbers, but those who can pay them the most, or in whom they are specially interested.

Nature of Occupations

Although organised industries have opened new fields of work for women, the kind and the number of occupations which are open to them are very limited. Women are employed on almost all tea gardens. Most of the mines, especially collieries, also employ women; but the prohibition of their work underground will eliminate a considerable number of them from mining work. In factories their work is confined mostly to textile mills and to seasonal factories connected with ginning and pressing cotton, pressing jute, milling rice, curing tea, and manufacturing shellac. The women workers in cotton ginning and pressing mills amount to half the total number of workers employed in these mills.

Women's work consists mostly of plucking on tea gardens; of carrying loads in coal, iron, and salt mines; of drying, spreading and turning rice, moving it from the hullers, and winnowing bran in rice mills; of stripping, grinding and sieving in shellac factories; and of drawing, roving, and moving receivers and hand-sewing in jute mills. Only in those districts where there is a scarcity of labour are women found in other departments of a jute mill.

In mills women are employed in a variety of occupations, such as winding, reeling, ring spinning, slubbing, mixing, carding, and warping,[59] but by far the largest number are employed in the first three occupations. Out of 12,072 women employed in 16 mills in Bombay in 1926, for instance, 4,691 or 38 per cent were winders, 3,140 or 26 per cent ring spinners, and 2,097 or 17 per cent reelers, as shown in the table below. In other words, over four-fifths of the women workers were employed in these three departments of cotton mills.

TABLE 7.8 Women's Occupations in Bombay Cotton Mills*

Department	*Number of women*	*Per cent of total*
Winding	4,691	38
Ring spinning	3,140	26
Reeling	2,097	17
Others	2,144	19
Total	12,072	100

Note: * Adapted from *Report of an Enquiry into Wages and Hours of Labour in the Cotton Mill Industry in 1926*, p. 80. Bombay, Government Central Press, 1930.

In certain kinds of work women's labour is preferable to that of men, but the main reason why women are employed in organised industries is the cheapness of their labour. Sometimes they are preferred to children because of their steadiness. A certain number of women also seem to be necessary to keep the men content.[60] This limitation of occupations for women lessens the demand for their labour and reduces the scale of their wages.

Conclusions

From the foregoing analysis it will be seen that women in India contribute as much to the production of national wealth as those in other industrially advanced countries. Of the women gainfully occupied, about one-third are wage-paid workers, and of the latter only a small proportion is engaged in organised industries. The advent of even so small a number of women in modern industries has given rise to several economic, political, and social problems.

It must be pointed out, first of all, that organised industries are a great boon to women themselves. Their most beneficial effects are as follows. In the first place, they have opened up new sources of income to many women who are in urgent need of supplementing their family income or of supporting themselves and their dependents. In the second place, economic independence has given women a better chance of self-expression. Being always dependent upon their fathers, husbands, or sons, most Indian women have scarcely any opportunity for an independent existence either in thought or in action. Independent living, away from the native place, often saves them from the tyranny of social custom, which closely regulates every step of their lives. What is of more importance is that industrial centres offer larger social contact, more new ideas, and greater educational facilities, which are themselves a great stimulus to the growth of their individuality. In the third place, the class struggles, common in all modern industries, have awakened class consciousness and class solidarity even among women, who take an important part in all industrial disputes and make common cause in all affairs of class interest. This growing power for concerted action has special significance in the struggle for civic rights and duties in industrial centres where most of them live.

These economic, social, and political benefits to women are not without their special significance for society as a whole. In the first place, the increasing pressure on land and the decline of cottage industries have created extensive under-employment among both men and women. Organised industries have not only created new industrial opportunities for the people but also equipped them with the modern tools and technique of production, which alone can make them industrially efficient against foreign competition. In the second place, organised industries have already helped in breakdown of the caste system, untouchability, the *purdah* system, the joint family system, and child marriage, which have so long retarded the progress of society. In the third place, struggles for civic rights and duties, which have become a common feature in all industrial centres, have given rise to a new civic consciousness even among women, and thus have paved the way for the growth of modern democracy in India.

However beneficial organised industries may be to women, they are not without great danger to society, even to women themselves, unless some of the problems raised by the entry of women into modern industries are adequately solved. Insanitary conditions, fatal accidents, long hours, low wages and sweating, especially for women, and overcrowding and congestion have already appeared in almost all the industrial centres of India. These problems may be conveniently considered from three distinct points of views, namely: (1) working conditions; (2) living conditions; and (3) social policy.

The most important problems of working conditions are those relating to age of employment, recruitment, sanitation, safety, hours, wages, and insurance. Legislative measures were undertaken by the Government in connection with these questions as early as 1863 for plantation women, 1891 for factory women, and 1901 for mining women. Since the inauguration of the International Labour Office and the adoption by the International Labour Conference of the various Conventions and Recommendations, Indian labour legislation has been revised and amended with special reference to the work of women so as to bring it into harmony with the standard set up by the Conference.

An important change needed for labour legislation is the regulation of the minimum age for the employment of children on plantations and the creation of half-time workers on plantations and in mines on the same basis as in the case of factories, where boys and girls between the ages of 12 and 15 are so employed. Plantation legislation has not yet put any restriction on the employment of children. Some of them begin work even at the age of 5 or 6. Mining legislation prohibits the employment of children under 13 and allows them to work full time after that age. The main object of this provision was the prohibition of underground employment of children, especially of girls under that age. But underground employment is in process of elimination and the time has come for the creation of half-time workers in surface work in mines.

That the age of 12 is too low for the employment of children cannot be denied, but the minimum age of employment and maximum age of compulsory education should be raised gradually for the sake of convenience.

What India chiefly needs to-day is free and compulsory primary education, the principles of which have already been accepted and applied to a limited extent. In order to be worth while, education should be compulsory up to the age of 12 and the maximum age of primary education and the minimum age of employment should be raised gradually up to 14 as early as possible.

The system of recruitment, whether direct or indirect, entailing as it does waste and corruption, shows the necessity for labour exchanges to be established by the Government. Provisions for sanitation and safety are inadequate, and need the introduction of newer methods, in accordance with the latest discoveries and inventions. Moreover, the time has come to reduce hours of work, which in the Washington Hours Convention of 1919 were provisionally fixed at 60 a week as a special concession to India, as compared with 57 hours a week for Japan and 48 hours a week for other countries.

The rate of wages is a very complicated question, as it, is in general outside the scope of labour legislation. But, in view of the fact that women are often 'sweated' in many industries and are unable to make collective bargains, it is the duty of the Government to fix a minimum wage, such as is already in existence in several countries, and has recently been recommended by the International Labour Conference. Moreover, the customs of long intervals and delay in wage payment, and of deductions by way of fines, are questions entirely within the scope of Government regulation.

As regards social insurance, it might be said that the scope of workmen's compensation is too much limited. The gradual separation of workers from their homesteads and the breakdown of the joint family system, in which the disabled, destitute, and even workless always found an asylum with some of their relatives, however distant, have made it imperative for the existing Workmen's Compensation Act to be extended and elaborated into a general social insurance system, covering all kinds of risk, including unemployment.

Administration of the labour law is another problem. It has been noted that the system of inspection is very inadequate, especially in mines and plantations. Labour legislation has no value unless it is enforced. Moreover, there is a necessity for employing women inspectors and women doctors in all industries.

The extension of the scope of the existing legislation is still another problem. It has been noted that labour legislation in India was enacted with special reference to particular industries and particular provinces. The time has come to consolidate all these measures into a series of general labour laws, covering groups of similar and kindred industries, and extending the scope of each to smaller establishments.

What is still more important is the improvement of the general conditions of life, including housing, education, recreation and other kinds of social activities for enriching life and increasing moral and spiritual values.

Among these conditions the most important is housing. After the primary needs of food and clothing, a woman requires a house where she can build up a home for her children as well as for herself and her husband. A home is in fact one of the best expressions of a woman's life. The lack of proper housing is the cause of high infant mortality, and of the low female population in the industrial centres, the prevalence of immorality, drunkenness, and gambling among men, the migratory habit of the working population, and the shortage of skilful and reliable workers.

The supply of housing accommodation by employers leads to the growth of a servile mentality and its supply by landlords tends to rack-renting. Nor can the workers be expected to build their own houses in large cities like Calcutta and Bombay. It therefore behoves the public and semi-public organisations to supply housing for industrial workers in large cities, where the workers can live without the fear of eviction and on payment of an economic rent.

A further question is the supply of accommodation for single women, including girls. For lack of proper facilities, many women in all industrial centres have become victims of unscrupulous men, both morally and economically. What is needed is that employers should be made to build dormitories for such women, and to employ responsible women for their care and supervision. The improvement of the living conditions of single women will not only raise the moral standard in industrial centres, but will also attract a large number of women from the country and help to solve the question of labour supply.

That housing accommodation must be accompanied by the provisions of proper sanitation, including adequate drainage, sanitary conservancy, and sufficient drinking water, goes without saying. What is equally important is to provide educational and recreational facilities, which are essential for the physical, intellectual, and moral development of women workers. While the undertaking of such work by the workers themselves must be encouraged their own efforts in this direction may scarcely be sufficient for the purpose.

Welfare work should therefore be undertaken by social service workers at the expense and under the supervision of all municipal governments.

But behind all these questions lies the development of a social policy towards women workers in modern industries. The work of women in modern industries is not only beneficial to women themselves and to society, as noted before, but it has become inevitable. India is already an industrially important country, and, with increasing political and economic independence, industrialisation is bound to grow at a rapid rate in India, drawing a larger and larger number of women into modern organised industries.

The underlying principle of this social policy must be the fact that in spite of biological distinctions between the sexes, indicating functional differences in certain life processes, and in spite of the existing inferior position of women in most communities, which is more or less historical and accidental, men and women are equal partners in society, and social progress depends largely upon the fullest expression of both in all social, political, and industrial spheres of life. This implies that women should not only enjoy the rights and privileges, but should also undertake all the duties and responsibilities of society. The realisation of this fact has led to a rapid improvement in all kinds of women's activities in all advanced countries, benefiting not only women themselves but also the communities of which they form a part. The static and backward condition of India is to no mean extent due to the inferior position of her women. It is thus a question not only of social justice but also of imperative necessity that India should adopt a policy tending to equalise social, political, and industrial opportunities for men and women alike.

The problem of developing this social policy towards women workers is a complicated one under the present social, political, and economic conditions of India, and involves several measures, of which the most important are as follows:

1. Free and compulsory education—both general and industrial—for girls, with co-education especially in the primary school, up to the minimum age of employment; provision for continuation or extension schools for all half-time working girls until the minimum age of marriage, which is at present 14;
2. The creation of new industrial opportunities for women by regulating working conditions with special reference to their ability and aptitude;

3. The abolition of child marriage, the purdah system, and the caste system with a view to giving women opportunities for devoting their childhood and early youth to the development of body and mind and to the achievement of character and individuality;
4. The political enfranchisement of women on the same basis as men, with a view to developing among them the sense of civic responsibility on the one hand and the power of taking the initiative in improving their own social and economic conditions on the other.

In short, the object of this social policy should be the elevation of the political, social, and industrial status of women, so that they may become not only wage earners but also good mothers, intelligent citizens, and responsible members of society.

Notes

1. In the preparation of this article, the writer has utilised his works on *Factory Labour in India*, Berlin, 1923; and *Plantation Labour in India*, Calcutta, 1931. Since the writing of the article, the *Report of the Royal Commission on Labour in India* has been published (London, H.M. Stationery Office, 1931). Due reference has been made below to the few changes made in consequence.
2. *Census Report of India*, 1921, vol. I, p. 285.
3. Compiled from *Annuaire Statistique* (Paris), 1929, pp. 204–5.The figures for Germany refer to the year 1925.
4. Besides the above figures, there are also workers employed on roads, railways and docks, and 'the fluid mass of the general labour available for any kind of unskilled employment'. The total number of such workers has been estimated at 6 million, but nothing is known as to the exact proportion of women workers.
5. *Census Report of India*, 1921, vol. I, p. 279.
6. *Ibid.*, p. 266.
7. Compiled from *Annuaire Statistique* (Paris), 1929, pp. 204–5.
8. Comprising Rs 12.90 crores invested by companies registered in British India and £29 millions invested by companies registered elsewhere. Cf. *Statistical Abstract for British India*, 1931, pp. 625 and 620.
9. *Review of the Trade of India*, 1928–29, pp. 163–4.
10. Consisting of 4,714 tea gardens (1929), 3,371 coffee estates (1929–30), and 2,782 rubber estates (1928). See the annual statistics published by the Government of India (supplement to the *Indian Trade Journal*) for these industries for the respective years.

11. *Census Report of India*, 1921, vol. I, p. 285.
12. Including Indian states. The figures for coffee estates refer to the year 1929–30. See the annual statistics for these industries.
13. Compiled from the annual statistics for the respective industries.
14. *Indian Tea Statistics*, 1929, p. 6.
15. This number is the average for two months of the total number of women on the books. Compiled from the *Reports on Immigrant Labour in the Province of Assam*, 1929.
16. Compiled from the *Reports on Immigrant Labour in the Province of Assam*, 1921–22.
17. A.G. Clow, *The State and Industry*, pp. 164–5, Calcutta, Government of India.
18. *Imperial Gazetteer of India*, 1908, vol. 3, pp. 197 and 205.
19. *Statistical Abstract for British India*, 1931, pp. 681 and 691.
20. *Statistics of British India*, 1921, vol. I, pp. 55 and 74; *Statistical Abstract for British India*, 1931, pp. 681–2.
21. *Statistical Abstract for British India*, 1900–01, p. 265; *Statistics of Factories subject to the Indian Factories Act*, 1930, p. 17. It must be remembered that this increase in the number of factories has been brought about partly by the extension of the scope of the Factories Act to the smaller establishments, and partly by the growth of new establishments.
22. Out of 1,936,249 factory workers in Japan in 1928, 987,373 were women. Cf. *Japanese Year Book*, 1931, p. 385.
23. Out of 991,323 textile workers in Japan in 1927, 803,358 were women. Cf. Japan, Department of Commerce and Industry, *Factory Statistics*, 1920, p. 26.
24. Compiled from *Census Report of India*, 1921, vol. I, p. 270. The actual number was 1,931,071.
25. See the present writer's *Factory Legislation in India* (Berlin, 1923), p. 83.
26. This sum consisted of Rs 39 crores invested by companies registered in British India and £81 million invested by companies registered elsewhere but at work in British India. Cf. *Statistical Abstract for British India*, 1931, pp. 625 and 629.
27. *Indian Mineral Production in 1929*, p.1.
28. *Indian Coal Statistics*, 1929, p. 1.
29. *Annual Report of the Chief Inspector of Mines in India*, 1929, pp. 97 and 107.
30. Compiled from *Annual Report of the Chief Inspector of Mines in India*, 1929, p. 47.
31. *Annual Report of the Chief Inspector of Mines in India*, 1929, p. 2.
32. Cf. the present writer's article on 'Labour Legislation in India', in *International Labour Review*, vol. XXII, no. 5, November 1930.
33. *Reports on Immigrant Labour in the Province of Assam*, 1930, pp. 2–5.

34. Government of Bombay, *Memorandum to the Royal Commission on Labour*, 1929, p. 250.
35. Compiled from *Reports on Immigrant Labour in the Province of Assam*, 1930.
36. The total number of inspections amounted to 2,388. Cf. *Annual Report of the Chief Inspector of Mines in India*, 1929, p. 107.
37. *Statistics of Factories subject to the Indian Factories Act*, 1928, p. 31.
38. Compiled from the *Annual Report of the Chief Inspector of Mines in India*, and *Statistics of Factories Subject to the Indian Factories Act*, for the respective years.
39. Out of an adult labour force of 625,310 in Assam gardens, in 1929, only 60,716 were Assamese.
40. Evidence of Mr Amrit Lal Ogha, MLC, Member of the Mining Board, before the Royal Commission on Labour in India.
41. Evidence of Mr J.B. Wardlaw, Agent, Bengal Coal Company Limited, before the Royal Commission on Labour in India.
42. In 1921 only 16 per cent of the inhabitants had been born in the city, and out of its 1,175,914 inhabitants, 235,566 came from Ratnagiri. Cf. Government of Bombay, *Memorandum to the Royal Commission on Labour*, p. 3.
43. B. Foley, ICS, *Report on Labour in Bengal*, p. 14, Calcutta, 1906.
44. *Memorandum by the Tata Iron and Steel Works to the Royal Commission on Indian Labour*, pp. 2–3, 1930.
45. In 1921 only 20 per cent of the inhabitants of Ahmedabad had been born in the city, 25 per cent came from the district other than the city, 20 per cent from Baroda State, and the rest from other provinces. Cf. Government of Bombay, *Memorandum to the Royal Commission on Labour*, p. 2.
46. Ibid., p. 119.
47. 'It might be said that a very large majority of the labour force is permanent, although workers without any connection with the villages form about only 20 per cent of the working class population.' Government of Bombay, *Memorandum to the Royal Commission on Labour*, p. 7.
48. Dagmar F. Curjel, *Women's Labour in Bengal Industries*, p. 6. *Bulletin of Indian Industries and Labour*, no. 31. Calcutta, Government Printing Press, 1923.
49. *Report of the Royal Commission on Labour in India*, p. 355.
50. *Report of the Assam Labour Board*, 1930, p. 2.
51. *Census Report of India*, 1921, vol. I, p. 293; *Report of the Royal Commission on Labour in India*, pp. 116 and 119.
52. *Census Report of India*, 1921, vol. I, pp. 92 and 273.
53. Government of Bombay, *Memorandum to the Royal Commission on Labour*, pp. 8 and 9.
54. *Report of the Royal Commission on Labour in India*, pp. 118, 364–5.
55. *Annual Report of the Chief Inspector of Mines in India*, 1929, p. 5.
56. *Report of the Royal Commission on Labour in India*, pp. 355 and 359.

57. *Memorandum of the Bombay Textile Labour Union to the Royal Commission on Indian Labour*, 1930, p. 9. The *Memorandum* also points out (p. 10) that some of the jobbers recruit children by entering into a contract with their parents to pay Rs 30 per annum to the parents, and to feed, clothe and house the children in return for their services.
58. Ibid., p. 7.
59. There are practically no women in weaving departments in the Bombay Presidency. Only two women are reported to be employed in the weaving department of the Sholapur mills.
60. Dagmar F. Curjel, *op. cit.*, p. 6.

Radhakamal Mukherjee (1889–1968)

Source: Professor Ajit Kumar Singh, Giri Institute of Development Studies, Lucknow.

Radhakamal Mukherjee was born in Berhampur in Bengal in 1889. Having obtained his BA Honours degree in English and history from Presidency College, Calcutta, in 1908, he proceeded to do his MA in economics, seeking, as he was to note later, 'scientific and adequate answers to the grave national issues of Indian misery, exploitation and subjection'. He passed his MA in 1910 coming first in the university and in the first division. Mukherjee taught at Krishnanath College in Berhampur from 1910 to 1915, but left Berhampur in 1915 as he had reason to fear political persecution as an alleged revolutionary. After a short spell as Principal of Sanatan Dharma College, Lahore, he was appointed special lecturer in economics at the University. In 1921 Mukherjee became the first professor of economics and sociology at Lucknow University and remained in this position until 1951. He was Vice-Chancellor of the University for over two years in the mid-1950s. Mukherjee travelled widely and lectured in many universities around the world. He died in 1968.

Mukherjee's publications are truly remarkable for their number, range, and quality. About seventy of his publications were identified by the Radhakamal Mukherjee Memorial Society, probably an underestimation. They cover a wide range of subjects and fields, including economics, sociology, psychology, ecology, history, philosophy, art and culture. Even within the broad field of economics, Mukherjee wrote on many topics, including rural and land problems, labour and migration, food planning, and economic history. His first book, *The Foundations of Indian Economics*, was published in 1916. It was based on considerable fieldwork in rural India, but Mukherjee's early views on development were quite controversial. His position on these issues changed somewhat over the years. I have included a critique in 1919 by Brij Narain in this volume (Chapter 3).

Today, Mukherjee is widely regarded as a pioneer of environmental economics, as indeed of several other topics. In his work he developed interdisciplinary approaches, focused on institutional factors, and extended the boundaries of whatever subject he took up. His contributions to demography, labour economics, and migration are also considerable, and perhaps the most interesting feature of his work was that he linked up all these issues within a larger framework. He was also one of the first to undertake the analysis of food planning. It is not possible to do justice to all his contributions within this short note.

Any attempt to select one piece by Mukherjee for a volume of this kind faces the problem of an embarrassment of riches. Almost any choice is likely to be faulted in these circumstances. I have decided to select a piece which I believe ties up his work on population, agriculture, and ecology and showcases his most remarkable skills.

Major Biographical Sources: Radhakamal Mukherjee, *Dawn of a New Era (An Autobiography)*, New Delhi, Radha Publications, 1997; Baljit Singh, 'Mukherjee as a Pioneer in Indian Economics', in Baljit Singh (ed.) *The Frontiers of Social Science—In Honour of Radhakamal Mukherjee*, London, Macmillan and Co, 1957.

According to Mukherjee an interactive process was under way in the Ganges valley, involving reduced rainfall and desertification, soil erosion, destruction of forests and grasslands, overgrazing, and more frequent droughts and floods. He argued that 'the alternation of drought and floods in Northern India is merely a symptom of such loss of ecological balance which man has periodically brought about by excessive increase of numbers or abuse of vegetation in dry and semi-dry areas of the plain'.

The concentration of population in the fertile Gangetic alluvial plain had, he believed, led to exhaustion and loss of fertility of the soil. Looking at the long-term impact of human settlement in the Ganges valley, Mukherjee felt that the Ganges valley, like the Indus valley, might lose its fertility.

Mukherjee sought to link ecological variables with population. For Etawah and Cawnpore districts he demonstrated that birth rates and cropped area tended to move in the same direction, while death rates and cropped area tended to move in opposite directions. In his view, the fertility and mortality rates of a population interacted with ecological factors. When a particular district reached equilibrium or saturation density in relation to agricultural and hydrographical conditions, death rates rose or birth rates permanently fell, leading to decline in the vital index. (The vital index was defined as 100 times the ratio of births to deaths; a ratio of above 100 indicated a healthy and growing population; a ratio below 100 indicated an unhealthy and declining population.)

In an exercise for six districts of present-day Uttar Pradesh, he compared the 'vital index' before and after saturation density was reached and during epidemics. He identified 1901 as the year of the attainment of saturation density in the six districts and showed that the above-100 vital index before 1900 indicated a 'healthy population' and the below-100 vital index for 1901, 1911, and 1921 indicated an 'unhealthy population'. Also the epidemic years 1905, 1908, and 1918 were marked by unhealthy, below-100, vital indices.

This essay is important for the way in which Mukherjee related human variables with ecological variables in complex interactive relationships.* However, the analysis of economic–demographic interactions is less convincing, given the poor quality of registration data and in the light of subsequent events. After 1921, it was public health measures in India that led to reduced mortality. The pressure of a growing population on

* Radhakamal Mukherjee (1934): 'The Broken Balance of Population, Land and Water', from *Indian Journal of Economics*, vol. 14, issue 54, 1934, pp. 255–66.

the available cultivable area after 1921had adverse ecological impacts, but it did not result in an increase in mortality in relation to fertility.

Mukherjee, through his own work and that of his associates, explored in depth the relationships between man and his environment. Ramachandra Guha (1992) has pointed out that Mukherjee in his book, *The Regional Balance of Man: An Ecological Theory of Population* (1938), provided 'a veritable Green Charter for India', listing a number of dos and don'ts aimed at preventing social regression and fostering social evolution. Many of these points can be traced to the paper selected for this volume and have become part of the thinking apparatus of the development economist of today, concerned about the environmental impact of development projects and programmes.

8

The Broken Balance of Population, Land and Water

Radhakamal Mukherjee

As we follow the course of the historic river Ganges towards the delta, the rainfall, the climate, the agriculture, and the density of population improve. It is significant that agricultural prosperity which is so closely bound up with the river system fluctuates with the vicissitudes of the rivers, streams and drainage. Everything points to a steady decline of old alluvial tracts and the emergence into prosperity and numbers of new alluvial tracts farthest towards the delta. Thus the Himalayan rivers which must once have built up with silt deposit the upper plains of the Gangetic valley have now cut deep channels in the very plains which they originally formed, and not only cease to fertilise them with fresh deposit, but actually erode and gradually but continuously carry away the silt which they once laid on them. This work of destruction is assisted by the numerous feeders which are cutting more deeply every year into the rich layers of deposit and carrying the most fertile elements of the old silt into the Ganges, Jumna and other large rivers. There goes on in the old alluvial plains a continual process of destruction and renewal. At each bend the concave bank is being eroded, while the opposite shore receives a new alluvial deposit to fill up the void left by the receding river. After a period of years the process is reversed, or the river suddenly cuts a new bed for itself. Between these processes, however, there is an enormous wastage of soil.

In Tahsils Etawah and Bharthana, district Etawah which is flanked by the rivers Jumna and the Chambal there are 41,077 and 40,634 acres respectively of waste, the proportions being 15.06 and 15.27 per cent of the total areas.

The wastage in the district as a whole has been estimated to be not less than 11 cubic feet of soil per second, equivalent to a steady outflow of earth in a stream 13 feet wide and 2 feet deep flowing at the rate of three miles per hour. The processes of erosion and ravine formation commenced within the last four centuries. From the prevalence of old stone sugar mills, the alignment of the old Mughal Imperial road still to be traced by its *kos* marks, the examination of old wells of known antiquity as well as from the study of ancient records it would seem probable that most of the erosion has occurred during the last 400 years. Along the Jumna, old stone sugar mills are found in thousands. In two villages alone over 500 mills were found, in one 600 and is another over 250. The loss of fertile soil that has been carried from different districts into the larger rivers during the last three or four centuries is incalculable. It is in the Chambal-Jumna tract that the tangle of wild and sterile ravines sloping from the uplands to the river bank shows its worst features. There is a rough country along the Chambal which drains the Native States of Gwalior and Dholpur and finally joins the Jumna below Etawah. As far as can be seen one meets here a labyrinth of rugged ravines and green valleys covered with acàcia jungle, every prominent bluff showing the ruins of some robber stronghold. This has been for centuries a No Man's Land occupied by wild Rajput tribes, robbers and raiders by profession, who settled on the flank of the Imperial highway through the Doab and were a thorn in the side of the Mussalman administration.[1]

The process of ravine formation is aided by the fact that as a result of concentration of population we find in a mature valley very little of forest belt left on the banks of the rivers which might protect them against erosion during the monsoon rains. In all ravine tracts the village communities are accordingly found to check erosion by building dams where the ravines are wide enough and the sides too have often been carefully terraced. Though such areas often provide excellent pasturage for domesticated stocks and have led as in Etawah to great development of the dairy industry yet the onslaught of these beasts against the inadequate vegetative cover further aggravates the dangers of scour and overdrainage. Thus, the gain to cattle-breeding and dairy may be offset by further loss of culturable land. The ravines present a further danger to the village population in the shelter it easily affords to bands of robbers and bandits, especially in its inaccessible portions. The intensity of grazing will be evident from the fact that one million animals grazed over 5,000 square miles only in the forests of the United Provinces.

An onslaught of herds and flocks continued for generations cannot but lead to the deterioration of vegetation thereby facilitating soil erosion. There is often a thin covering of scrub jungle, which hardly can absorb any portion of the excess water during the heavy rains. With the hardening effect of the tread of animals and rapid drainage, the monsoon rains penetrate to a depth of few inches only, and this quickly dries, leaving a soil almost destitute of moisture down to the underground spring water level 100 feet or more below. This has reacted very unfavourably upon the agricultural population. The gradual loss of fertile lands caused by the extension of ravines along the banks of the Ganges and the Jumna and their tributaries is on the aggregate serious. It has been estimated that the total area of such desert-like and inhospitable ravines in the United Provinces alone is between half a million and a million acres.

The destruction of forests and indiscriminate extermination of grassland increase both floods and droughts, alter both the time and duration of the river flood, factors of great importance to agricultural prosperity; while the silting up of river bottoms spells decline of the mature portion of the valley and especially the delta region. Nowhere are forests and grasslands more important for agriculture than the tropical and subtropical regions where the vegetation not only conserves the moisture and ensures fertility by spreading a cover of silt but also prevents the ground from being over-heated and rendered dry by the sun.[2] Deforestation in these regions is particularly harmful in its effects towards upsetting the balance between the factors which determine climate and hydrographical conditions. The alternation of drought and floods in Northern India is merely a symptom of such loss of ecologic balance which man has periodically brought about by either excessive increase of numbers or abuse of vegetation in dry and semi-dry areas of the plain.[3]

The great densely population Gangetic plain is now practically bare of forest growth. It is inevitable that with the disappearance of the forests, the meteorological conditions of the Gangetic valley gradually would change. It has been estimated that of the water-vapour which is condensed as rainfall over the land, about two-thirds is provided by evaporation over the oceans, and the remaining third by evaporation and transpiration over the land. The latter contribution is made up of evaporation of rainfall intercepted by foliage, evaporation from the soil and transpiration, and estimates are made of these three factors for forest, crops or grass land, and bare soil. The figures are expressed as percentages of an average rainfall of 30 inches a year; for forests they give interception, 15; evaporation from soil, 7; transpiration, 25; total, 47 per cent. For crops evaporation from soil, 17; transpiration 37; total 54 per cent. For bare soil evaporation 30 per cent. Thus the replacement of forests by field crops or grassland would tend to increase the supply of moisture to the air and, therefore, the general rainfall slightly; replacement by bare soils, would decrease the general rainfall slightly. The changes in the run-off are likely to be more noticeable, replacement of forests by crops would decrease the run-off by 15 per cent, and make it less regular, replacement by bare soil would increase the run-off but would make it highly irregular. A forest 30 feet high may be considered as adding about 30 feet to the effective height of the ground, and this should increase the local orographical rainfall by 1 or 2 per cent.[4] The role of forest and grass in reducing run-off and erosion has been proved also by studies of Lowdermilk on cultivated field and temple forests in China, in which a ratio of 59: 1 was found. More recently in the chaparral of Southern California Lowdermilk and associates found a ratio as high as 100: 1.[5] The greater friction of the wind with tree surface compared with open ground is another factor. To this may be added, in favourable mountain situations, an increased supply of water collected mechanically from clouds which envelop the forests. Forests drawing their water-supply from deep sources possibly exercise a slight mitigating effect on droughts. On account of the widespread destruction of forests, throughout the heavily populated Ganges valley the rainfall in some parts is already becoming more scanty and the heat of the hot weather months more intolerable. It is not improbable that in some distant future the Ganges valley may share the fate of the Indus valley, where once there was smiling plenty. The traces of ancient river beds and sand-buried cities extended over a vast space in the desert country east of the Indus testify to the gradual desiccation of a once fertile region. The debris and mounds vestiges of a forgotten civilization recently excavated in the sandy deserts of Harappa whisper a tragedy of famine, despair and abandonment. In the south-western portions of the Doab the desert has already appeared. Further towards the north-west we have the semi-desert tract where can be marked the abandoned bed of one of the greater Punjab rivers, the Hakra, which was a live river probably up to early Muhammadan times and then lost itself in the sands. It appears that the watering of the Punjab rivers gradually transferred the Sutlej from the Hakra system to the

Indus system, the Saraswati and its associated rivers were then unable to maintain a flow to the Hakra Channel and dried up. The much discussed 'westing' of the Punjab is due to nothing more than the capture of the rivers in the sands. Thus the India's desert extends north-east to broad sandy wastes which merge into the scrub covered plains characteristic of the south-western portion of the United Provinces. This region was formerly productive and well watered, and composed of large and prosperous towns which are now insignificant and dependent for such prosperity as they enjoy upon modern irrigation canals. The change in meteorological conditions is probably due to long continued human settlement and increase of numbers, extension of cultivation and contraction of forests which formerly protected the head-waters and drainage area generally of the Hakra, the Sutlej and the Jumna, and their associated rivers. For not far distant is Kurukshetra which was the first permanent home of the Indo-Aryans, the centre from which their culture gradually spread towards the east and the south-west.

There is yet another way in which population pressure has brought injury to man, making barren what was once a fertile region. Throughout the Gangetic plain, apart from land which has been rendered barren by erosion there are vast stretches of what are called Usar land. These alkali lands cover about two million acres in the United Provinces alone; they are to be found mainly in the country between the Jumna and the Ganges, and between the Ganges and the Gogra. In those tracts of the United Provinces and Bihar where the soil is close in texture long human settlement has meant an intensive perennial irrigation coupled with surface tillage. This has produced vast expanses of dead alkali land.

We thus realize that the concentration of population in the fertile alluvial plain itself leads to exhaustion and loss of fertility of the soil in various ways. Even in the most fertile tracts deserts and barren lands appear reacting most unfavourably upon both the economic condition and the well-being of man. Due to continuous exhaustion of both tilled and pasture lands the soil becomes depleted of certain mineral ingredients. In considerable parts of the plain phosphorus is deficient in the soil and its effects on the health of both cattle and human population are far-reaching. Ill-nourished cattle become less efficient for drawing the plough and lifting the water for irrigation and yield less milk. On account of imperfect cultivation and inadequate manuring crops suffer both in quality and quantity. Thus fewer animals are kept by the cultivator and he himself suffers due to faulty nutrition. Malnutrition thus pursues its harmful course in an ever-widening vicious circle; the cultivator is too often ill-nourished and ravaged by disease due commonly to lack of nourishment; his beasts likewise obtain inadequate nourishment while both toil wearily[6] in a heartless effort to extract from the ill-nourished earth enough to keep them from starvation.

Both man's ignorance and improvidence as well as natural causes check the aggregation of population beyond a certain stage. Thus the population tends to advance onward along the course of the rivers towards the more fertile region of softer alluvium. On the other hand, in the older and harder alluvium the excessive pressure of population leads to a change of hydrographical and agricultural conditions for the worse, upsetting the ecologic equilibrium and bringing about, first, a decline of the standard of vegetation and of fauna, and then of human numbers and living standards. The continuous expansion of agriculture and irrigation due to population pressure in the south-western portion of the plain has led to the depletion of subsoil water-reservoirs and decline of the water level; while the encroachment on marshes, grasslands, and forests has decreased humidity as well as fertility of land, letting loose the forces of erosion and run-off. The process of desiccation has already told on the breed and mortality of cattle which can stand neither the increased strain due to the fall of the well water level nor the chronic fodder famine. The diminution of the numbers of live stock and the deterioration of their breed are found associated with agricultural decline and general lowering of vitality of the human population in areas which were once smiling with milk and honey. There can be no surer evidence of population pressure than a close correspondence between the rates of reproduction and mortality and the fluctuations of the cropped area, as shown in two central districts of the upper plain. [Charts I and II have not been reproduced.]

Nature has a safety valve in the forces of natality and mortality which would not permit animal and human populations to multiply up to the extreme limits of food-supply, for no system of living community can work unless there is some adjustment to the needs of the future.[7] With animals as well as humans migration in response to an unfavourable habitat acts as a sort of safety valve reducing the chances of starvation and resulting in a readjustment of the density of numbers in different places. Elton, indeed, emphasises the importance of the migratory tendency of animals as contributing towards a solution of the animal population problem and offering a means of enormously increasing the possibilities of adaptive radiation.[8] The study of human numbers in the congested Ganges plain, where migration may be roughly estimated as amounting to only 5 per cent of the total population seems to support the older hypothesis that adaptation is produced by the elimination of the unfit from a *stationary* population of animals in which new hereditary variations are constantly being produced. Both natality and mortality are here matters of ecologic adjustment striking out a normal balance of numbers with the ecological area, where the evolutionary processes are at work with whole and more or less sedentary populations.[9] Thus the movement of population in certain areas of the Ganges valley is similar to that of bacterial population confined in a test tube, or of rodent population in a certain range of territory, tending to follow Pearl's logistic curve. In what decade the equilibrium density has been reached in a particular district depends upon agricultural and, especially, hydrographic conditions. But no sooner is it reached than we find the tendency towards a decrease of density either through a decreasing survival rate or through a permanent lowering of the birth-rate. Thus the population trend seems to be alike in human and animal and bacterial populations when they reach saturation density.[10] Statistical evidence of this is further furnished by some of the congested districts of the Ganges valley where the population after reaching a saturation density tends to show a lower biological rigour as indicated by the 'vital index' (100 births/deaths.) This constant has been effectively used by Pearl to measure the biological health of a population and to indicate its probable future course. If the ratio 100 births/deaths is greater than 100, the population is in a growing and in so far a healthy condition. If it is less than 100 the population is biologically unhealthy. No single measure gives so sensitive a measure of the vitality of a population. From the vital indices we may easily conclude that populations, after having over-stepped the saturation density, have become biologically unhealthy. The damage done by the epidemics to these populations is much severer than elsewhere.

Notes

1. Crooke: *North-Western Provinces of India*, p. 26; also *District Gazetteer*, Etawah, Agra and Muttra.
2. Report on Agriculture of the United Provinces submitted by the Royal Commission on Agriculture.
3. The writer's *The Concepts of Balance and Organisation in Social Economy*, *Sociology and Social Research*, August 1932.

4. C.E.P. Brooks: 'The Influence of Forests on Rainfall and Run-off', *Meteorological Magazine*, December 1927.
5. W.C. Lowdermilk: *The Changing Evaporation Precipitation Cycles of North China.* Proceedings of the Engineering Society of China, 1925, quoted by Clements.
6. See Mc Garrison's evidence, *Report of Royal Agricultural Commission*, vol. I, pt. II.
7. The writer's *Population Balance and Optimum*, Proceedings of the International Population Congress, Rome, 1932.
8. Elton: *Animal Ecology and Evolution.*
9. The writer's 'Optimum and Overpopulation', *The Indian Journal of Economics*, January 1930.
10. The writer's 'The Criterion of Optimum Population', *The American Journal of Sociology*, March 1933.

Appendix 8.1

Districts	*Years of saturation density*	*Vital indices before the year of saturation density*				*Vital indices in the years of epidemic outbursts*			*Vital indices after the year of saturation density*							
		1881	*1886*	*1891*	*1896*	*1905*	*1908*	*1918*	*1901*	*1906*	*1911*	*1916*	*1921*	*1926*	*1930*
Agra	1901	145.5	100	165	133	52	54	79	142	94	98	161	108	146	162
Aligarh	1901	180	96	143	150	92	52	31	153	121	90	185	105	138	155
Cawnpore	1901	106	109	92	121	86	86	42	126	63	94	155	84	130	123
Etawah	1901	126	92	110	155	118	62	43	150	75	93	161	88	132	146
Lucknow	1901	125	121	99	113	75	59	44	113	103	93	896	97	152	92
Muttra	1901	138	90	136	147	36	39	28	118	98	98	189	116	129	129

Gyanchand (1893–1983)

Source: Courtesy N.K. Chowdhury, from a painting in Patna College, Patna.

Gyanchand was born in 1893 in Loralai, Baluchistan, in present-day Pakistan. He obtained his MA degree from Government College, Lahore. In 1920 he joined the Benares Hindu University and taught economics there until 1926. His reputation in the field of Indian public finance was established when he published his first major book, *The Financial System of India*, in 1926. This book has recently been republished in 2000. Gyanchand was invited to deliver the prestigious Banaili readership lecture at Patna University in 1926, which was published as *Financial Reconstruction of India* in 1931. He joined Patna University in 1926 as assistant professor at Patna College, a postgraduate teaching institution catering at that time to the whole of Bihar and Orissa. In 1930, he published another major work, *The Essential of Indian Federal Finance*. In the same year he went to the London School of Economics to work for his Ph.D. on Indian local finance, a relatively under-researched subject. He returned to India in 1932, having secured his Ph.D. degree, and was promoted in the Bihar Education Service to the rank of professor.

Gyanchand continued as professor and head of the department of economics at Patna College until 1946, when he joined the International Monetary Fund in Washington. He was recalled by Jawaharlal Nehru to join the government as the head of the economic section of the cabinet secretariat in New Delhi, but he left the post in 1951, apparently on account of differences with the bureaucracy on Indian planning (see Bose 1981). C.D. Deshmukh, the Finance Minister at the time, gives a different reason: he felt planning was not a field in which Gyanchand had much to contribute, and he had therefore recruited J.J. Anjaria and K.N. Raj to work on techniques of planning (Deshmukh 1974). Gyanchand later served for a year as economic adviser to the government of British Guyana in 1962.

Gyanchand is remembered, even today, as a great teacher and economist who made major contributions in public finance and population studies. Among his important writings, perhaps his *India's Teeming Millions*, published in 1939, is one of the best known. Like Radhakamal Mukherjee, he was one of the earliest professional economists to argue strongly for policies to reduce fertility.

One of Gyanchand's finest moments was when he gave evidence before the Fiscal Commission in 1923. A young and relatively unknown Indian economist facing an august and formidable body, he argued that protection was not India's prime need; what she needed was a policy of state encouragement and support for industry.

Gyanchand was a strong believer in socialism and was close to the leaders of the Indian socialist movement in the 1930s and 1940s. Early in his career as a government employee, he appears to have kept his political views to himself. This is apparent in the paper I have selected as an example of his writing. However, later on, he did not conceal his ideological position and sympathies. During the Quit India Movement in 1942, at great risk to his career, he continued to maintain contact with socialist leaders who had gone underground. He visited the Soviet Union in 1932 and again in 1948 and then most of the Soviet Bloc countries. He was a great admirer of China's economic progress, and based on two visits wrote his *New Economy of China*, published in 1958. His views on Indian development were spelled out in his book, *Socialist Transformation of the Indian Economy*, published in 1965. Gyanchand died in 1983.

Major biographical source: S.K. Bose, 'Gyanchand—A Biographical Note', in S.K. Bose (ed.) *Essays in Honour of Dr Gyanchand—He that Blazed the Trail*, New Delhi, People's Publishing House, 1981.

The idea that India should be a planned economy had gained currency in the 1930s. It was partly a response to the ongoing process of planning being attempted in the Soviet Union and partly reflected a widespread desire for greater coordination in economic activity in India. Industrialists, civil servants, and several Indian economists took up the question of planning and expressed their views on how it should be conducted.

Gyanchand* observed that everybody in India appeared to want planning, but he doubted if many had clear ideas of what planning meant and what was required to carry it out. He felt it had to be a programme of economic reconstruction, not merely of recovery, and it had to address the problem of poverty.

Analysing the situation in India in the mid-1930s, Gyanchand argued that the state was passing though difficult times due to the introduction of provincial autonomy and 'federation with safeguards', which would, he believed, release new and unpredictable forces in the country. A government with the power to carry through the required measures of both economic and social reconstruction did not exist.

Gyanchand criticized G.D. Birla, a representative of industrialists, who argued that India should seek 'maximum prosperity with a reasonable amount of effort'. The goal, he argued, was to see that the vast majority of the population was endowed with enough surpluses to enjoy collective security and creative social activities. Economic development, in itself, would not eliminate poverty:

'The general standard of living of the masses cannot be raised merely by the economic development of the country. It will be necessary, if that end is to be achieved, to make the masses the principal beneficiaries of economic progress'.

* Gyanchand (1935): 'The Essentials of Economic Planning for India', from *Indian Journal of Economics*, vol. 15, issue 59, 1935, pp. 409–22.

This led him to reject any gradualist approach to development:

> Planning and the maintenance of *status quo* are mutually incompatible propositions. We must be prepared for a complete economic and social reconstruction; and whatever be the method by which we try to reach that goal, it will essentially involve a revolution of our whole national life, and revolutions can never be carried out without a shift in the centre of gravity of social economy and realignment of social, economic and political factors of national life.

Gyanchand was advocating a revolution, but wording it rather carefully.

Looking at agriculture he felt that unless the problem of small and fragmented holdings was tackled, other measures to promote efficient agriculture would have little impact. He felt that the lack of surplus in the hands of agriculturists would limit, from the demand side, the scope for rapid modern industrial development.

Many development economists today would agree with Gyanchand that planning cannot succeed in a country like India without structural and far-reaching social and economic changes. Again, many would agree with him that slow agricultural growth could act as a constraint on industrial growth. Gyanchand believed that growth must be accompanied by poverty reduction. He was clearly rejecting the belief that the benefits of economic growth would, in due course, 'trickle down' to the poor. These are issues which come up repeatedly in the context of current discussions on Indian planning and indeed of development strategies in general.

9

The Essentials of Economic Planning for India

Gyanchand

'We may not all be socialists now, but we are certainly (nearly) all planners'. These words of Professor Robinson must be accepted as a fair statement of the present position of the public opinion all over the world. In India the Government has often been blamed for not being sufficiently solicitious of the economic interest of the country, but in the matter of planning the Government, instead of following public opinion, has undertaken to lead it and already the proposals are under way the avowed object of which is the introduction of planned economy into India. The portfolios of Governor-General's Executive Council are to be redistributed. The functions of the Tariff Board are to be enlarged and it is likely to be placed on a permanent basis. The Indian Tariff Act is to be consolidated, revised and put in a more convenient form. The proposal for having an Economic General Staff has been put off for the time being, but besides the Punjab, which has had a Board of Economic Enquiry for a long period, the United Provinces and Bengal have set up the Boards of Economic Enquiry and the other Provinces are expected to follow suit. The existing commercial treaties are to be overhauled and new ones concluded to promote the commercial interests of India. The deliberations of the two Inter-Provincial Conferences have resulted in the proposals for the establishment of the Central Industrial Intelligence Research Bureau, a scheme for developing the hand-loom industry and another for marketing surveys and the appointment of Senior and Junior Marketing Officers. Bengal has introduced a scheme for the restriction of jute cultivation and restriction of the production of tea and rubber are already in force. The UP Government has gone further and accepted the resolution for the formulation of Five Year Plans and commercial interests, European and Indian, are all for planned economy.

The unanimity of opinion on the subject of planning is as remarkable as it is impressive and if it is to be taken at its face value, it is an index to the growing desire of every section in India to join hands for the common good of all. The Governments, Central and Provincial, the Chambers of Commerce, European, Indian and National, all school of public thought, the Directors of Industries and Agriculture and experts of every kind are all ready to pool their knowledge, experiences and resources to establish a new economic order in this country. We in India are all, and not nearly all, planners. There is no resistance to overcome, no parties to be 'co-ordinated', no contradictions, problems or classes to be 'liquidated'. In America Roosevelt has carried out his measures in a constitutional manner, but has had to reckon with opposition, passive or active; and though his personal popularity may still be the same, the prospect of his going further with the momentum of his start is very doubtful and criticism of his policies and opposition to their execution are gaining in volume and intensity. In India we are starting under better auspices and all measures taken so far have received full measure of public support and have only had the effects of whetting the appetite for more of the same kind. The state of Government finances makes it necessary for them to tread very warily, but once the specious days return, nothing need be in the way of our going ahead 'on our way' and enrich the country with the full benefits of the planned economy.

Knowing as we do the difficulties of concerted action in every other sphere of national life, this imposing façade of common agreement is, on a little reflection, likely to give rise to doubts as to whether it is as substantial as it is imposing. We are all for planning, but we have to make sure that we have a clear understanding of its meaning and implication and have the means at our disposal to take adequate measures to carry out the policy and programme of planned economy. The necessity of planning all the world over is taken to have arisen because there is economic distress in spite of the plenty of material goods and it is necessary to solve the problem of distribution when the problem of production has been solved. Does this apply to India as well? Have we solved the problem of production? The answer does not admit of any difference of opinion in view of the low level of productive efficiency all round and utterly insufficient national income of our people. If that is so, the policy of restriction as a general measure of economic improvement is obviously out of place in this country. Where we are producing for the world markets, a temporary reduction of particular commodities may be necessary to adjust supply to demand; but as we want more, far more, wealth and not less, it is absolutely wrong to organize scarcity in this country as a measure of long-range planning. With all the poverty that we have, not only in this country, but in every other country of the world organised scarcity as a way out of the existing appalling situation can only be accepted as a tragic illustration of the distributive fallacy practised on a scale which points to the bankruptcy of economic thought and statesmanship. But in this country, of all countries, to plan in order to restrict is so obviously out of accord with the facts and needs of the situation that it should not be at all necessary to stress the point.

Planning in India, we have to remember, has to be a measure of economic reconstruction and not merely recovery, for recovery in this country to the 1929 or 1926 or any other selected level may alleviate the present acute distress but is no remedy for the chronic and abject poverty of our people. We have to plan in order to change their standard of living out of all recognition to their present miserable existence.

India is suffering from the effects of the world crisis and improvement of her economic position is limited by the international situation. But her real ills are due to the fundamental defects of her economic life and can only be cured by measures devised for their removal. Even if the rise and stability of prices can be brought about and trade barriers removed or made much less obnoxious than they are to-day, of which, humanly speaking there is no chance, that will not reduce the grinding poverty of the masses or bring hope and cheer into their lives. The vast multitude for whom we have got to plan are living on the very lowest margin of subsistence, and if our efforts have to bear fruit within the time that matters to them, we have to deal with the basic facts of their existence and so increase their productivity and purchasing power that they can feel a sense of well-being and security which may make their lives worth living to themselves and the community.

It may, however, be urged that all the measures, which have so far been adopted or are contemplated, have just this object in view. The immediate cause of the general appreciation of the need for planning may be the depression and the example of other countries, but its object is permanent and appreciable improvement in the economic condition of the masses; and the fact that there is such a large measure of common consent in favour of making a mass attack on poverty has to be taken as an asset of first-rate importance. That it would be if one could have an assurance that this common consent is based on a common goal and the conditions for reaching it are in existence.

Let us take the latter point first. It will be readily admitted that if planning for any country—much more so for India with its 350 millions of population—is to be attempted, our essential pre-requisite is that the state, which has to be the prime mover in the formulation and execution of all plans, must be sure of its present position and future. In saying this I am not avowing any sympathy, sneaking or otherwise, for dictatorship of any kind. The countries in which planning has been successful to any extent are all, it is true, being governed by dictators. Roosevelt's New Deal, which may be cited as an exception, has been put through mainly owing to the assumption by him of quasi-dictatorial power; and even the best friends of democracy admit that its future depends upon it showing capacity for decisive action at a time when it is being challenged from all sides—a capacity of which it has not given any convincing proofs in the past. But I am not dealing with that point at all. My point is that India is passing through a period of extreme political uncertainty and doubt. The Government of India is stable enough as things are and will not become less so under the new constitution. But the introduction of provincial autonomy and federation with safeguards, whatever that may mean or amount to, will bring into play new political forces about the alignment or effects of which no forecast is possible. The White Paper, even if it is coming, is, it is quite clear, not bringing political peace with it and the Government of India and the leaders of public opinion in India will be pre-occupied in years to come with matters relating to the division or transfer of political power and will not be able to use the latter for the purpose of introducing planned economy in the sense in which the phrase has come to be used in recent years. Whatever our hopes may be about the future, it cannot be denied that we are passing through a period of twilight in our political history and during such a period economic planning which, above everything else, must require on the part of the Government a firm grip of political situation and the prospect of being able to proceed further on an even keel, cannot be successfully attempted, much less carried to its full consummation. With the very best intention in the world the rulers of India to-day or their prospective successors cannot therefore take in hand the task of economic planning for India.

If the above view is correct, our essential condition for the introduction of economic planning in India is non-existent. But there is another, which is no less essential, about whose non-existence also there can be no doubt. Planned economy is a phrase which in the country of its origin has acquired a significance that carries with the necessity for changes in the very foundations of social life. But even if the Marxian connotation of the phrase is not accepted, it cannot but be admitted that for carrying out economic change of the kind and the range, that must be involved in planning of any kind, corresponding changes in all important spheres of social life cannot be avoided. Economic reconstruction without social reconstruction will not only be not fruitful but give rise to internal stresses which will have very undesirable reactions on the whole social economy. We will not only not resolve old contradictions but create new ones, and to the waste of efforts will be added the greater lack of harmony in the different aspects of social life which will have a further disruptive effect on the latter.

When the practical issues, which are absorbing the attention and energy of the nation, turned round questions like a few seats more or less in the legislature, share of the different communities in the public services and entry of the depressed classes into temples, the stage cannot be said to have been set for introducing or carrying out any programme of economic planning. Many acid tests have been prescribed for knowing whether we really combine together for our common ends, but the application of the one test, which would make all others unnecessary, i.e., our willingness to subordinate every other interest to the paramount need for raising the plane on which our people are living, is still not practical politics. In saying this I ought to add, I am not raising any deterministic issue and under-rating the importance of one social factor or magnifying that of another. But there must be an order of precedence in practical affairs whatever may be the consideration which may lead us to fix it. Economic planning is a big task, big enough to take all our time, ability and resources, and if we are really serious about it, we should rise to the height of the occasion and declare our determination to concentrate our entire energy on its completion. We should do so not only because it is ever so much more worth while than most other things that are in the fore-front of public life, but also because it is a matter of extreme urgency that it should be done. As I have said above we cannot adopt this course because we are dissipating our limited resources, material and moral, in tilting against social and political windmills. For economic planning, as for planning of any sort, we require, if I may use a phrase which is overworked but convenient, the right sense of values and that we are lacking in altogether. The ultimate values are important; but if, in a paper read at the Economic Conference, nothing ultimate is to be referred to, we must have contingent values to shape our policy and choose our course. But we are off the mark of economic planning altogether and, therefore, all this talk of economic planning is merely an exercise in creating a delusive atmosphere.

Besides these conditions which are essential for economic planning we have to consider the question of the goal. As Sir Arthur Salter said a few years ago at a meeting of the American Political Academy that if we would re-mould the world after our heart's desire, we must know what our heart's desire is. One may even go further and say that it is not enough to know what we want but also be sure about why we want it. 'We need,' to quote from J.M. Keynes, 'by an effort of the mind to elucidate our own feelings....We need a new set of convictions which spring naturally from a candid examination of our inner feelings in relation to the outside facts.' This is what is needed everywhere economic planning is sought to be seriously attempted; but here in India where owing to our political subjection our whole trend of national thought has been more negative than positive, the need of first clarifying our feelings and then elucidating them with an effort of the mind is all the more urgent for effective action. The fact that people of widely divergent points of view and interest are all for economic planning is due to our having fallen victim to the lure of a catching phrase. The Russians may be entirely mistaken, but they at least have merit of being coherent in their emotions, thoughts and actions. They are out to establish a classless society and their method is the dictatorship of the proletariat. That gives an integrity to their plans and a purpose to their policies. Hitler, in spite of his obsessions and crude methods of propaganda, also knows what he is about. He is essentially positive and realises that 'Underlying philosophy is decisive for the construction of the state'. His philosophy has been built upon a race-myth but has given him and the movement which he leads a new set of convictions. Convictions can be right or wrong; and the wrong ones cannot, according to the age-old belief of men, be made the basis of an enduring social order. But in a world in which nothing endures in the long run and the truth is relative, convictions which contain an element of the truth, howsoever relative, can give a point and decisiveness to actions and make it correct from the pragmatic standpoint.

For economic planning, in other words, we want a determined objective and that is just what we have not got. Mr G.D. Birla is his speech on economic planning delivered at the annual session of the Federation of the Indian Chamber of Commerce held at Delhi on 1 April 1934, also emphasised the supreme importance of being clear about the goal and then proceeded to define it in what he called 'a layman's language' by saying that 'the object of economic plan...should be to bring about maximum prosperity with a reasonable amount of effort'. Here we have, in plain words, what we should aim at and most other planners in India would, if pressed to state the object of planning, probably say something to the same effect and also feel convinced that if that does not satisfy the delegates or any one of the delegates to the Economic Conference, it is because the academic mind acquires the incorrigible habit of indulging in the niceties of thought and expression for their own sake. What can be clearer than maximum prosperity as the goal of economic planning and who can feel any hesitation in co-operating in 'reasonable effort' to attain it? We all want prosperity and the more of it, the better. But we must, of course, remember that human nature being what it is we must not expect too much of it or strain it beyond the point of endurance. That comes to saying, what Mr G.D. Birla has said for us in a layman's language already, that our efforts must be reasonable.

Maximum prosperity is a laudable and even unexceptionable goal of economic planning; but the trouble about it is that it can mean all things to all men. That prosperity in itself cannot give us economic security or even fair standard of living for the people in general has been very recently demonstrated by the experience of the United States of America in the period of prosperity and adversity which she has known. When Hoover rode to the White House on the crest of prosperity, he and most Americans were, as is well-known, buoyant enough to believe that in one country at least poverty had been permanently banished.

Then came the chastening experience of the depression and Hoover's successor realized that wide diffusion of purchasing power and its increase in the hands of the masses was an essential condition of production sustained at a high level of efficiency, and since then he, the NRA, the AAA, and the other bodies that he has created have been struggling valiantly but so far unsuccessfully with the dilemma of high real wages without high costs. They have, it may be admitted, been successful in creating an atmosphere of manly endeavour in face of overwhelming difficulties and believe that planning is necessary; but considerable increase of purchasing power in the hands of the masses has still to come. It is no use labouring the point. Prosperity, a high level of prosperity, in itself has so far meant extreme contrasts of wealth and poverty and very precarious economic life.

In fairness to Mr Birla and most other planners in India it must be stated that they realize the need for having a broad base for prosperity; but the general standard of living of the masses cannot be raised merely by economic development of the country. It will be necessary, if that end is to be achieved, to make the masses the principal beneficiary of economic progress. And if that is to be made the main object of economic planning and it will be easy to get for it a large measure of general assent—we will be brought up against one or two stark facts of the economic situation in the country which make anything like adequate increase in the purchasing power of the masses a practical impossibility. The increase to be adequate, it may be repeated, has to change radically and very much for the better the plane of economic existence at which the vast majority of our people are living, and for that we have to create surplus in the hands of the people to enable them to provide themselves with the necessaries of efficiency, health and culture and contribute to the public funds enough to enable the state to develop social services for providing collective security and creative social activities of the highest order. In order to do that we have to multiply wealth in their hands many—and—very manifold to replace grovelling squalid want by a condition fit for a people who may be taken to have a future worthy of their past.

The multiplication of wealth in India in the hands of our people is limited by many factors but among them the one which dominates the rest is the size of holdings of the cultivators and the conditions of the land tenures under which they hold them. In the landlord provinces not only the size of the holdings is small and they are fragmented, as is the case all over the country, but the conditions of tenure leave no scope for the enterprise of the landlords even if they can be awakened to the need of justifying their existence, which seems to be well-nigh impossible, and the cultivators have got to carry a burden of obligation which is as prejudicial to their self-respect as to their economic position and prospects. In the other provinces the fact that the owners of land are not subject to the onerous obligation of paying rent makes their position relatively better; but judged from the absolute standard—not the one which is suggested by the comparison of the condition of our people with that of the people of any other country, but by the irreducible minimum, for which provision must be made in economic planning—not only the minimum is not attained but it cannot be attained. Improvements is marketing conditions, the establishment of land mortgage banks, agricultural research and selection of better-yielding and disease-resistent varieties of seeds—the proposals which have been in the fore of late—will, apart from being slow in operation—make only a slight impression on the stubborn realities of the rural economy which are determined by the small and fragmented size of the holding—the size which is bound to grow smaller owing to the enormous growth of numbers which has taken place and is continuing—and any hope that these measures in themselves will give us an India without the dismal condition of to-day must be regarded more or less illusory. Every province has its system of land-tenures which has become ossified by the practice of centuries and its growing class of landless labourers for whom no provision can possibly be made in the present framework of agricultural life. If the importance of these elementary facts is duly appreciated and its bearing on the possibilities of economic development understood, we are driven to the conclusion that the surplus in the hands of our agricultural population—surplus adequate enough to find a basis of life on a much higher plane of economic existence—cannot be found.

The same fact is of over-shadowing importance for the prospect of developing large or small industries in this country. At present less than one per cent of people are making their living in the organised industries. The condition of workers in these industries is hardly any better than the condition which they permanently or for the time being leave behind and, therefore, the quantitative increase in the number and size of industries cannot give us the qualitative minimum without which we ought not to be satisfied. But even if that aspect of the matter is not to be considered, the development must be limited in India by the surplus in the hands of our agricultural class. The measure of the size of potential markets in India is not the area of the country or its teeming millions but their buying powers. It may be possible with efforts, which at present cannot be put forth owing to the lack of industrial capital, experience and organisation, to increase the percentage of our industrial population from one to say three per cent of our total population, in 10 years, but even then capacity to sell and, therefore, the level and stability of their economic life, must depend upon the capacity to buy of the remaining 97 per cent of our population; and as by far the largest part of it is and must remain agricultural, the inexorable facts of their economic situation, which rendered the prospect of any considerable increase in their purchasing power so very remote as to be hardly of any practical value, govern the industrial situation as they do the agricultural. What is true of large industries is also true of small industries. They have to, even if they can hold their own against the competition of machine-made goods, which is very doubtful, find their market in the villages, which cannot be done because of the present and potential purchasing power of the masses being extremely limited. Industries, therefore, not only cannot materially reduce the pressure on the land but cannot be established on secure foundations owing to the fundamental difficulties of our rural economy.

The whole discussion of economic planning has so far taken place on the facile assumption that we can introduce planned economy in this country without in any way changing the standards, motives or orbits of economic life. This assumption, which is a pure delusion, is more than anything else responsible for the chorus of approval with which the proposals for economic planning have been received and supported. But when it is realized that economic planning means planned economy and planned economy must mean a new economic and, therefore, a new social order, we shall understand the full import of this new fashion in our public life. Planned economy and the maintenance of the *status quo* are mutually incompatible propositions and if we want to keep step with the rest of the world in its march, real or simulated, towards planned economy, we must be prepared for a complete economic and social reconstruction; and whatever be the method by which we try to reach the goal, it will essentially involve a revolution in our whole national life, and revolutions can never be carried out without a shift in the centre of gravity of social economy and realignment of social, economic and political factors of national life. The India of planned economy, and the same statement is true of the world as a whole, must, in its mechanism and informing purpose, be entirely different from the India of today; and when this truth is borne in upon those who now have joined in this grand orchestra of economic planning, what looks like symphony of many notes will resolve itself into the most jarring disharmony of discordant notes in widely different pitches and keys.

The line of argument followed in this paper has, it must have been clear from the beginning, been adopted in order to point to the conclusion that the proposed measures of economic planning for India involve confusion of ideas, policy and practice and we shall not get anywhere by them. The conclusion is negative; but lest it be dismissed as being purely destructive of all that is being said or done, I must in concluding this paper, state my position briefly but clearly. I am not at all for drift or fate. I am for social control, with a definite, determined objective. That is to say I am for economic planning for India. But I see that neither we have clearly understood what it means and involves nor we have the means at our disposal for carrying out a far-reaching and comprehensive change like planned economy. I am also not for standing still. Let us by all means re-distribute

Government portfolios, enlarge the functions and utility of the Tariff Board, appoint marketing officers, and carry out economic surveys, make use of the fiscal convention to get better terms in international exchange, establish land mortgage banks and have demonstrations of improved methods of cultivation. These are all useful measures and they will have ameliorative effect. But let us not confuse the issues. If the peculiar conditions of our national life or some immutable laws of being make gradualness inevitable, let us proceed gradually, step by step, from precedent to precedent and build slowly but surely. I am not for all or nothing. But if we permit ourselves to hope that we will, thereby, in a measurable time, bring economic planning into full operation, we shall only be laying in store for our people a disillusionment of the worst kind. The pace at which the world events are moving, is already disturbing enough and it does not look as if any country will be in a position to choose its own tempo of change of progress. But even if we can withstand the impact of these forces, we certainly cannot raise false hopes and build upon unity of professions without any unity of thought, purpose and action.

P.J. Thomas
(1895–1965)

Source: Rajkumar, P.V. (ed.) (1978), *Economics is Not All: Dr B. Natarajan 67th Birthday Commemoration Volume*, Madras.

Parakunnel Joseph Thomas was born in Kuravilangadu in present-day Kerala in 1895. He obtained his BA Honours from St Joseph's College, Trichinopoly in 1916 and then taught at the Maharaja's College in Trivandrum. He went to Balliol College, Oxford, in 1920 and did his B. Litt. on the 'Calico Trade and its Influence on British History'. Published in 1926 as *Mercantilism and the East India Trade,* this highly original work was reviewed very favourably by A. P. Usher in the *American Economic Review* in 1927. For his D.Phil. at Oxford, he worked on Indian federal finance, which he developed into a book, *Growth of Federal Finance in India*, published in 1939. This became a standard account of the subject.

Between 1924 and 1927, Thomas worked in Ceylon where he became professor of economics at the Ceylon University College. He returned to India in 1927 as professor of economics in Madras University, a post he continued to hold until 1946. He had worked with the Bowley-Robertson Committee in the early 1930s on a scheme for an economic census. In 1937 he presided over the Indian Economic Association Conference. In 1937 he became a member of the Madras Legislative Council and economic adviser to the chief minister. In 1942 he moved to Delhi as Economic Adviser in the department of finance. In the same year he also became Chairman of the Fact-Finding Committee (Handloom and Mills), which produced an excellent report. He attended the inaugural session of the UN as member of the Indian delegation. He was Chairman of the Indian Post-war Planning Committee. In 1948 he returned to Kerala and was active in public life, becoming a member of the Rajya Sabha in 1957. He died in 1965.

Thomas published several books and many articles on a wide range of subjects, including economic depression and recovery, prices and statistics, village studies, prohibition, the stock market, Indian industry, and mercantilism. Among his important papers was one published in the *Economic Journal* in 1935 on India and the World Economic Depression, as well as the essay, that I have selected for inclusion in this volume.

Major Biographical Source: *http://www.palai.com/personalities/thomas.htm*

India suffered greatly during the worldwide depression of the 1930s. The slump in the prices of primary products led to a breakdown of purchasing power and the terms of trade moved against agriculture. This led to decline in production, income, and employment in agriculture as well as in transport and banking and public revenue. The government, as Thomas* noted, maintained balanced budgets by retrenchment and reduction in public expenditure, particularly on construction. All this resulted in a vicious downward spiral.

Thomas observed that in most European countries 'orthodox canons of public expenditure have been abandoned' and loan-financed public capital works were being started to help maintain purchasing power. He made a strong case for capital expenditure on public works in India to inject purchasing power and revive business activity. He used the arguments of Kahn and Keynes to stress that the initial public expenditure would have multiplier effects on employment, especially if the labour content was high and materials were locally procured.

In the Indian case, unlike that of developed countries, there was 'infinite room' for carrying out such capital works, which would build infrastructure and general amenities and meet 'the most essential human needs, like drinking water, light, housing, and drainage'. Thomas argued that this would promote social and economic development and that the government could borrow the required amounts without difficulty. The primary employment created would be equalled by secondary employment creation through the multiplier.

Looking at the past, Thomas pointed out that public works were used to combat depression between 1825 and 1850 in some parts of the country. Later this approach was used to tackle the aftermath of drought, and the procedures for this were embodied in the famine codes.

Public works needed to be well organized, with minimal leakage, good monitoring, and maximum feasible use of labour. He also noted the need to have a mix of large and small works. Each province would have to carry out public works programmes over a five- to ten-year period. This would not only strengthen the capital base of the economy but induce an upward spiral in economic activities, resulting in recovery. As a result of increased expenditure on public works, the demand for foodstuffs and clothing would increase; prices would begin to gently rise; agricultural and industrial employment would go up; trade would grow; and public revenues would expand.

Thomas's case for government intervention in the form of loan-financed public works was a bold and novel approach to lift India out of the impasse created by the world economic situation and the orthodox budgetary policies of the colonial government. The argument for greater public expenditure and investment in development-related activities was obviously not a new one; this had been a major contention of nationalist economists and thinkers for many years. However, Thomas saw expanded public works, in the specific context of the depression of the mid-1930s, as an ideal way to revive the Indian economy and promote agriculture and industry. As he observed, most European countries had adopted this approach. Unfortunately it was not taken up by the colonial government. Until the Second World War, the government remained wedded to conservative finance and did not favour Keynesian-type solutions.

* P.J. Thomas (1935): 'A Plan for Economic Recovery', from *Indian Journal of Economics*, vol. 15, issue 59, pp. 447–57.

10

A Plan for Economic Recovery

P.J. Thomas

In this paper, I have shown that the breakdown of purchasing power, which is the most disquieting factor in the present economic situation, can be remedied by a suitable programme of public works, which will not only increase employment and purchasing power, but will also provide the country with a better economic equipment. This is one of the most important aspects of economic planning to-day. A more comprehensive type of planning may not be practicable in the circumstances of India, but no serious objection can be urged against a cautious policy of loan expenditure on urgently needed works of public utility.

Perhaps the most disquieting feature of India's economic position to-day is *the breakdown of purchasing power* which has resulted from the heavy slump in the price of primary products since 1929. While the prices of manufactured goods have fallen only about 27 per cent on an average, those of primary products fell more than 50 per cent, and 'fixed' charges—land revenue, rent and interest payments—remain nearly where they were in 1929. The diminution of purchasing power in the country can be gauged by the fact while the value of the principal crops came to Rs 1,018 crores in 1929, it was only Rs 534 crores (or 52.5 per cent) in 1933. The prices of commodities that agriculturists sell slumped by about 50 per cent, but the prices of many things which they buy fell only 20 to 30 per cent. In result:—(i) consumption has slackened in many lines; e.g., the annual *per capita* consumption of white sugar, which was 7.7 lbs, for 5 years before 1930, fell to 5.8 lbs, in 1932–33—a feature which sugar manufacturers must take into account; (ii) agricultural production has diminished in several lines, thus increasing rural unemployment; (iii) the standard of living, which had been steadily rising before the depression, has since fallen; (iv) the earnings of railways, commercial firms, banks and of all business have diminished; and (v) the public revenue under customs, excise, stamps, registration fees, etc., have fallen, to the great detriment of the central, provincial and local authorities. The whole phenomenon may be described as a vicious downward spiral. When prices fell, incomes diminished, and with diminished incomes, the buying power has contracted, and business got slackened. Thus the public fisc as well as the private purse came to be affected seriously.

Government's efforts, while effective in maintaining its own financial position, have not been equally effective in maintaining the country's purchasing power. In spite of dwindling business and falling revenues, the Government of India has balanced its budget, partly by retrenchment and partly by increased taxation, and largely by the copious outflow of gold that came as a godsend. India's dues in England have been punctually met, the burden of her debt has been reduced and the balance of trade in favour of India, which had become slender at the end of 1932, has again become substantial. Consequently, India's credit to-day stands high among the nations of the world, public borrowing is easy and Government is now in a position to boldly launch forth the long-expected Reserve Bank. Government has also taken steps to safeguard India's trade, both external and internal, and to this the two trade agreements, the Crop-Planning Conference and the marketing scheme bear ample testimony. In addition, several provincial governments have made revenue remissions and some have granted relief by debt conciliation and other measures.

But it is well to remember that Government's budget has been balanced, by unbalancing private budgets to some extent. The scheme of retrenchment, whether by the central government or by the provincial governments, was carried out at the expense of employment and purchasing power. Before 1929, a large constructional activity was going on all over the country. There was a large capital programme on the railways; the provincial governments were engaged on an active policy of road-making and irrigation works. Thus Government, which was already the largest single employer of labour in the country took upon itself a great responsibility. But since 1930, these public works programmes were drastically curtailed and that has seriously affected the purchasing power of the country.

For the three years ending 1929–30, the total works expenditure on Indian railways amounted to Rs 124 crores or Rs 41 crores annually, but for the last three financial years (1931–32 to 1933–34) the total has fallen to Rs 27 crores, or Rs 9 crores annually. If we take capital expenditure alone, the fall was from Rs 101 crores in the first period to Rs 6¾ crores in the second. The expenditure on new constructions in the last two financial years was only Rs 57 lakhs and Rs 22 lakhs respectively. This curtailment may be partly due to a wise change of policy, but we are here considering only its results on employment. The total provincial expenditure on civil works which amounted to Rs 9.3 crores in 1928–29 fell to Rs 5.4 crores in 1932–33—a fall of 41 per cent; and the expenditure not charged to revenue (excluding Burma) fell from Rs 97 lakhs to Rs 6 lakhs—a fall of 94 per cent. At the same time, local authorities also severely restricted their outlay on works. Taking only the total central and provincial expenditure on public works, the fall may be seen from Table 10.1.

TABLE 10.1

	Total works expenditure on railway (Rs lakhs)	*Provincial civil works (Rs lakhs)*	*Total (Rs lakhs)*
1928–29	38.35	10.23	48.58
1932–33	6.42	5.58	12.00
Percentage decline	83%	46%	75%

[*Note*: The figures on provincial works do not correspond to those in the text. Ed.]

We have not got ample statistical data for accurately measuring the resultant fall in employment and purchasing power, but some general idea may be formed from the fact that in the case of most works 50 to 70 per cent goes directly to labour and even the rest goes indirectly to labour, seeing that the stores are increasingly purchased within India.

We must remember that such a severe cut by Government coincided with the disbanding and repatriation of labourers from Malaya and Ceylon and the closing of many of the tea, and of the rubber, plantations within this country. Not only did the large inflow of remittances from Ceylon and Malaya cease since 1930, but the labourers who hitherto made those remittances came back home to aggravate the unemployment situation in the country. The cumulative result of all this was the setting in motion of a vicious downward spiral with all its attendant consequences.

How to convert the downward spiral into an upward spiral of economic recovery? Unfortunately, the critics of Government, whether politicians or economists, have concentrated their attention on exchange depreciation, but currency manipulations are either risky or ineffective in the present circumstances, particularly of India. As Keynes naively puts it: 'You cannot get fat by buying a larger belt'. An increase of currency can only be effective if it is accompanied by an increase of spending power in the pockets of the people, and spending power can only increase by more extended employment. The demand for goods must be sustained and business activity must be revived, and this alone will set in motion an upward spiral. Such activity cannot come by private initiative in times like the present; the public authority must give the start, and then private agency will follow up. This has been recognized in most European countries, and public works expenditure is no longer a side-show but has become the central feature of their economic policy. Orthodox canons of public expenditure have been abandoned, and in several countries, loans have been raised for carrying out capital works with a view to maintaining purchasing power.

The scheme of public expenditure now put forward is materially different from the relief works which used to be urged by some for 'making work'. The aim now is to time the capital undertakings of public authorities in such a manner as to concentrate them in the trough of the depression and to curtail activity when business improves. Thereby, purchasing power can be injected and business activity revived in times of depression. The works would directly employ many persons and then more will be employed when industry and trade expand, as they are bound to, by the growing demand for consumption goods.

The secondary employment resulting from public works has been mathematically analysed by Keynes, Kahn, and other writers.[1] According to Keynes, for every two men employed on public works, at least one man will be employed on secondary employment. Kahn estimates the ratio of primary to secondary employment in the least favourable case at 1:0.67, and similar results are reported by the German Statistisches Reichsamt. The most favourable results are obtained from works in the case of which wages contribute a high proportion of costs, and for which raw material comes mostly from within the country. Road-making, and earthworks of all kinds are therefore greatly helpful in the reflation of economic activity.

In the case of India, public works expenditure is particularly desirable, feasible and beneficial, at the present juncture.

The chief objection raised in England and certain other Western countries against public expenditure is that the opportunities for fresh development of capital works are limited. Large sums were spent in the last decade for increasing general amenities, and more cannot be spent in a productive manner. Obviously, this objection cannot be urged about any part of India. There is in this country infinite room for carrying out works, not only for providing general amenities, but for supplying the most essential human needs—drinking water, light, housing, and drainage. The country is also in need of roads, bridges, irrigation works of all kinds, reclamation of waste lands and water-logged areas, construction of electric plant, and erection of earth works for protection against floods. Most of these works are directly remunerative, and others indirectly. Such works will not only increase purchasing power, and give a stimulus to economic activity, but will also protect the country from debt, disease and drought. They will also increase public revenues and improve the economic equipment of the country. More village roads are needed for efficient marketing and cheaper power supply will expand industrial facilities. Better housing, cleaner drinking water and better drainage are required in villages as well as in towns, and these will lead not only to greater physical comfort but to greater economic efficiency.

There cannot be a more opportune time than the present for undertaking such works of public utility. We are apparently at the bottom of the depression, and this is just the time when loan expenditure is most effective. Government's credit stands high, and capital can be had to-day at unusually favourable rates. India can now borrow on terms more favourable than those on which Germany, Japan, and even France are able to borrow. Labour is also plentiful and cheap. There are large numbers of unemployed and under-employed labourers eagerly looking for work.

When the spending power of labourers is increased, they will buy more of foodstuffs and clothes and all kinds of consumable commodities. Judging from the agricultural family budgets collected in various parts of India, about 60 to 70 per cent of the total expenditure of the common people is on foodstuffs, and nearly 95 per cent of the goods they consume are from within the country. In this respect, conditions are different in the more advanced Western countries, which depend more largely on imported foodstuffs and raw material. A larger amount spent on wages in England may bring about a greater demand for goods that are rather luxuries, while in India, with its large numbers of underfed persons, a bigger wage bill will expand the demand for necessaries. The law of equi-marginal returns demands that a country which consumes hardly 15 yards of cotton cloth (including kadar) and 15 lbs of sugar (including gur) *per capita* per annum will have to largely increase its consumption of such goods before thinking of silks and diamonds. Therefore, the results of increased expenditure on public works in India will be (i) a greater demand for foodstuffs and clothing, (ii) a gentle upwards trend of prices, (iii) greater employment in agriculture and industries, (iv) expansion of trade and (v) increase of public revenues, central, provincial and local. In this expansion, not only manual workers, but intellectual workers will also find increased employment. I have estimated that for four man newly employed on public works, at least three and perhaps four may be absorbed in secondary employment. Therefore, the secondary employment from public works must be larger in the case of India.

Public works have already served such a purpose in the past, even in this country. A hundred years ago, 1825–50, there was a prolonged depression in Southern and Western India; prices fell rapidly, agriculturists suffered, weavers lost their occupation and public revenues diminished. After much hesitation, the Government of Madras launched on schemes of irrigation works and road-making, and as a result money circulated in the country, prices gently rose after 1850, public revenues improved and prosperity revived. Sir Arthur Cotton was greatly instrumental in carrying out this forward policy, and in 1850, the Madras Public Works Commissioners showed in their report how 'a vast stimulus' was given 'to industry and production by the employment of labour and circulation of capital' in poverty stricken districts. Subsequently, railways and factories were constructed, and tea plantations were opened and much money flowed into the country. But the initial stimulus came from the public works policy of Government. Later, the same policy was adapted to famine relief, and became the core of the famine code which came into operation after 1880. This was how Government in India planned long before 'planning' was heard of.[2]

The Scheme must be carefully devised. Public works in the past have not always been used to the greatest advantage of the country. Too much of the money went into the pockets of contractors and other middlemen, and too little into those of labourers, with the result that the effect on purchasing power has not been sufficiently great. An effort must therefore be made to direct and control such activities. An expert committee must be appointed in every province (with the Finance Member as Chairman) for scrutinizing schemes sent up by local authorities, and for watching wage-schedules and conditions of labour; provision must also be made for a periodical survey of economic results by competent persons.

In selecting schemes, preference must be given to works that require a maximum of human labour and minimum of capital goods. It is not enough to have a few large works; we must rather have a large number of small works scattered about the country, especially in 'depressed' rural areas where purchasing power is parched up. Minor works like wells, tanks, canals and village roads will put some money into the pockets of the agricultural labourers in upcountry villages, and there is extensive room for the expansion of their consuming capacity.

Some difficulties in the way. The question of increasing public works expenditure was discussed at the Provincial Economic Conference at Delhi last April, and the Government of India has already offered to lend to the provincial governments for carrying out schemes of public works. Particular attention is being paid to road development. In order to induce the provincial governments to launch on road-making schemes, a resolution was passed in the Legislative Assembly last March making provision for provincial grants from the Road Fund being utilized for the services of loans raised for the construction of new roads and for their maintenance. However, the provinces are slow in moving, and have their own doubts about the financial soundness of raising loans for road development. Indeed roads will increase revenue collections, but the central revenues will benefit at least as much as provincial revenues. Is it not fair then, ask some, that the central government also share in the financial burden of road development? The question will therefore have to be more seriously faced by both governments, and it is hoped that the ensuing Road Congress will result in the satisfactory settlement of this important question.

A stable recovery. Each province must now plan and carry out a programme of public works, ranging over a period of five to ten years. The immediate expenditure must be the largest, but with improving economic conditions private agencies will revive and the State's outlay may be diminished. Schemes of commodity restriction and currency manipulations are of doubtful value and, as experience elsewhere has shown, it is extremely difficult to control the reactions of such policies; but the carrying out of public works which are directly or indirectly remunerative has no such serious risks. If public expenditure is to be effectively used for counteracting booms and slumps, credit must be carefully controlled, and now that the foundations of our Reserve Bank have been firmly laid, we can boldly go ahead with a suitable programme of public works. Such a programme, if properly carried out, will not only improve the economic equipment of the country, but will set in motion an upward spiral, with gently rising prices, increasing employment and purchasing power, expanding trade and rising public revenues. Thus it will lead on to a stable economic recovery.

Notes

1. Keynes, *Means to Prosperity*; R.F. Kahn, in the *Economic Journal* (June 1931); Mitnitsky, in the *International Labour Review* (October 1934).
2. See the paper on *Economic Depression in the Madras Presidency* (1830–50) read at the last year's Conference.

P.S. Lokanathan (1894–1972)

Source: Courtesy Professor L. Subramaniam and Mr L. Swaminathan.

Palamadai Samu Lokanathan was born in 1894. After graduating from Madras University, he worked as a research student with Gilbert Slater doing fieldwork in Tirunelveli district. In 1927, Lokanathan was appointed reader in economics at the university and acted as professor of economics from April to September 1935 and again from 1941 to 1942. One of the earliest economic journalists in India, he became editor of the Delhi newspaper, *Hindustan Times* and subsequently of the financial journal, *Eastern Economist*. In 1947, he was elected President of the Indian Economic Association. Lokanathan was appointed the first Secretary-General of the UN Economic Commission for Asia and the Far East (ECAFE) in Shanghai in 1946, a position he held until 1956. Returning to India he served as the first Director-General of the newly founded National Council for Applied Economic Research in New Delhi from 1956 to 1967. Lokanathan died in 1972.

Lokanathan's first major publication was *Industrial Welfare in India*, brought out by the University of Madras in 1929. He is, however, better known for his classic work on the Indian managing agency system, *Industrial Organization in India*, based on his London Ph.D., and published in 1935. This was generally regarded as a highly original piece of work. Austin Robinson, in his review in the *Economic Journal* in 1935 described the book 'as the product of real research, and deals in first-rate fashion with real problems'. Lokanathan produced several other books and articles and was a leading Indian economist of the post-Independence period. The selection that follows is, not surprisingly, from his *Industrial Organization in India*.

Major Biographical Sources: The bulk of the information has been obtained from: *http://www.ncaer.org/downloads/Brochures/GoldenJubileeBrochure.pdf.*

http://www.palamadai.net/eminent.html.

http://www.unescap.org/oes/lokanathan.asp.

Gilbert Slater, *Southern India: Its Political and Economic Problems*, London, George Allen and Unwin, 1936.

As Lokanathan observed, the actual methods by which industrial units in India were organized and floated were rarely discussed. The role of the promoter, as distinguished from the entrepreneur, was important. Also the system had evolved in response to the special conditions in India. Modern industry was promoted, developed, and controlled by British merchants representing British trading firms as well as by Indian cotton merchants in Bombay, Ahmedabad, and elsewhere. He then documented several important cases of the promotional role of managing agents.*

Managing agents typically began with one industry and then moved on to develop other industries based on inter-industry linkages. Beginning as family concerns many graduated into limited-liability companies. Some partners worked mainly in India while others worked in the UK. They would develop a new enterprise and when it reached a certain point they would convert it into a joint-stock company and sell off their holding but retain control through a management contract. The activities of the British managing agencies were designed to get the maximum benefit from the limited number of their own people in India. They played a role as a conduit for British capital and helped it to respond to market opportunities available in the context of the shortage of Indian entrepreneurs.

In Bombay, in the latter half of the nineteenth century, Indian merchants began to pioneer, promote, finance, and manage textile mills. While many companies were joint-stock enterprises, Lokanathan noted that the managing agents maintained tight control, thereby combining 'the virtues of unity of management of proprietary or partnership concern with the ampler resources of a joint-stock company'.

He showed how the managing agency firms were formed, looking at a number of cases. There was a very close relationship between the agency and the concern in the form of a long-term contract. While the managing agent looked after the business side and knew the market very well, they imported experts for technical work. Managing agents obtained remuneration from their role as managing agents as well as profits as shareholders.

Lokanathan concluded that the floating of new units had generally been sound and economical. Managing agents acted as 'universal providers of industry, being promoters, financiers, and managers of the venture they established'. They also retained a continued interest in the success of the venture, especially when they retained a significant portion of the company's shares. Further, by nurturing the company before selling off the shares to private investors, they helped to reduce the risk for the latter. However, Lokanathan did not minimize the problems that arose when the managing agent focused on short-term gains, or sought to hoodwink investors. He argued for greater cooperation among managing agents to improve their overall performance.

Like L.C. Jain's work on indigenous banking, Lokanathan's work on the managing agency system was extremely balanced in its assessment. An important contribution of Lokanathan was his thesis that this system was the right solution in the unique setting for industrial development in late nineteenth-century India. He also made the extremely important point towards the end of his book that the existing institution of managing agencies still had a role to play. It would be unwise to dismantle existing institutions which had played a role in the past because they had some defects; in the medium term they could be moulded to serve emerging needs in new and better ways. Of course, in the long run such institutions would have to be transformed or replaced.

* P.S. Lokanathan (1935): 'Pioneering of Industry in India', from P.S. Lokanathan, *Industrial Organization in India*, London, George Allen and Unwin, 1935, pp. 13–40.

11

Pioneering of Industry in India

P.S. Lokanathan

Although the history of the development of Indian industry has been the subject of many recent books, the actual methods by which the individual units in each of the important industries are organized and floated have so far received little attention. Yet the pioneering and promoting of industry in India reveal some distinct and almost unique features which differ from those of company promotion in other countries and are almost without parallel in any part of the world. The neglect by Indian economists of this aspect of organization may be explained partly by the general tendency, until recently, to ignore the role of the promoter, as his function was not sufficiently differentiated from that of the entrepreneur. Although with the growth of joint-stock forms of organization the promoter-entrepreneur has been largely replaced by a Board of Directors in most countries, it was thought that the methods of setting up a business and floating it were not sufficiently distinctive to invite special study. In countries, however, in which there arose a separate class of 'promoters' whose main function was that of starting or organizing a business, and who very often were not interested in its further career and development, some attention has been given and judgment formed as to their soundness and economy. In India, although here and there a few men of the professional promoter type have floated industrial concerns—and their activities were pronounced during the boom period 1919–21—it cannot be said that the promoting function has become sufficiently specialized to have brought into the field a new and separate class of promoters.

Another reason for neglect was that Indian economists did not fully realize the exceptional and distinctive features of a system which evolved in the special circumstances of the country and which was accepted as perfectly normal by them. It is only in recent years that they have realized that the differences between the system in India and elsewhere are much greater than the similarities, and that it is necessary not merely to explain the Indian system but to examine its features from the point of view of past conditions and future requirements.

There is no doubt that one of the factors on which the success of an industrial unit depends is the careful planning of the scheme and its launching under favourable conditions. This requires great constructive ability on the part of the organizer, and a country rich in such talents will be able to achieve industrial success sooner than one which, however well endowed with natural resources, is lacking in the supply of initiative and enterprise. Modern industry in India owed its development primarily to two classes of people; British merchants who had come out to represent British trading firms, and the cotton merchants of Bombay and, latterly, of Ahmedabad and other centres. These, directly or indirectly, were responsible for much of the development that has occurred. India was fortunate in having in the country British merchants with wide experience and considerable financial resources who were able to pioneer and establish new industrial concerns. But the peculiarity of the system lay in the fact that enterprises were promoted and controlled by persons who belonged to what are known as Managing Agency firms or, as more popularly known, managing agents. Even when, as in western India, Indian merchants pioneered the cotton industry, the same system was developed, although there were differences in the circumstances that gave rise to it.

The significant role played by managing agents in the development and organization of industry will be marked in almost every chapter of this book, but we are now concerned with their role as promoters or undertakers of business.

British Managing Agents

It is not possible to trace the origin of the managing agency system, as it was the result of gradual evolution. The history of some of the managing agents like Martin & Co., Andrew Yule & Co., Killick, Nixon & Co., or W.H. Brady & Co., shows how much the system owes to the enterprise and ability of the individual men who came out to India as representatives of some trading companies. They were men who were first engaged in the general trading business, but soon turned their attention to other lines of activity. They found a country with vast undeveloped resources; but unlike

Canada or Australia, India had a large consuming population and a plentiful labour supply. They found that the country was lacking in industrial leaders, in fact, in any industries in the modern acceptation of the term, and that they had the whole field clear to themselves. The experience they had gained in their general merchandise business was such as was capable of being utilized in the organization and advancement of industrial concerns, and they were fully prepared to engage experts for technical purposes. Thus industrial advancement in India was in the hands of men who were keen business men and not technical experts. Being pioneers, they realized such profits in each line of business that they could afford to make mistakes without burning their fingers. From one industry they turned to another, not only because the experience gained in the one was equally valuable in the other, so that all that they needed was to get experts versed in the technique of each industry, but also because each line of business opened the way for another, and the market for the products of one line of business was found in another. Thus managing agents of jute mills started colliery concerns, and found that the jute mills were good customers for their coal. Then again, when some of them floated boating and inland steamer companies, these latter were able to get their own jute mills and colliery companies and tea estates to send their goods by their line of steamers. It was thus a great thing for them to know that they had a market which was controlled by themselves, and thus one line of activity naturally led to another. That is why in India managing agency firms have neither specialized in one or two industries nor developed a vertical form of organization. They have used their knowledge in developing quite a miscellaneous range of enterprises, including jute mills, tea gardens, flour mills, coal companies, shipping companies, insurance agencies, etc. But though managing agents usually concerned themselves with a variety of enterprises there are a few firms specializing in one branch of industry, and these may be regarded as specialist managing firms. The main reason for such growth was that the field open to them was large and had to be shared out only among a limited number of firms.

Organization of Managing Agents

For the purpose of promoting the different concerns in which they were interested, these pioneers formed themselves into partnerships. In many cases they merely comprised a few members of the family with one or two outsiders. More recently, the tendency has been to form limited liability companies with shares privately held. Thus about six firms in Bengal are limited companies. English managing agency firms are generally servants of the corresponding firms in England, or, in these days of income-tax difficulty and differentiation of the legal systems in the two countries, are technically separate, though actually the firms in England are able to exercise general control by means of their capital invested therein.[1] The evolution of family agency concerns into private limited liability companies is rather interesting. It often happens that the sons of some of the family concerns are not willing to spend their time in India and are therefore eager to avail themselves of the services of able assistants.[2] The assistants are engaged in London, often University men, through the University Appointments Board, or technical men gathered from British industrial firms. The 'sons' get pushed on, but often prefer to spend their inherited money in England, and the assistant gets his chance, stimulated by the fact that he has to make his own way in the world. The men among the staff who have made good are brought into the concerns as partners, and in this way not merely is the firm energized and vitalized, but the knowledge that such opportunities are more easily available in India than elsewhere has led to some of the abler youths of England taking up junior posts with prospects of rising to the position of partners. Retirement at a comparatively early age also holds out prospects of early promotion for the younger men. The opportunities which Indian industry has thus afforded to the young brains of England are quite exceptional, and India has served as a good training-ground for business talents. There are again instances of some managing agency firms making a definite rule against having as partners or employees, more than a limited number of persons belonging to one family. Thus in a firm of managing agents in Calcutta, the founder of the firm which has 15 partners, of whom 6 were serving in India, and 9 in England in 1926, made a definite rule prohibiting the taking in of relatives.[3] On the whole it may be said that although family influences predominate and the partnership is carried on among the same families from generation to generation, there has always been plenty of scope for the more enterprising and ambitious of the junior assistants to look forward to becoming ultimately partners and in many instances heads of firms;[4] succeeding frequently after retirement to the headship of the associated London firm. Thus the infusion of 'outside' blood in British firms in India has been stimulating and fruitful. The responsibilities abroad are great, and even a desire to see a son in a prominent position does not always outweigh the father's desire not to have his business ruined. In a few instances managing agency concerns have been turned into joint-stock public limited companies, although the shares are held by only a limited number of persons.[5] There is no uniform practice in regard to the number of partners in each concern. The number depends upon the extent and sphere of influence of each agency firm and the number of enterprises it has to manage. From 3 to 15 is quite common, though it sometimes goes up to the maximum of 20. Some of them work in India, while others work in England, and, as the Industrial Commission stated, the system arose out of the 'difficulty in the case of companies under European control of finding among the relatively small class of leading men of business available in India directors, especially managing directors, who will remain in the country long enough to guarantee the continuous supervision requisite for the successful conduct of such businesses. An agency firm as a rule comprises several partners, some of whom are taking their turn of duty in India, while the others attend to the firm's affairs in London or elsewhere'.[6] But this view of the constant interchange of partners between India and England is not borne out by actual facts. The practice seems to be for some partners to serve in India throughout the period of their service and then to retire from India, either permanently or with a view to working in England. Similarly, those who serve in England pay occasional visits to India.

From the point of view of starting a new concern, what is more important to note is that in India at the time when the system was evolving itself there was hardly any investing class as such. Capital could not be attracted from the people of India, and the managing agents were prepared to put in a large capital. After the concerns were established and shown to be working profitably, it was possible to attract investors to them, and thus build up in India an investing public. They thus nursed a large number of enterprises in their early years of struggle and till they could come out into the open market for capital. In some cases a long interval has occurred between the starting of a concern and its conversion into a joint-stock public company, during the whole of which the managing agents have nursed the enterprise. As a writer put it in the *Capital, Trade Supplement,* December 1932, 'the managing agents nourished the growth of new enterprises and carefully nursed the young and immature'. When the time was opportune for the conversion into public companies, the managing agents got the bulk of their capital out by selling a large portion of their interests, and having unloosened their capital were ready to enter into fresh enterprises.

But in each case in parting with their interests they were careful to retain their power and control either by securing a long fixed tenure of management or by including in the articles of agreement terms ensuring their permanence and rendering it extremely difficult for anyone to turn them out.[7] In theory, 51 per cent of the shares is needed to secure absolute control of a concern, and there are some concerns where the agency firms do have as much as that.[8] But as is more usually the case, their holdings are far less, but even with a 25 or 30 per cent of the holdings in one hand they are able to control the destinies of the concerns as effectually as if they were absolute masters. The Indian Company Law of 1882, favoured the growth of the system of managing agents by the very elastic nature of its provisions. Up till 1913 the law did not compel the constitution of an elected Board of Directors; still less did it require the creation of a managing director. It was, therefore, possible to evolve a system by which the persons interested in the enterprise constituted themselves managing agents. When, later on, the law required the constitution of a Board of Directors, the managing agents had no difficulty in getting together a few friends as directors from among their business associates, who were perfectly aware that their continuance on the Board depended on their loyalty to the managing agents who had the power to choose their own friends. Thus although outwardly many of the concerns were joint-stock companies with Boards of Directors, in effect they were more akin to partnerships with control in the hands of the managing agents. At its best the system was eminently suited to the needs of the country and the limitations under which British capitalists had to work. On the one hand there was the fact that owing to climatic and other conditions it would have been difficult for British capitalists to work continuously in India and to find for every concern competent men who could serve as directors and as managing directors. The system of managing agents made it possible to administer and manage industrial ventures with a few able leaders, and thus it was possible to effect great economy in the labour of higher grade administrative staff. On the other hand the flow of British capital to Indian industry was greatly facilitated by a system which enabled control to be vested in British hands, though there was a leavening of Indian element in some of the concerns. The English managing agents in Bengal, Assam, and other provinces constituted a sort of bottle-neck through which British capital flowed to India and got distributed among the varied enterprises promoted by the British managing agents. But for the managing agency system the pace of industrial development in India would have been slower, and the opportunities for British capital and British enterprise to function in India would have been limited. Thus England and India both gained. The lack of indigenous capital and Indian industrial leadership gave the British merchants their opportunity. The available British capital seeking investment found among these British merchants just the right sort of men who could safely be entrusted with it. Once the system came into existence its very success led to its growth and development.

Indian Managing Agents

If, therefore, the managing agency system grew up, particularly in Bengal and Upper India, out of the special economic conditions in which British merchants and officers representing British trading firms in India found themselves, for reasons slightly different but essentially the same, there evolved a similar system on the western side of India. There, too, the merchants who were engaged in general trade, and more particularly in the cotton trade, began to take interest in the development of industry, and were helped considerably by the resident English representatives of British machine-manufacturing firms. They were also faced by the same set of facts. Capital was extremely limited and, such as it was, remained entirely with a few wealthy merchants like themselves engaged in commerce. The wealth acquired during the American Civil War formed, indeed, the basis for the promotion of cotton companies in Bombay city.[9] There was no large investing class in the country, and industrial leadership was lacking. As in Lancashire, where the wealth acquired in commerce became the basis for the starting of the textile industry, so in Bombay the merchants who amassed fortunes in trade and commerce pioneered the new industry. There have been instances where men who had once been 'Bardan carriers'[10] and became rich by trading in cotton and cotton yarn, used their wealth in the development of the industry.[11] Thus it was inevitable that the pioneering and promoting of industry in western India was undertaken by a few wealthy merchant communities such as the Parsis and the Bhatias. The first successful cotton company in India, the Oriental Mill, was promoted by a wealthy Parsi merchant and converted into a joint-stock company in 1858, and was managed by Messrs Framji & Co., who were appointed as Secretaries and agents. Thus began the system of management by managing agents in the cotton-mill industry in India.[12] Later, wealthy merchants belonging to other communities followed. The money required for the cotton mills was subscribed by the promoters and their friends, and those who had large financial interests in the concerns constituted themselves as managing agents. While in Bengal the difficulty of finding among the few British residents a sufficient number of able men to serve as directors and managing directors was partly responsible for the growth of the managing agency system, in the Bombay Presidency the scarcity of industrial leaders in the country led to similar results. The whole task of pioneering, financing, and managing the mills fell on the shoulders of a few merchants, and although with a view of getting a certain amount of additional capital they were prepared to take in some from outside, they always took care that control remained in their own hands. Thus a form of organization was evolved which, while formally joint stock, was in reality largely proprietary in character, and the managing agency system tended to combine the virtues of the unity of management of a proprietary or partnership concern with the ampler resources of a joint-stock company. To a foreign student of Indian industry it might appear paradoxical that the most important of its organized industries, like cotton, jute, coal mining, flour, and tea companies, should have been organized on a joint-stock basis when everyone knows that there had been a dearth of managerial and directing ability, and that capital seeking investment was limited and confined to only a few wealthy groups. But the explanation for this apparent paradox lies in the evolution of the managing agency system. The managing agents retained a considerable share in the interests of the firms they promoted, and took in a few rich capitalists as shareholders with a view to getting an increase of capital. As will be noticed when studying the system as it works in Ahmedabad, many of the so-called public joint-stock companies are essentially private in character, the bulk of the shares being held by only half a dozen persons. How far this type of organization was efficient in the past, and developed on proper lines, and how far it should prove beneficial in the future we shall consider later; but that in the early stages of its evolution it fitted the country admirably, and that, indeed, there was no alternative to it, cannot be doubted. Everything began to adjust itself to the system. Investors who had any money to invest in industries were willing to put their money in any enterprise promoted or backed by a reputable firm of managing agents. The imprimatur of a managing agent was found essential for the successful flotation of any public company in India. Even at a time of depression, as in 1931–2, when capital was justifiably shy, many new sugar companies were successfully floated by managing agents because of the confidence of the public in the promoters. The banking organization of the country came to be adapted to the development of the managing agency system to such an extent that credit was often refused to an industrial concern unless guaranteed by the managing agents. This was most general in Bombay, though in Bengal the managing agents did not have to give their personal guarantee in the case of bank loans and overdrafts.[13] Thus industrial finance was entirely provided either directly by the agents or indirectly through their guaranteeing the banks. In short, managing agents became the pivot of the whole industrial system.

Steps in the Formation of Managing Agency Firms

It is now necessary to consider in greater detail the actual steps in the formation of managing agency firms and the nature of the agreements entered into between them and the concerns they manage. As was already pointed out, managing agents started either as family concerns like Messrs Tata, Sons & Co., Nowrosji Wadia & Sons, and Currimbhai Ebrahim & Sons, Ltd., which later were converted into partnerships, or more often directly as partnerships comprising 3 to 15, or even up to the maximum of 20 persons.[14] When such a limited liability company is formed, the major portion of the shares is held by the persons who have promoted it, and the outside public are allowed to come in for a limited number of shares, generally up to 25 per cent. It is necessary broadly to distinguish between three types of managing agency firms, each type predominating in certain parts of India. Thus the British managing agency firms in India, the Indian agency firms in Bombay, and those in Ahmedabad show some differences in organization. In all three one finds proprietary firms, partnerships with unlimited liability, limited companies with shares privately held, and in a very few cases also public joint-stock limited liability companies.[15] In Bombay, where partnership agency firms predominate, the partners agree to take over a certain minimum number of shares, and usually about 25 per cent of the mill companies' shares are owned by the partners taken together.[16] The usual method of organizing a managing agency firm with a view to floating a cotton-mill company in Ahmedabad is for a limited liability company to be formed with a nominal capital of Rs 1,000, there being 1,000 shares of Re 1 each. To buy this one-rupee share, a person has to lay down Rs 5,000, partly in the share of the mill company, and partly in cash deposits with the mill. 'Anyone who comes forward with Rs 5,000, i.e. Rs 3,000 in the shape of ordinary share capital and Rs 2,000 in the shape of deposits for a fixed period of seven years, is given one share of the managing agency or one-thousandth part of the agency commission.[17] This one-rupee share has considerably more value than its nominal value, and in some cases it is said to fetch a premium of Rs 700 or 800. Formerly the managing agents used to take into their agency firms any person or persons who supplied a certain amount of capital as something like sleeping partners, but now most of the agencies have been made into limited liability concerns and shares are issued, a portion of which the holders may sell at their discretion. In the past it was also the practice when loans were taken from private firms of Shroffs, to grant them a share in the managing agency commission in addition to the usual interest on the loan. When a cotton mill is floated as a joint-stock company, the several partners of the managing agency firm subscribe to the shares of the company and take them up fully in some agreed proportion. Although the shares are nominally open to the public, it is the partners that are responsible for a certain percentage of the shares, and it is open to any partner to distribute the shares later among his friends or the outside public. These latter do not come in directly in the beginning, but only when a partner unloads the shares.[18] But even when he does, he gets his usual commission based on the total holding, while the owners of the shares get only the declared dividend. The partnership agreement is non-terminable for at least eighty years. In cases where a partner desires to transfer his rights, the other partners must be given the first choice to buy him out.

It will thus be evident that in each type mentioned above, the relation between the managing agents and the concerns floated by them is very intimate. When an agreement is entered into between a mill company and a managing agent, it is in effect an agreement between themselves in their dual capacity. The managing agents are the leading shareholders of the concern, and so the agreement is between themselves as (a) managers and (b) shareholders. Of course, in so far as shares are gradually taken up by outsiders, and as managing agents unload their capital on the market, the agreement becomes more real and has consequences of great economic and social importance. The draft of the agreement is settled by the Board of Directors, who again are the individuals comprising the managing agency firm or their friends. The agreements contain various features which differ greatly in detail done from another. In many cases the agreement provides for a long fixed tenure of management extending to twenty or thirty years. In Ahmedabad the agency cannot be terminated at all, and the only circumstance in which it can change hands is when a concern does not work well, and is unable to find the requisite finance, in which case the agency is voluntarily surrendered to a new firm of partners. But even in terminable agreements care is taken to ensure that managing agents are not turned out easily. Some of the provisions state the conditions under which the managing agency agreement may be terminated, and it will be noticed that except in cases of gross mismanagement or incompetence they cannot be turned out, and even so a two-thirds majority is often required. Since managing agents retain a certain percentage of shares, it is not easy to get such a large majority against them. Again, the agreement sometimes requires a minimum share amount to be held by the managing agents, and this in turn ensures their continuance.

Promotion of Concerns in the Cotton Industry

The early cotton mills in India were first established in Bombay city and owed their existence, as already stated, to the enterprise and energy of a few wealthy Parsi merchants and bankers who were assisted by the agents of British machine-making firms. Soon after the Hindu community of Bhatias entered the field as promoters and started mills with the aid of their own resources and those of their friends. Although they were ignorant of the technical conditions of the industry they were men who had an intimate knowledge of the cotton trade and gave personal attention to the details of the working of the mill companies. Their want of technical experience was made up by the importing of skilled technical labour, and but for the Lancashire men who came out as managers to supervise Lancashire machinery, the cotton industry could not have developed so rapidly in India. The mills started in the earlier period were all adequately financed and equipped. The profits that were earned by them were such as to invite more and more mill promotions. But the later entrants were of the type well known in all countries. They were the speculative class of company promoters who had little experience and less resources of their own. They held out much promise of high profits to investors, and their interest was only to win substantial gains by floating the companies. The system of remuneration based on output increased the number of concerns floated. A mill agent assured of a minimum commission on production (quarter anna per lb of yarn) had every inducement to promote a mill because, whatever be the ultimate success or failure of the concern, the commission would enable him to recover the capital he had put in. By holding out promises of buying stores, supplies, machinery, etc., and by offering to utilize their services for building and construction, various persons were persuaded to take up shares in the mill agents' concern. Thus apart from the mill agents themselves, the chief shareholders were the friends and relations of the agents, the machinery and store suppliers, the coal dealer, the cotton merchant, the broker, the maccadam, the building contractor—all who were in a greater or lesser degree obliged to the agents and drawing benefit directly from the new enterprise.[19] In many cases, even before the engines emitted steam, the companies had to wind up.[20] Instances were not unknown when a few people sought to start a company with only the vaguest notion of how to work a cotton mill, and governed only by the motive of making enormous profit by selling out their interest in the concern. As one lawyer remarked, speaking of the prospectus of a mill company shown to him, 'this company is being formed to purchase the land of B at a fabulous price, to build a cotton mill thereon for the benefit of B and to appoint him and his nominees as agents for life and secure employment for their friends and relations.[21] Companies projected on these lines often did not reach the stage of registration or the issue of a prospectus, while those which could gather a little capital from unwary investors soon came to grief. But these cannot be regarded as the normal feature. On the other hand, in many cases the methods of promotion were characterized by careful investigation and prudent planning. The industry owed much to the pioneering work of men like J.N. Tata, who went over to England to study the working of the mills in Lancashire, and to obtain machinery suitable for spinning and weaving in the different climate conditions of India. The influence of Greaves, Cotton & Co., Ltd., who became managing agents of several cotton mills, and of Bradbury, Brady & Co., who were machinery agents, and who advised the mills in regard to equipment, was also important in the development of the cotton industry. But when cotton mills came to be floated by smaller capitalists and less well-known managing agents, whose only motive was to get the agency commission, certain serious evils came to be associated with the system of flotation which led to fluctuations in the progress of the industry. By holding out promises of buying materials from cotton merchants, coal dealers, store suppliers, etc., sufficient funds were secured for the company from such persons, but the mills suffered greatly owing to the poor quality of the goods delivered and the obligation to buy from those who had subscribed to the shares of the company on such assurances.[22] The contract for the cartage of the company's cotton, machinery, and other goods was given to those who took a large number of shares, while the building contractor had to accept a substantial sum in script for his work in lieu of cash. Again, part of the subscription to mill shares came from the local agents of machinery firms,[23] and machinery was purchased only from those who were prepared not only to supply it on credit but also willing to make a contribution to the share capital. The machinery agents could afford to subscribe initially to the shares of a company and gradually unload their capital because with machinery costing about Rs 7 to 8 lakhs for a moderately sized mill, the commission amounted to Rs 50,000, part of which they could easily invest in the mill. But such a system of mill flotation meant the import of unsuitable machinery, and mills started sometimes with a load of debt to the machine-markers, which they could not repay. Some of them therefore became 'the museum of all kinds of obsolete machinery'[24] and had to close down or to be reorganized. There was enormous waste in such a system of promotion, but luckily it became rarer with the passage of time. The public came to look with suspicion upon such methods, and soon it was made impossible for any but influential mill agents of ability and prestige to float cotton mills with success. But this is not to say that even to-day wasteful and unsound methods of flotation do not exist. In the boom period of 1919 to 1921 many a concern was started in India which had not the least title to public support.[25] Professional promoters sprang up all over the country, holding out absurd promises of huge profits, with the result that an enormous amount of capital was wasted. Mills were transferred from one agency to another and capitalized at enormously inflated values. But on the whole the agency system of mill flotation has ensured to India a certain economy, and the flotation of wild-cat enterprises has been rendered less easy.

The methods of promoting cotton mills in Ahmedabad and elsewhere have differed from those prevalent in Bombay. In Ahmedabad, as has already been pointed out in a general way, the mills have been started, controlled, and financed by the managing agents who, together with some of their friends, practically owned the mills. Unlike the cotton merchants of Bombay, the mill agents of Ahmedabad were financiers and capitalists who, with the profits of money-lending and banking, became the pioneers of the mill industry. The public were invited to come into the industry only after a lapse of time, and on the whole their confidence in the mill industry had been such that they were not only willing to take shares but to make heavy deposits with the mill companies.

Jute Mills

As with the cotton industry where Lancashire men came out to run the cotton mills and train Indian workers to tend the machinery, so in the jute industry Dundee mill overseers came out to look after the machinery in the mills in Bengal. The first jute mill was started by one Acland with the help of an Indian financial agent,[26] and these two partners managed the mill. Even when the first limited liability company in the jute industry was started, it is significant that it was managed by a firm of managing agents (Messrs Borradaile, Schiller & Co.) although there was also a managing director in the concern. The history of the flotation of jute mills in Bengal shows the part played by individual merchants who later founded the managing agency firms in their own names or in those of local agents of British firms. Although the first jute mill had a chequered career and was restarted in 1868 as a new company, and the managing agency transferred to a new firm, the industry was so prosperous that many new mills were floated between 1872 and 1873. Indeed, in that period it was only necessary to issue a prospectus for the shares to be fully subscribed forthwith. Naturally some of the new companies were conceived rather hastily and started with insufficient resources and equipment. They became moribund and had to be reorganized and restarted under new names and new management.[27] The pioneers of the jute mills belonged to two or three distinct classes of people. Some of them were men who had come out as representatives of British firms and started jute mills, with the help of a few partners and founded managing agency firms in their own name. There were instances of the servants and officers of the managing agency firms persuading their head office to float new concerns, and in this way some mills were floated. The Borneo Jute Company was started in 1859 at the instance of the local agents of the Borneo Company. On the other hand the Gouripore mill was started by a Doctor Barrie representing Messrs Scott, Thomson & Co. in conjunction with one Smith representing a sugar refining company. Thus either the old agency firms went on promoting new mills, or new agency partnership firms were organized by persons representing British trading firms with a view specially to floating new concerns.

Iron and Steel Industry

Perhaps in no other industry has the extent or importance of the pioneering and experimenting work been revealed to a greater extent and the part played by managing agents seen in truer perspective than in the promotion of the Tata Iron and Steel Co.[28] From 1900 to 1907, when the company was actually floated, the time and money spent by J.N. Tata and his friends in the investigation of the suitable conditions for the manufacture of pig-iron and steel were enormous. After getting a prospecting licence in 1900 and arranging for the prospecting work to be done by some agents, he went over to Germany and America and realized that if his scheme was to mature it was necessary to spend a large amount in preliminary investigation and in a thorough and scientific survey of local conditions, raw materials, markets, etc. But nothing daunted him. An expert engineer was got out, and for the next two years an enormous amount of wandering, combined with great privation, marked the adventurous prospecting operations. The preliminary cost had reached the sum of £ 30,000, which would have been sheer loss if the enterprise had never reached the stage of successful flotation, and indeed the project on which Tata and the expert were engaged in prospecting was not destined to be started in his lifetime. It was the discovery of the rich ores in the lofty Gurumaishini Hill and the great assistance rendered by Mr P.N. Bose, a retired official of the Geological Survey Department, that finally led to the maturing of the project; and in 1907, after experiencing a great check in the attempt to float a company with British capital, the Tata Iron and Steel Co. was finally started with Indian capital. The industry owed its rise and development entirely to the initiative and ability of J.N. Tata, the head of the managing agency firm founded by him. But for the expenditure which he was prepared to risk in the enterprise, the steel company would never have been founded.

Promoters' Remuneration

Has the cost of promotion in India been excessive? It is difficult to answer this question with any exactness, as in the large majority of cases the remuneration to promoters takes the form of managing agency commissions and profits, and is not directly in the form of promoters' shares, thus identifying their interests not only with the promotion but also with the continuing prosperity of the concern. In return for organizing a business unit, the promoter enters into an agreement by which he becomes the managing agent of that concern for a definite period of time and cannot ordinarily be turned out. In a word, the return to the promoter is the right of managing the concern with all the privileges and rights pertaining to management, and, as we shall see later, these extend to the right of taking commissions on all kinds of activities pursued on behalf of the business. It is therefore difficult to separate the share belonging to him in his capacity of promoter from that accruing to him in his capacity as manager.

There have been cases where the promoters have sought to make money by the sale of their own properties to the business which they floated. But the Indian company law has ensured a certain amount of publicity by insisting that the names of all vendors from whom any property is acquired must be published, and by providing that full particulars of the nature and extent of the interests of every director in the promotion of the company and in the property proposed to be acquired by the company must be published in the prospectus. This has given a fair security against fraud and exploitation of the investors by the promoters.

A typical case of promoters' rights and privileges and the remuneration granted to them is the furnished by the agreement between Messrs Tata, Sons & Co. and Tata Iron and Steel Co., when the latter was started. 'All the ore fields, railway, and freight concessions, together with all the other privileges conceded by the Government of India, were handed over to the company by Messrs Tata, Sons & Co. in consideration of the allotment to them of 15 lakhs of rupees in ordinary shares, issued as fully paid up, and 5¼ lakhs of rupees in cash to reimburse them for their preliminary out-of-pocket outlay upon the scheme. This latter amount, with an addition of 4¾ lakhs of rupees of their own (making a total of 10 lakhs), the firm undertook to invest in the shares of the company and not to sell any of those shares for five years. The firm was also to receive a royalty of 4 annas per ton sold as ore in India or exported. The firm was also to act as agents for the company for a period of eighteen years, their remuneration being a commission of 5 per cent on annual net profits, after deducting interest on debentures and amount set aside for depreciation, with a minimum commission of Rs 50,000 per year.[29]

Since it is impossible to assess separately the amount of promoter's profits as it is absorbed in his profits of management, the question whether the promotion of industry is done economically is one intimately connected with the efficiency and economy of management, a question to be examined fully later. The managing agent gets profits in a dual capacity. As holder of a considerable amount of shares it is to his interest that the company is efficiently managed and that dividends are annually declared. But he is able to get paid in a number of other ways, and receives commission on purchase and sale, on insurance, and thus is in a position to make money even when the company is unable to declare any profit. Managing agency by itself tends, therefore, to secure a certain value because of its rights and privileges, apart from its ability to show profit in the concerns managed. It might happen, although such cases are undoubtedly exceptional, that the managing agents may be able to secure some income from the concerns for a considerable time, although the concerns they manage have been losing. But the nemesis comes ultimately, and the more enlightened among them are not willing to kill the goose that lays the golden eggs.

Conclusion

It will be clear from the above that the methods of floating industrial units in India have on the whole been sound and economical, and that the system of promoting concerns by managing agents has yielded fruitful results. It has for one thing kept away the parasitic type of company promoters, who, except in some abnormal years, were given short shrift. The men who pioneered the enterprise were persons with considerable financial resources, able and willing to command expert assistance for investigating and prospecting thoroughly any projects before trying to float them.[30] Large sums of money were spent on pioneering schemes which could not ultimately reach the stage of flotation, and the burden of such losses was borne by the managing agents, and the public were relieved of it. Thus managing agents performed services in India which issue houses were doing in other countries. They were, indeed, what may be termed universal providers of industry, being promoters, financiers, and mangers of the venture they established. The name of the managing agent was in itself a guarantee to the public of the soundness of the enterprise in which he was interested, and the absence of it in a public issue a presumption of its untrustworthiness. In this way the public came more and more to realize that they were not to risk their capital in ventures not backed by one or other well-known agency firms. A great deal of waste was thus avoided. True, there was danger even in this. A scheme sound in itself and promoted by a person not belonging to an agency firm might be unable to effect a successful flotation. When to this is added the fact that managing agents were sometimes unenterprising, it is obvious that some desirable ventures might have been crowded out. But on the whole there seems to be little doubt that the public would lose less by putting a brake upon the activities of even able promoters than by encouraging too freely the brilliant but resourceless and opportunist promoters. The system of promotion by managing agents was thus a distinct gain to industry.

Second, since managing agents had a deeper interest in the concern than a mere promoter would have had, they were not only interested in successful flotation but their interests were linked up with the fortunes of the concerns they started. They were at least believers in their own offspring, and being endowed with more than average ability there was every chance of their enterprise turning out to be a success. Most of them owned, at least in the early years of the company, the bulk of the shares in the concerns for which they were managing agents. Failure of the ventures meant not loss of dividend and agency commission but, what is even more important, it implied loss of credit. This close association of ownership and control has resulted in a unity of aim and motive, and the common defects of joint-stock enterprise arising from diffused authority were obviated by a system in which the managing agents who had the greatest interest were able to work with a single-minded purpose and free from the shackles of control by a Board of Directors. The inertia that sometimes characterizes the management of a joint-stock company because of the unwillingness of the Board to take risks is absent in a system of management in which the management is assured of a long tenure. The 'golden rule of capitalism' that 'where the risk lies, control must lie' is satisfied in the scheme of organization in India. But the special feature of the system arises when the managing agent ceases to have a majority or even a considerable portion of the shares of the company, and then arises conflict of interest between him and the shareholders. It is the emergence of this conflict in recent years in the system of managing agency as it works in Bombay city that has caused all the difficulty and brought discredit to the system. But further consideration of all this must be deferred to a later chapter dealing with an estimate of the work and future of the Indian managing agency system.

Third, industrial enterprises were nursed for a long time by managing agents until they felt they could be safely launched out and thrown open to public subscription. This has been specially so in regard to concerns floated by British managing agents. The Indian Paper Mill Company was started years ago, and still continues as a private company, because Messrs Andrew Yule & Co. would not float it as a public company until absolutely assured of success.[31] It has been said that owing to doubts in the mind of the investor about the value and character of any new proposition placed before him there exists a gap between the sources of demand for capital and the sources of supply which constitutes an 'economic distance' in every country,[32] and in India this distance is bridged in a fairly effective way by the managing agent, who has proved a helpful intermediary. What is more, since the concern had previously been working successfully in a small way the investors could be certain of a safe and sound investment.

It is not, however, to be understood that the flotation of industrial concerns was not sometimes attended with waste or that there were not cases of ill-conceived and even fraudulent promotion. The number of companies that were wound up within a year of their starting is some measure of the amount of capital running to waste each year. There have been cases where unscrupulous promoters organized themselves into so-called managing agents with a view to hoodwinking the investors; but the only resemblance between them and the old and well-known agency firms was the name 'managing agents'. Fortunately, such people have never had a long innings. Again, in the hectic years of 1920 and 1921, some cases of mill reorganization occurred where the promoters made enormous profit at the expense of the investors. An instance of this character is given in the Report of the Bombay Stock Exchange Enquiry Committee, p. 52, and it reveals the fact that managing agents were not wholly immune from the charge of wasteful promotion and reorganization.

Further, while the fullest credit may be given to the pioneering work of managing agents there is increasing justification for the view that in recent years they have been rather unwilling to pioneer and risk in new enterprises[33] where the profits might neither be large nor certain. It must be admitted, of course, that whether a new business is to be started or not is a matter which must really be left to the discretion of the managing agents. But the point is that in a country where the public look for leadership to the managing agents, any conservatism and narrow-mindedness in the latter may have serious effects on the economic development of the country. While from their personal point of view there may be justification for their concentrating attention on routine lines of business activity, and on pursuit of certain gains, it may be that the country would have been better served if its industrial leaders had been more adventurous, and if they had not shown a tendency to rest on their oars and to be content to earn from old investments rather than embark on new and uncertain ventures. However successful the managing agency system of promotion might have been in the past, it cannot be concluded that it is so at present, or will continue to be so in the future. The past was the golden age of Indian industrial development. There was such a vast, unexplored field that the way was very smooth, and men of ordinary ability and initiative were able to pioneer in those years. Now that the task is less easy because of the greater obstacles to encounter, one is not so certain that the managing agents will justify their permanent existence. Since the country is largely dependent upon the agency system for its industrial development, the extent to which it is capable of fulfilling its functions by continuously supplying itself with fresh talents and new blood is not a mere private matter but an important social problem on which some light must be thrown.

Again, there has not been enough co-operative endeavour among managing agents in floating concerns which may be either too big or too risky for any one individual firm to undertake. The only way of overcoming the existing defect is for them to co-operate with another in floating big enterprises. Further, it is also unfortunate that the Indian and European managing agents have been working on parallel and often in separate fields. They have not fully co-operated in the common purpose of advancing industrial development. The differences in methods and organization between the Indian and British managing agents will engage our attention later.

Notes

1. Thus the managing agents of the Bengal Paper Mill Co., Ltd., are Balmer, Lawrie & Co., Ltd. Their London correspondents are Alexander Lawrie & Co., Ltd. The partners of this latter firm are partners of the Calcutta firm, and thus control the Bengal Paper Mill Co. *Indian Tariff Board*: *Paper and Paper Pulp Industries*, Evidence, 1932,vol. I, p. 462.
2. Sir C. Rhodes's letter to the writer dated 19 September 1933.
3. *Indian Tariff Board: Cotton Industry*, Evidence, 1927, vol. 3, p. 324.
4. The names of Sir Percy Newson, Sir Campbell Rhodes, and Sir Alexander Murray, who, however, was only the head of the Indian branch, may be cited as examples.
5. Burn & Co., Ltd. is a public limited company which has been amalgamated with Martin & Co., and which manages the Indian Iron & Steel Co., Indian Standard Wagon Co., etc.
6. *Report of the Indian Industrial Commission*, 1916–18, p. 13.
7. The following extracts from the Articles of Association relating to two mills managed by Messrs Andrew Yule & Co. will show how the agents secure a permanent right of management:
   (*a*) *Budge-Budge Mills*—'The firm of Messrs Andrew Yule & Co. and their successors in business under that or any other name or style and their

assignees shall be and continue to be the managing agents of the Company and shall as such managing agents be remunerated by a commission of 5 per cent on the net profits of the Company and Rs 500 per month for a suitable office and establishment in Calcutta to be provided by the agents, but in case such net profits and the said sum of Rs 500 per month shall not amount to Rs 42,000 per annum the remuneration shall be made up to Rs 42,000.'

(*b*) *Central Jute Mills*—'The firm of Messrs Andrew Yule & Co. and their successors in business under that or any other name or style, already irrevocably declared by the Memorandum of Association to be the managing agent of the Company shall as such managing agent be remunerated by a Commission of 2 per cent on the gross proceeds of sales of goods made by the Company, but in case the said 2 per cent on the sales shall not amount to Rs 30,000, then the remuneration shall be made up to Rs 30,000 in any year.'

Quoted from the *Capital*, Calcutta, by the *Indian Textile Journal*, March 1904, p. 188.

8. See Appendix 11.1 at the end of the chapter, where the holdings of some of the managing agents in those companies which they manage are given.
9. 'The merchants reaped a rich harvest of profits. These came mostly in the shape of nuggets of gold and silver authentically recorded at 51 crores of rupees'. D.E. Wacha, *Life of Tata*, 1918, p. 17.
10. 'Bardan carriers' are persons who carry cotton bales.
11. *Indian Textile Journal*, October 1893.
12. S.M. Rutnagur, *The Cotton Mills, 1927*, p. 9.
13. *Indian Central Banking Enquiry Committee*, Report, 1931, vol. I, p. 276.
14. *Indian Tariff Board: Cotton Industry*, 1927, vol. 3, Evidence of the Ahmedabad Mill Owners' Association, p. 441. The company law prohibited the formation of limited or unlimited partnerships of more than twenty persons.
15. *Indian Central Banking Enquiry Committee*, Report, p. 643. Out of thirty-six firms whose names appear in the Calcutta Stock Exchange list, only seven are limited companies and the rest are private firms.

    Family Concerns

    Most of the Ahmedabad mill agency companies are more or less family concerns. In Bombay, Morarji Gokuldass & Co. is a private partnership with only one person from outside (Sir D.E. Wacha). Messrs Thackersey, Mooljee & Co., Mathradass Gokuldass & Co., D.M. Petit, Sons & Co., Nowrosjee Wadia & Sons, C.N. Wadia & Co., and Narottam Morarjee & Co. are all more or less family concerns, though legally they are private partnerships.

    Public Limited Companies

    (*a*) Messrs W.H. Brady & Co., Ltd., was registered as a joint-stock company (Bombay) in June 1913. No shares were offered to the public, and the conversion into a public limited company involved no change either in the management or policy. The business which was established in 1893 had since grown very much, thus necessitating the change of organization (*Indian Textile Journal*, June 1913, p. 299).

(*b*) Binny & Co., Ltd., became a public limited company with 1350 lakhs of capital (Madras).

(*c*) Burn & Co., Ltd., public limited company (Calcutta).

(*d*) Steel Bros. Co., Ltd., public limited company (Calcutta).

(*e*) Stanes Co., Ltd., public limited company (Madras).

Private Limited Companies

(1) Messrs Tata, Sons & Co., Ltd., registered in 1917 with a capital of Rs 117 lakhs, Bombay.

(2) Messrs E.D. Sassoon & Co., Ltd., registered in 1920 with a capital of Rs 100 lakhs, Bombay.

(3) Messrs Cowasji Jehangir & Co., Ltd., registered in 1920 with a capital of Rs 100 lakhs, Bombay.

(4) Messrs Currimbhai Ebrahim & Sons, Ltd., registered in 1916 with a capital of Rs 93 lakhs, Bombay.

(5) Messrs Andrew Yule & Co., registered in 1919, paid up capital Rs 180 lakhs, Calcutta.

(6) Messrs Birla Bros. Co., registered in 1918, paid up capital Rs 50 lakhs, Calcutta.

(7) Messrs Begg, Dunlop & Co., registered in 1922, paid up capital Rs 51 lakhs, Calcutta.

(8) Messrs Balmer, Lawrie & Co., registered in 1924, authorized capital Rs 60 lakhs, Calcutta.

(9) Messrs Villiers & Co., Ltd., registered in 1919, authorized capital Rs 20 lakhs, Calcutta.

(10) Messrs Low & Co., registered in 1919, authorized capital Rs 30 lakhs, Calcutta.

The above information relating to public and private limited companies was extracted from *The Investor's India Year Book*, 1930–1, and from Pat Lovett, *The Mirror of Investment*, 1927.

16. 'I began business in 1883 with a share in the agency of the Bombay Cotton Manufacturing Co., and *thereby* incurred a liability to take up shares of the value of Rs 30,000'. Letter left behind by a mill agent who committed suicide, quoted in the *Indian Textile Journal*, September 1909.
17. *Indian Central Banking Enquiry Committee*, Report, 1931, vol. I, p. 277.
18. *Indian Central Banking Enquiry Committee*, Evidence of the Ahmedabad Mill Owners' Association, vol. 2, p. 480.
19. *Indian Textile Journal*, December 1904, p. 73.
20. S.M. Rutnagur, *The Cotton Mills*, 1927, p. 47.

21. *Ibid.*
22. In Lancashire, too, the mills sometimes had credit from merchants and became 'tied' to them with the same adverse consequences. *Committee on Industry and Trade, Survey of Textile Industries*, 1928, p. 27.
23. S.M. Rutnagar, *The Cotton Mills*, p. 47.

    In Ahmedabad, too, the system by which local agents of British machinery firms were asked to subscribe to the shares of the concern was no means exceptional.

    Indian Textile Journal, July 1904, p. 324: 'By an agreement made on 19th April, 1895, by the Ahmedabad Advance Spinning and Weaving Co., Ltd., with one Mr T. Ralph Douse, in consideration of a sum of £33,000 he was to supply to the company 15,000 spindles and 300 looms with all preparatory machinery, engines and boilers, and it was arranged that the sum of £33,000 should be paid *half* in cash and *half in fully paid up* shares in the Company'.

    Out of a total of 799 shares of Rs 1,000 each in the Queen Mills, Mr Abdul Husen Abdul Karim became the owner of 592 shares, and these were shares given to him in lieu of cash for supplying machinery (*Indian Textile Journal*, September 1909, p. 434).
24. Arno Pearse, *The Cotton Industry of India*, 1930, p. 8.
25. *Report of the Bombay Stock Exchange Enquiry Committee*, 1924.
26. D.R. Wallace, *The Romance of Jute*, 2nd edition, 1928, p. 11.
27. *Ibid.*, p. 31.
28. For the pioneering work of J.N. Tata the reader is referred to the admirable works: D.E. Wacha, *Life of J.N. Tata*, 1918, and F.R. Harris, *Life of J.N. Tata*, 1925.
29. F.R. Harris, *Life of J.N. Tata*, 1925, p. 203.
30. For example, 'In regard to the Katni Cement Company, we first started a syndicate putting in 5 or 6 lakhs of rupees and tried and risked money; finding that it was successful we finally started the concern and threw it open for public subscription. We asked our machinery agents to give us different kinds of machinery and got from Germany experts and paid them all at our risk' (Sir Fazulbhoy Currimbhai, *Industrial Commission*, Evidence, vol. 3, p. 98).
31. *Indian Tariff Board: Paper and Paper Pulp Industries*, Evidence tendered by applicants for protection, 1925, p. 311. Also Report, 1931, p. 99.
32. F. Lavington, *British Capital Market*, 1921, p. 103.
33. *Report of the Indian Industrial Commission*, p. 13.

APPENDIX 11.1

Holdings of Messrs Tata, Sons & Co., Ltd., in the Tata Iron and Steel Co., Ltd.

	Par Value
Before 1914, 32,800 ordinary shares and 3,000 deferred shares	Rs 25,50,000
In 1924, 32,600 ordinary shares, 4,500 deferred, and 2,800 second preference shares	Rs 28,60,000

This out of a total called capital in March 1922 of 946.80 lakhs amounts to less than 3 per cent (*Indian Tariff Board: Steel Industry*, 1924, vol. I, Evidence, p. 219).

Percentage Holdings of F.W. Heilgers & Co., Managing Agents of Titaghur Paper Mills

	Per cent
Ordinary Shares	11.5
Preference, old issue	0.3
Preference, new issue	0.6
Deferred	60.8

The percentage of total capital held by managing agents is 13.1 (*Indian Tariff Board: Paper and Pulp Industries*, 1932, vol. I, p. 325).

Holdings of the Managing Agents of Deccan Paper Mills, Ltd.

They hold Rs 5 to 6 lakhs out of a total paid-up capital of Rs 9.25 lakhs, i.e., nearly 60 per cent of the shares (Ibid., p. 580).

V.K.R.V. Rao (1908–1991)

Source: Institute for Social and Economic Change, Bangalore.

Vijendra Kasturi Ranga Varadaraja Rao was born in 1908 in Kancheepuram in present-day Tamil Nadu. He did his BA (Honours) and MA in economics from Bombay University. His MA thesis under the supervision of Professor C.N. Vakil was published in 1931 as *Taxation of Income in India* and was well received. Rao went to Cambridge in 1933 after having taught for a couple of years at Wilson College. In Cambridge he interacted with some of the greatest economists of the period, including Keynes, Dobb, Kahn, and Joan Robinson. As a member of the prestigious Political Economy Club, he read two papers. After obtaining a first class in his economics tripos in 1934, he went on to do his Ph.D. with Colin Clark on India's national income. Rao won the prestigious Adam Smith Prize in 1935. In 1936, he was among the earliest to be awarded the Ph.D. degree from Cambridge. His dissertation was a pioneering exercise in estimating India's national income, which became a classic soon after its publication in 1940 and provided the basis for national income estimation for many decades thereafter.

Rao returned to India and in 1937 joined L.D. Arts College in Ahmedabad as Principal. Delhi University selected him as its first professor of economics, a post he assumed in 1942 and held until his retirement in 1961. Before Independence he worked for a while in the Food Department of the government. A major achievement was the creation of the Delhi School of Economics in 1949, which became a premier centre for the study of economics. Later, in 1958, he founded the Institute of Economic Growth in Delhi and in 1972, the Institute for Social and Economic Change in Bangalore. Rao made major contributions to education and research as Director of the Delhi School of Economics (1948–57), Vice-Chancellor of Delhi University (1957–60), Director of the Institute of Economic Growth (1960–63) and the Institute for Social and Economic Change (1972–77). In 1985 he was accorded the title of National Professor.

After Independence he served on numerous important national commissions and committees and was Chairman of the UN Sub-commission for Economic Development (1947–50). Between 1963 and 1971, V.K.R.V. Rao held high national positions as Member of the Planning Commission and then as Cabinet Minister. He died in 1991.

Among his numerous books and articles, pride of place would probably go to *The National Income of British India, 1931–32*, published in 1940. This is one of the classics in Indian economics of the twentieth century. Rao also had several important publications in the *Economic Journal* and the *Indian Economic Review*.

Major Biographical Sources: S.L. Rao (ed.), *The Partial Memories of V.K.R.V. Rao*, New Delhi, Oxford University Press, 2002; Kiran Mishra, *V.K.R.V. Rao: His Life and Times*, New Delhi, Vikas, 1996. Also the website of the Institute for Social and Economic Change, http://www.isec.ac.in.

This paper applied, for the first time, the concept of disguised unemployment to an underdeveloped country like India.* Rao's paper appeared well before Rosenstein-Rodan's 1943 paper in the *Economic Journal*, which is usually credited with the first use of the term, disguised unemployment, in the development literature. The discussion that followed the presentation of Rao's paper during the Indian Economic Conference has also been included as the opinions expressed anticipated many modern ideas on employment and unemployment.

Rao acknowledged that Joan Robinson had introduced the concept of disguised unemployment in the context of depression in developed countries; he then proceeded to show how it could be used in relation to India. Rao first defined unemployment as '[the] loss of employment of workers who were previously employed and inability to obtain employment by these and others who might not have been previously employed but who now seek for employment at existing levels of wages or slightly lower levels'.

In the Indian context, Rao proceeded to distinguish between four kinds of unemployment: frictional unemployment, which was not a serious problem in India; cyclical unemployment, which existed but was not serious; seasonal unemployment, which was a major problem, especially in agriculture where it was difficult to spread work opportunities over the year; and, disguised unemployment, involving 'the diversion of labour from more productive to less productive occupations'.

Rao estimated that 48 million out the 91 million persons working in India were seasonally employed. He did not estimate the magnitude of disguised unemployment, but asserted that it was large and growing. In this context he clearly stated that the withdrawal of the labour of the disguisedly unemployed from the land would not adversely affect agricultural output:

> It is a well known fact that *there are on the land a number of people who do not really contribute to the production of agricultural output and that if they give up agriculture, output would remain much the same.* They are the disguised unemployed of India, and their numbers are large enough to constitute a major problem in India's economy [italics added].

Rao was considering the situation in India under colonial rule where workers in handicrafts had lost their jobs and were, in the absence of a better alternative, taking to agriculture. This led him to describe such persons as the disguisedly unemployed. However, later in his paper, he moved to a more general view that all those in agriculture who could be removed from it without affecting its output, were disguisedly unemployed.

Rao's views are similar to those of Ambedkar who implied that labour withdrawal from agriculture would reduce 'predation' and create surplus for capital formation. (See Chapter 2 and my paper, 'The Indian Antecedents of Disguised Unemployment and

* V.K.R.V. Rao (1938): 'The Problem of Unemployment in India', from *Indian Journal of Economics*, 1938, issue 71, pp. 627–34 and pp. 676–79 (discussion).

Surplus Labour', *Indian Journal of Labour Economics*, Vol. 51, No. 1, January–March 2008, pp. 53–62.) Rao set out more explicitly and in modern terms, the assumed condition for labour shifts from agriculture to non-agriculture, viz. that agricultural output should not fall. He also defined availability for work more precisely, not in relation to any expected wage, but to going rates of remuneration. Given that this paper appeared in 1938 and applied for the first time the concept of disguised unemployment in relation to economic development, its contribution to modern development economics deserves to be recognized.

In the discussion that followed Rao's presentation at the Indian Economic Conference in 1938, P.S. Lokanathan pointed out that population growth could also be a factor responsible for the growth of disguised unemployment and argued that the solution lay in raising productivity. H.L. Dey, in his intervention, anticipated the modern income concept of work, noting that there was the problem of extremely low earnings for the majority of the population. Interestingly, the demand constraint on employment expansion was not considered.

12

The Problem of Unemployment in India

V.K.R.V. Rao

Various definitions have been attempted of the phrase 'full employment' and 'unemployment,' and these have shown how difficult it is to draw the line at the point where unemployment ceases and voluntary choice of leisure takes its place. In actual fact, given a high enough wage rate or a marked fall in the pain of labour such as, e.g., accompanies patriotic outbursts on the part of the nation, there will be a great addition to the number of people seeking work; and given a big enough fall in wage rates or a marked rise in the feeling of pain associated with labour, there will be a great addition to the number of people not seeking work. From this point of view, full employment is reached only when even an indefinite rise in wages no longer results in an increase in the supply of labour offering itself for employment or to put it in a different way, when the slightest fall in wages will lead to a contraction in the supply of labour offering itself for employment. From this point of view, there is no community where there is no unemployment.

It is clear therefore that full employment and unemployment involve somewhat different sets of concepts and that while unemployment means absence of full employment, full employment means more than absence of unemployment. What then is unemployment? Unemployment may be described as loss of employment by those who are already in employment. But it is not necessary, as Mrs Robinson points out, that an unemployed person need necessarily be an unoccupied person; for the dismissed worker may, as an alternative to suicide scratch up a living somehow or other by his own efforts. In such a case, a decline of effective demand would lead to a diversion of labour from occupations in which productivity is higher to others where it is lower; this Mrs Robinson terms 'disguised unemployment'.

In addition, there is a class of unemployment that does not come under the scope of our definition; and that is the juvenile and adolescent labour, which has never known employment. In order to include them as well we may add to the category of the unemployed also those young persons who want work at the existing levels of wages or even at slightly lower levels but who cannot get work. There are also those other members of the community who might suddenly find themselves deprived of an unearned income and might therefore seek employment at existing levels of wages or at slightly lower levels, but are unable to get it. These also could be described as a part of the unemployed. We might now define unemployment as 'loss of employment of workers who were previously employed and inability to obtain employment by these and others who might not have been previously employed but who now seek for employment at existing levels of wages or at slightly lower levels'. This excludes from the category of the unemployed those members of the community who do not want employment at present wage levels but who would do so at higher rates; for unemployment of this kind will be found in every community. I am also quite conscious of the fact that I am connecting up unemployment with inability to obtain work at a *particular wage level*; but I am doing this deliberately. Given certain assumptions and a low enough wage rate, there could not be much unemployment, just as given a low enough price there would be few commodities suffering from deficiency of demand. It is therefore no solution of unemployment to suggest that wages should be lowered indefinitely till full employment is reached.

Unemployment may be described as of the following four kinds:

1. Frictional
2. Cyclical
3. Seasonal
4. Disguised

Frictional unemployment is that which arises from the fact that it takes time for different kinds of labour supply to adjust themselves to changes in demand, the total demand remaining constant. This is inevitable in any community where there are changes in tastes or in technique. This kind of unemployment is temporary; but even this can be obviated to a considerable extent by instituting labour exchanges and a labour intelligence service of which parents can take advantage in choosing vocations for their children.

Cyclical unemployment is the unemployment which results from periodic fluctuations in total demand; and it is this kind of unemployment which has attracted the attention of economists the most. This kind of unemployment is more peculiar to industrially developed countries which have their economy organised on a capitalistic basis. It is not such a serious problem in the case of India. But it cannot be denied that it exists; and will probably increase in importance with the growth of industrialisation.

Seasonal unemployment is unemployment which is due to technical conditions of production. It is true that seasonal unemployment may also be the result of seasonal demand; but in this case, it would be possible, with conscious effort, to spread the work over the whole year; such a course, however, is not possible when the employment is determined by the technical conditions of industry. The most typical example of such an industry is agriculture, particularly in places where it is solely dependent on the rainfall. It is needless to say therefore that this kind of unemployment is a major problem in an agricultural country like ours.

Disguised unemployment is a new category added to the existing list by Mrs Robinson; and in my opinion, it is a very important addition. By disguised unemployment is meant diversion of labour from more productive to less productive occupations. It can be described by a situation like, e.g., when a country loses its export market for the products of its skilled labour, thereby leading to an addition in the numbers of its unskilled labour; or when a country is in a process of industrial decay. It would also describe a situation when the handicrafts of a country give way before mill products, but the labour thus released gets no employment in the more productive factory occupations, but has to fall back upon trades or occupations less remunerative than the handicrafts in which it was previously engaged. The last situation would really describe what has been happening in India.

We may now turn to the problem of unemployment in India. Our problems are mainly those of seasonal and of disguised unemployment. Not that we do not have frictional unemployment in some of the bigger cities. It is also not true to suggest that industrial or cyclical unemployment of the type found in the west is not to be found in India. The recent depression has provided solid proof to the contrary as can be seen from Table 12.1.

The fall in what may be termed organised industrial employment during the four years of the slump was as much as 314,000 or a little less than 12 per cent of the total labour employed. It is obvious therefore that cyclical unemployment has also begun to make its appearance in India; but compared to the total employed or employable population in India, the numbers of

TABLE 12.1 Numbers employed

(Figures in '000s)

	In mines	*In railways*	*In factories*	*Total of columns 2, 3, and 4*
1929	365	818	1,553	2,736
1933	316	701	1,405	2,422

the cyclically unemployed are negligible. They do not constitute India's major problem.

It we turn to the number of workers engaged in agriculture, we really get to the heart of the problem. The relevant statistics are given in Table 12.2.

TABLE 12.2 Numbers Following as Principal Occupation

(Figures in '000s)

	Males	*Females*	*Total*
Cultivating owners	16,468	1,696	18,164
Tenant cultivators	20,070	3,444	23,514
Agricultural labourers	12,477	7,717	20,194

This entire population of nearly 62 million persons who are engaged in agriculture, whether as employers or as employees, is variously estimated to be unoccupied from 60 to 150 days in a year. The Royal Commission on Agriculture themselves opine that persons engaged in agriculture in India have from 2 to 5 months of pure leisure. In strict theory, one should say that the 20 million agricultural labourers are unemployed for a part of the year, while the 42 million cultivating owners and tenant cultivators have leisure during the same period. But in practice, there is not much distinction between some of the cultivating owners and tenant cultivators, especially of those whose holdings are very small, and most of the agricultural labourers; and a number of these so-called employers would come under the category of persons wanting work but unable to get it during the seasonal periods of apparent leisure. If we estimate this number at one half—and that would be a conservative estimate—of the employer class in agriculture we get 21 million cultivating owners and tenant cultivators as persons who are unoccupied for a part of the year and who would like to get some remunerative employment during that period. The total number of persons seeking employment—including in this number those who are unemployed as also those who are unoccupied—comes to 41 millions; and these are unemployed for a part of the year. Seasonal unemployment therefore accounts for 41 millions out of a total of 98 millions of workers in the country, assuming that those engaged in trade, transport and industry find work during the whole of the year. In other words, more that 40 per cent of India's occupied persons are seasonally unemployed.

It is more difficult to make any estimate of the volume of disguised unemployment in the country. That there is a large volume there can be no doubt. The progressive ruralization seen during the five decades preceding 1921 has brought to the land several millions who were previously employed in handicrafts, urban industries and other non-agricultural pursuits. It is a well known fact that there are on the land a number of people who really do not contribute to the production of agricultural output, and that if they give up agriculture, output would remain about much the same. These are the disguised unemployed of India, and their numbers are large enough to constitute a major problem in India's economy.

To sum up, India is suffering today from the two serious problems of seasonal unemployment and of disguised unemployment; and these are threatening to become a permanent feature of Indian economy. The combined result of both is to make production much less than what it could be; and the nation's standard of life gets unduly depressed. It is my belief that the presence of seasonal unemployment, particularly on such a large scale, is an economic fact of major importance; and must be taken into account in determining economic policy.

What is the best way of dealing with the question of seasonal unemployment? I think it can be met in two ways:

1. Remove the seasonal character of the employment by changing the relevant technical conditions in such a way as to provide work for the whole year.
2. Provide seasonal employment of such a kind as to be only available during the period when these 41 millions are free from their main occupation; this would in effect mean employment for the whole of the year, but it would be in two different occupations.

The first alternative is not so impossible as it may appear at first sight. In fact, even today, cultivators who can get a double crop and others who grow garden crops do find work for the whole of the year. There are at present nearly 35 million acres which are sown more than once; and assuming one worker per 4.3 acres (dividing the total area sown by 62 millions), this area must be providing whole-year employment to at least 8 million persons engaged in agriculture. To give similar employment to the 41 millions who are seasonally unemployed would require an area of at least 176 millions acres to be double-cropped. This is not possible. With the best effort in the world, it is not possible to increase the area under irrigation by anything like even another 50 millions acres; and without irrigation, one cannot normally take up double cropping. It is not possible to do away with the seasonal character of India's agricultural industry. All the same, there is no doubt that the area under irrigation, particularly irrigation by wells and tanks, could be substantially increased; and it is the duty of the new provincial governments to take up this work as early as possible, for the problem of India's unemployment is urgent and should brook no delay.

The other alternative left to us was that of providing seasonal employment so timed as to do away with the seasonal unemployment of these 41 millions. In most parts of the country, this would probably mean employment during the months of February, March and April. To do this means the development of certain *types of industries* the nature of which we shall now proceed to examine. First the industries must be such as can be profitably worked for 3 to 4 months during the year; in other words, the fact of their machinery or equipment being idle during the greater part of the year must not result in the industry proving a losing proposition. Interpreted in economic terms, this condition means that capital investment in such industries should be very small, and other overhead charges also should be very low. We can put the same thing in a different way by saying that these industries must be such that prime costs form the largest part of the cost of production of their output, and overheads, only a small proportion. This means in turn that the industries must be as little capitalistic as possible, using the phrase 'capitalistic' in the sense of 'involving the use of capital'. Industries in which labour charges form the largest part of costs are usually the handicrafts. The building industry, particularly that branch of it which deals with repairs of buildings and roads, and construction of roads, cleaning of tanks, canals etc., can also be a very good seasonal industry.

The other condition to be satisfied if the seasonal employment were to be taken advantage of is that the skill required on the part of the workers employed should not be very high. It must not be forgotten that the type of labour for whom this employment is intended has as its major occupation another industry, *viz.*, agriculture; and that therefore the work offered to them should be simple and easy to understand. The handicrafts therefore must be of such a kind as not only to involve little capital to run them but should also be such as can be run by comparatively unskilled labour.

A third and obvious condition is that these industries must be located in rural centres to which agricultural labour can easily and inexpensively resort when it finds itself unemployed. The growth of urban handicrafts can at best be only a partial solution to the problem of India's seasonally unemployed and care must therefore be taken to see that the handicrafts encouraged are located in villages or at least in such small towns as really form the centre of a group of villages. I conclude therefore that there is a clear economic case for handicrafts in this country. Handicrafts located in rural centres and working for a part of the year constitute the best way of providing seasonal employment to the 41 million persons engaged in agriculture who regularly experience seasonal unemployment. I suggest that Government have a special responsibility in this matter; and popularly constituted as they now are in the provinces, they would also be able to obtain public support for any schemes which they may undertake. It is therefore a matter for congratulation to find that at any rate some of the new provincial governments are showing a keen interest in the promotion of handicrafts in their respective provinces. My only criticism would be that their policy is not positive enough in this direction. It is not merely sufficient to give financial or other support to the existing handicrafts. It is necessary to see that the industrial development of the country proceeds on such lines that additions to its industrial production take place mainly through the medium of handicrafts. At any rate, all new industrial establishments can be licensed and permitted to operate only if they are located in rural centres. Government can also concentrate the constructional part of their rural development programme such as road repairs, building of new roads, clearing up tanks and canals, putting up and repairing fences, etc., entirely during those months when agricultural labour is unemployed. In the meanwhile, vigorous research work should be undertaken to find such substitutes for imports as can be produced by handicrafts. Government should also go ahead with the task of extending the area under irrigation, particularly by giving subsidies to villages, building new tanks, etc. In these ways, the state may do something towards meeting the problem of unemployment in India. The private individual too, if he likes, can do his little bit by voluntarily extending his patronage to the products of handicrafts.

To sum up, unemployment in India is mainly of a seasonal kind. The number of those seasonally unemployed is estimated at 41 millions. To solve it, it is necessary, on the one hand to extend the area under irrigation, garden crops, etc.; on the other, to provide handicrafts in rural centres which will work only for 2 to 4 months in a year and provide employment to the seasonally unemployed just when they need it.

Conference Proceedings

Unemployment

Dr P.S. Lokanathan commenting on Dr V.K.R.V. Rao's paper said that while he did not deny the practical value of the concept of disguised unemployment, he could not agree that it was an independent factor explaining unemployment. Dr Rao had suggested that disguised unemployment like, for example, frictional, seasonal or cyclical unemployment, was a distinct type of unemployment of the same order of explanatory causes as those others. In the opinion of the speaker that was not the case at all. The cause that brought about unemployment had nothing whatever to do with disguised unemployment and those were the well-known factors of frictional, seasonal, cyclical and other types. The usefulness of the concept of disguised unemployment lay in the fact that it was a convenient term used by Mrs Robinson to explain an old phenomenon of a situation in which labour thrown out of work in certain industries got adjusted by employment in less remunerative trades. When, for example, the handicrafts of a country suffered a decline consequent upon the competition of mill products and the workers thrown out of employment, those that resorted to less remunerative employments, e.g., agriculture, were, no doubt, formally reemployed, but they were now engaged in less productive work and hence in one sense it might be said that their unemployment was disguised. But in any case the cause that had led to this result was entirely due to changes in the conditions of demand and should not be confused with the result itself. Disguised unemployment was therefore the result of changes in effective demand for or supply of labour and in no sense a cause of unemployment.

There was further a danger of exaggerating the value of this concept in its theoretical and practical aspects, especially as applied to old agricultural countries. Unemployment was essentially a problem arising out of a profit–wage relationship. Where there were independent producers, changes in effective demand brought about not unemployment but a decline in incomes. Perhaps the use of the term disguised unemployment to explain short period phenomena might be justified on the ground that here were people who either continued in an occupation which gave them less return than before or resorted to inferior trades. But if after full readjustment there were too many people occupied in particular industries, thus depressing their income, there would be no point in calling them as disguised unemployed. A more realistic view of the matter would be to regard the problem as one of low productivity and of taking steps to raise it. It was well-known that in India the number of people on land was far too many for the full utilisation of it and that any steps taken to relieve this pressure on the land would be very desirable indeed. Not all the surplus labour on land was the result of the displaced workers from other occupations taking to agriculture. A good deal of it was due to the increased population's inability to find alternative occupations of a more remunerative character. To say therefore, as Dr Rao did, that the large number of agriculturists who did not contribute to the production of agricultural output constituted the disguised unemployed might be formally correct; but in reality it did not explain the true nature of the problem which was low income and low productivity.

Referring to Dr Rao's paper, Dr H.L. Dey stated that while he agreed generally with the author, there was one point on which he had his doubts. Dr Rao had suggested that the remedy for seasonal unemployment would be the starting of such handicrafts in the village as would involve little capital and little skill. Theoretically, the suggestion was all right, but its technical limitation was that industries that required little skill, e.g., spinning, were those which produced simple and standardised goods that satisfied mass demand and which were exactly the industries that gave the largest advantages to machine production as against hand production. Dr Dey, therefore, thought that a better and more appropriate remedy would be the ruralisation of the lighter machine industries, subject to the condition that while during the agricultural season their operations would normally be on the single shift system, double shifts should be adopted in the slack season of agriculture so as to employ the agricultural labourers. Such ruralisation of industries would also mitigate the general underemployment in the rural areas and raise the average income of agricultural families. He pointed out that the Dhakeswari Cotton Mills at Narayanganj near Dacca had achieved a large measure of success in this direction.

Dr Rao defines unemployment as inability to find work at a particular wage level. The definition is sound, but the important point that matters is the level taken as the basis of an argument. In India even at the prevailing level of wages, there is an enormous amount of unemployment; but for a vast majority of people employment at the existing level of wages is no employment in the real sense of the word. They live in conditions of utter insecurity and suffer from acute distress. The average earnings of our people being what they are, a large majority of them are suffering from disguised unemployment—i.e., they are doing work which brings them much less than they are worth and much less than the minimum necessary to civilized existence.

In India the method of giving relief in the immediate future must be on the lines suggested by Dr Rao. We must introduce industries in rural areas which will enable people to use their spare time productively. Decentralization of factories, which is already going on to a certain extent, will not be a suitable measure because work in factories cannot be made a part-time or spare-time occupation. The most fruitful method of using the idle hours of agricultural classes is co-operative work to develop public amenities, and next best, work to producing commodities for self-use. Subsidiary occupations must be simple and their products disposable without raising the complicated problems of marketing and competition.

But the real problem of unemployment cannot be solved without a thorough reconstruction of our economic life. Unemployment among the educated class is only a by-product of unemployment among the masses and both problems can be solved if conditions favourable for a complete re-organization of our economic life can be created. I need not add that these conditions do not exist at present.

President's Remarks

The President (Dr Thomas) at the conclusion of the discussion, said: It is true that the statistics of unemployment in India are imperfect, but this need not delay action for relieving unemployment; for, that there is wide-spread unemployment and under-employment is clear on all accounts. Nor need we worry about attaining logical perfection in regard to the classification of unemployment. 'Disguised' unemployment may not be an independent class, as was pointed out; but that kind of unemployment is familiar to us in this country where for the last one hundred years handicraftsmen who formerly engaged themselves in skilled industrial work have drifted to less remunerative agricultural labour.

Different remedies are needed for the different types of unemployment prevalent in this country. Perennial under-employment and seasonal unemployment are our chief evils. The former must be tackled by the establishment of suitable home industries which the rural population can carry on, along with their principal occupation. In Japan, silk-reeling is a home industry and occupies men and women in their leisure hours. For seasonal unemployment, seasonal factories may be possible in many areas. It is also necessary to start medium-sized industries in congested rural areas, so that some of the under-employed persons may give up agriculture and become industrial labourers. In slack times, it may be advisable to have co-operative labour ventures for road-making, house-building, etc. Even in farming, co-operative labour can be employed. Co-operative tillage is a means by which the advantages of large-scale production may be reaped in agriculture.

No doubt large-scale industries are needed, but one may be sceptical about the unemployment problem being solved by the establishment of a few heavy industries. Our large-scale industries have lately expanded much, but the increase of employment has been small. For a thickly populated country like India, mainly engaged in agricultural occupations, it would be best to employ as large a proportion of labourers as possible in small and medium-sized industries not far from our farms.

B.P. Adarkar (1903–1988)

< *Source*: Courtesy Priya Adarkar.

Bhalchandra Pundlik Adarkar was born in Vengorla in present-day Maharashtra in 1903. After obtaining a B A (Honours) in Sanskrit and English from Bombay University in 1925, Adarkar took his economics tripos from Cambridge in 1930, securing a First Class First. In 1933 he became the first Indian to win the prestigious Adam Smith Prize in economic research. He researched for some time at the London School of Economics, working with Hugh Dalton and Herman Finer, and submitted his MA thesis at Cambridge. John Maynard Keynes thought highly of him and, in his letter supporting Adarkar's application for the post of Professor at Benares Hindu University, wrote: 'I consider him to be the most promising Indian student of economics, as far as original work is concerned, who has been in this country.' (Letter from Keynes, 21 June 1932, *Keynes Papers*, King's College, Cambridge.)

Between 1932 and 1936 Adarkar was professor of economics at Benares Hindu University and between 1936 and 1941 taught at Allahabad University. Thereafter he worked for the Government of India and produced a number of major studies and reports, including several for the Labour Investigation Committee during 1944–45. Two reports of Adarkar were particularly influential. One was the *Report on Health Insurance for Industrial Workers*, which formed the basis for the Employees' State Insurance Scheme adopted after Independence and the other was the *Report on Federal Finance in Australia,* written with B.K. Nehru, based on a study-visit to Australia in 1947. This contributed significantly to the development of the present system of five-yearly Finance Commissions.

After Independence Adarkar held senior positions in the Ministry of Finance and External Affairs, including several postings with Indian diplomatic missions. He also represented India as a member of several delegations to UN meetings and conferences. In 1959, he retired from government service.

Among his books, *The Principles and Problems of Federal Finance*, published in 1933, is regarded as a classic in its field. *The Theory of Monetary Policy*, published in 1939 with a foreword by Jawaharlal Nehru, was a contribution to Keynesian thought. *The Indian Fiscal Policy*, from which the extract here is taken, was published in 1941. Adarkar also published several papers in the *Economic Journal* over the 1930s on topics ranging from saving and usury to financial aspects of the 1935 Indian constitution. He was the managing editor of the *Indian Journal of Economics* from 1940 to 1942. Adarkar died in 1988.

Major Biographical Sources: 'Biographical Sketch of Professor B P Adarkar', prepared by him in the 1970s. (Courtesy: Priya Adarkar.) Anand G. Chandavarkar: *Keynes and India, A Study in Economics and Biography*, Basingstoke, Macmillan, 1989.

The extract I have selected is, I believe, a good example of B.P. Adarkar's writing.* It is a brief, pointed, and strong attack on critics of protection in India, like H.L. Dey and B.N. Adarkar, who had argued against it in the 1930s. He made a strong case for protection for infant and 'embryo' industries in India, as in other countries. Unlike Coyajee (see Chapter 4), Adarkar felt that protection was needed on a continuing basis. He argued that 'a basic level of protection would have to be maintained to create that atmosphere of confidence and stability which is essential to a programme of industrial development in a backward country possessing the necessary potentialities'.

Adarkar attacked economists who held protection responsible for India's failure to develop over the previous twenty years. The tardy development of industries was, in his words, 'due to the superficial aid given by the half-hearted, grudging concessions of a so-called "discriminating" protection'. Against their arguments for shifting attention to rationalization, internal planning, social and moral uplift, education, rural reconstruction, agriculture, mining, transport, banking, etc. Adarkar responded that none of these measures dealt with the real problem, which was to promote industrialization and economic development. Like many other Indian economists, Adarkar argued that agriculture could not be the solution for India given the pressure on cultivable land. Industrialization was tied to the promotion of scientific progress and defence capabilities; it would also mobilize Indian capital which was shy and locked up in gold hoards.

Adarkar did not accept the view that discriminating protection in India had led to regressive taxation. He believed that the lower degree of inequality in India than in the West made Indian taxation, which had about half the revenues coming from customs duties, comparatively less regressive. Again, in a poor country taxes had, of necessity, to fall on the poor to some extent. Progressive public expenditure policies could correct for this and ways of taxing the rich could be explored.

On the question of the burden of protection on consumers, Adarkar opened new ground in the Indian debate, by drawing attention to the impact through the multiplier process of the expansion in primary employment in the protected industry in terms of expanded secondary employment in other industries and agriculture. As Bhabatosh Datta (1978) observed, Adarkar wrote before the classic papers of Stolper and Samuelson (1941) and Scitovsky (1942) were available (in fact, Adarkar's arguments first appeared in an earlier paper published in the *Indian Journal of Economics* in April 1937).He could not therefore draw upon the important contributions made by these papers to the relationship between tariff and social welfare.

Adarkar disputed the view that once protection became effective, government revenues would decline. The growth of the industry and the increase in national dividend that follow would, in his view, provide new sources of tax revenue. While he accepted

* B.P. Adarkar (1941): 'Indian Protection—A Bird's-eye View', from B.P. Adarkar, *The Indian Fiscal Policy*, Allahabad, Kitabistan, 1941, pp. 15–27.

that protection might create vested interests, he saw this as a consequence of industrialization itself and believed it could be tackled.

Adarkar's contribution to the debate on protection took the form of a strong defence of protection as a development policy, rather than a temporary expedient. This was similar to the arguments of some nationalists who had also favoured protection on a wider and more enduring basis, but Adarkar argued his case as an economist, using the tools of modern economics of the late-1930s. After Independence the Fiscal Commission of 1949–50 also concluded that protection had not been viewed by the colonial government as an instrument of general economic development, but as a means of enabling particular industries to withstand foreign competition. It therefore recommended a policy of developmental protection.

13

Indian Protection—A Bird's-Eye View

B.P. Adarkar

Let us now turn to the question of India's fiscal policy, which has been already anticipated in the foregoing discussion at several points. Firstly, then, it is beyond doubt true that India fulfils all the requirements of what Pigou calls a backward 'agricultural country wishful to develop manufactures'. It is by now a commonplace in economics how the various important elements of productive power, such as industrial technique, organised systems of transport, banking and communications, trade connections and goodwill, an efficient labour-supply and a group of enterprising and far-seeing captains of industry, arise and are augmented in a cumulative manner under the aegis of a well-planned system of protection. The prosperity of Germany, the United States and several continental countries has been attributed even by leading free-trade authorities like Taussig and others to protectionist policies. Latest cases are Japan, Australia, Canada and South Africa. Those who deny the efficacy of protectionism would do well to peruse the industrial histories of these nations. The Indian Fiscal Commission has gone through this question with great power and far-seeing vision and decided that, for the sake of a rapid industrialisation, the country should take a step forward in the direction of protection. It was unfortunate that they recommended merely Discriminating Protection, i.e., for infant industries, which, even according to Pigou and free-trade authorities is more appropriate to develop industrial communities possessing such 'infants', than to agricultural countries with potentialities of an all-round industrial development. There is no doubt, at any rate at this date, that Discriminating Protection was merely a compromise formula devised by the majority to soothe external interests and the adjective 'discriminating' merely gave a semblance of respectability and level-headedness to the formula. And yet it must be remembered that the actual details of the formula restricted its scope to a far greater extent than necessary, while the administrative machinery set up for its execution by the Government came to be such that hurdles after hurdles were placed in the way of the applicant industries. Even a general system of protection can be 'discriminating' without excluding all but infant industries from its scope. Apart from established infant industries, new or 'embryo' industries would also have to be considered for selective protection, as was done in other protectionist countries, while a basic level of protection would have to be maintained to create that atmosphere of confidence and stability which is essential to a programme of industrial development in a backward country possessing the necessary potentialities. At present the Tariff Board has to work within the strait-jacket of the triple formula and exercise almost a valetudinarian caution in the prescription of its fiscal recipes. I do not think that this type of nibbling would help in the tremendous problem of industrialising a sub-continent like India.

The growth of population during recent years has been alarmingly rapid and the pressure on land is increasing day by day. Not only this but the fertility of the soil is rapidly dwindling, so that the fertility–acreage quota per head of population has also been, in recent years, falling very fast. The optimists have contented themselves with figures showing that *per capita* real production has increased. Such and other people, who (e.g.) look at superficial things like budget surpluses of Government, its credit abroad, etc., without pausing to think how these have been brought about, are living in a dreamland of hallucinating prosperity. But actually the situation in the country, for those who have eyes to see, is daily getting from bad to worse; unemployment is rapidly increasing, while poverty, destitution and indebtedness are stalking through the land. Throughout this period, the silent sufferer is the agriculturist whose responsibilities are growing out of all proportions to his capacities to bear the burden of feeding the country.

Table 13.1 shows the gravity of the situation:

TABLE 13.1

	1911	*1921*	*1931*	*1936*	*1938*	*1941*
Total population in millions	315	319	352	377*	386*	400*
Working population in millions	154	146	149	–	–	–
Employed in industries (millions)	15	16	17	–	–	–

Note: * Estimated.

The 'industrial' employment of the Census figures has to be discounted in so far as nearly 7 millions are engaged in the plantation industries, while the large-scale industrial establishments provide employment at present only for between 1.5 to 2 millions of workers. From 1921 to 1941, i.e., within a period of twenty years as the figures show the population will have grown by nearly 80 millions; if the increase of employable persons is taken to be about 20 millions, it is hardly probable that more than 2 millions will have been absorbed in the sugar, match-making, and cement industries apart from the old-established industries during these years. Thus it will be found that there is a great and growing maladjustment of the labour-supply of the country—a maladjustment which cannot be corrected until suitable industrial avenues are provided. What have our friends, the critics of protection, got to say about this? Here are the samples: 'Even on the most extravagant and optimistic (*sic*) supposition that there could be a doubling of industrial production during the next ten years, the additional industrial employment created thereby would absorb only 1.6 per cent of the agricultural workers. It is, therefore, clear that it would be a vain hope that a policy of industrial protection would effect any appreciable improvement...'[1] 'Statistics show that even if these industries develop to the farthest limit of expansion, they will not be able to absorb more than an insignificant proportion of our total population. Industrialisation by protection, is therefore, a chimerical proposition.'[2] The United States and Germany had, according to another writer, 'a much more equitable distribution of the population between agriculture and industry than obtains in India', and as 'these proportions are relevant (?) in balancing the gain against the loss' of protection, 'the actual volume of the sacrifice that India will have to make will be infinitely greater than that of these countries'.[3]

It is fine logic, indeed, to base conclusions such as these, regarding the failure of protection on figures of a tardy industrial development, when the obvious conclusion should have been that tardy development of industries itself was due to the superficial aid given by the half-hearted, grudging concessions of a so-called 'discriminating' protection! And in any case, to base conclusions as to possibilities of employment on the actualities of today is not only wrong logic but bad economics. The panaceas proposed by the critics themselves are rationalisation, internal planning, social and moral uplift, education, rural reconstruction, development of other departments of economic life such as agriculture, mining, transport, banking, etc. All this is well said, but the questions are (*i*) how rationalisation would hasten industrial development in this country, seeing that it can affect only the existing industries, (*ii*) secondly, whether such random shots at the 'bull's eye' of progress as social uplift, etc., would solve the crucial problem of population pressure and a low standard of life, (there is no objection, however, against these innocent, philanthropic items of social programme *per se*), (*iii*) thirdly, whether industrialisation can necessarily only take place at the expense of agriculture, (*iv*) fourthly, whether mining, transport and banking can develop at all without a rapid programme of industrialisation. There is no case on record of an agricultural country having successfully industrialised itself and raised its standards by merely tinkering with haphazard methods of social welfare which are clearly of a long-period character: these, indeed, have their place in the economic policy of a country, but they are more consumptional than productional in their aspect and they are slow business at best.

As regards the general question whether India should be an *Agrarstaat* or *Industriestaat*, at this distance of time there can hardly be any dispute that what we should aim at is a diversification of our economic life. This has been brought home to us particularly by the last Depression which caused a far greater proportionate fall in agricultural prices than in industrial prices, making our real ratio of trade seriously adverse. Owing to the slight recovery that is taking place in the world markets, the two sets of prices (agricultural and industrial) are again converging towards a new parity thus slightly improving our real ratio, but this much can be taken for granted that, owing to the tractor and the steam-engine, agriculture has been glutted and the real ratio might well worsen again. Moreover, a primary occupation like agriculture can never hold out any hope of a high standard of life for our growing millions with a diminishing fertility-acreage ratio; primary occupations are always associated with a low standard of life. Agriculture means backwardness and backwardness, again, is a cumulative process. Moreover, scientific progress is closely associated with industries and both these again with political supremacy; if 'defence is more important than opulence', modernisation on industrial lines is essential; it is essential if we are to have a place in the sun, especially in view of the new military responsibilities which are bound to devolve upon India in the near future. Moreover, there is no doubt whatever that industrialisation would mobilise our shy capital which has been locked up for centuries in the form of gold for want of a better investment, though the claim that industrialisation itself would cause an immediate growth in our capital resources may be regarded as erring on the side of optimism. It is hopeless to expect that this gold can be suitably invested in land, or in social uplift.

The Tariff Board has been handicapped in its operation in several ways: its constitution, its functions, its personnel have left much to be desired; its deliberations have been hindered by the strict implications of the triple formula; its recommendations have not infrequently been rejected; its reports have been on occasions shelved indefinitely; the Commerce Department has nipped many an industry in the bud by putting obstacles in the way of applicant industries and refusing to place their cases before the Board, thus pre-judging and prejudicially judging such issues as should have been the proper subjects for the Board itself to advise upon. In spite of all these impediments, the Tariff Board has, on the whole, discharged its responsibilities with vision, sagacity and impartially. If there is no humming prosperity in the country with thriving industries everywhere, the fault at any rate is not theirs. What little protection has been available after the combing process of the present machinery has more than justified itself. It may at once be admitted that the system as it has developed has contracted some defects: but what system is without defects? Moreover, in this case, they are undoubtedly the defects of the merits of Protection. Critics have exaggerated the defects and shut their eyes to the progress achieved by way of direct and indirect employment and the growth of the national income as a whole, thus willingly losing their perspective.

The first complaint of the critics is that discriminating protection has led to regressive taxation. Now it would be inaccurate to suggest that the system of Indian public finance leaves nothing to be desired; on the contrary, a majority of Indian economists have rightly condemned it both for its inequities of burdens and its wastefulness of expenditures. There are, however, one or two points which we have to bear in mind in this connection. In the first place, it must be remembered that the inequality of distribution in this country is not so great as in the West, so that a scheme of taxes (in which, say, the customs duties are 53 per cent of the total tax burden) is bound to be less regressive in its effects in India than in the Western countries. Second, without prejudice to a general conclusion that reform can make the system somewhat less regressive than it actually is, it must be pointed out that as the majority of our countrymen are poor, to run any government whatever on modern lines, the tax burden will have to fall mostly upon the poor. Third, a system of finance may be regressive as to taxation, but if it is progressive as to expenditure, the evil effects of regression will be sufficiently compensated for in the other direction. This is the first relativity aspect. Fourth, regression or progression is a relative idea; if owing to customs duties, the tax system has become regressive, there are two ways in which this can be corrected: either to reduce customs taxation, thus relieving the poor, or to raise more revenue from taxes which fall specifically upon the rich. If protective duties can be justified on broader grounds, such as that the national income would increase,[4] then clearly the former course is not the wiser, for if national income as a whole grows, the later distributional aspects can be taken care of by the Government. In brief, let the 'heap' (*pace* Stamp) of national resources first be greater; its sharing can well be our next preoccupation. On the other hand any student of Indian public finance can tell us that there is a vast scope for taxation of the upper strata of incomes, so as to make the bias of the tax system more progressive or less regressive than it is today. Reform of income taxation, taxation of the incomes from land, taxation of inheritance, succession and legacies, taxation of property (both movable and immovable) of joint and separate families, and of transfer of property,—these and several other sources will have to be tapped. Though the difficulties, principally legal and administrative, are great here, our authorities on taxation have generally agreed that the country is insufficiently taxed in these directions as well as on the whole. We shall be reaching the optimum size of public finance in India by increasing our public activities rather than by curtailing them: if this is so, there is no case for reducing customs duties but only for exploring the other avenues of taxing the rich. Finally, and this is a theoretical point, it is not correct to suppose that regression reduces economic welfare under all circumstances whatever. It might do so, if the actual absolute taxation paid in by the poor individual is greater in amount than what the rich individual pays; for the rest, the theory of public finance does not make any deliverance on the question. Although it may well be granted that a greater element of progression will make the maximum number of us happier than we are, there is no proof that in India the poor actually pay in taxation less than the rich or that the rich benefit actually by expenditure more than the poor; and hence the conclusion is that there still takes place a transference of wealth from the rich to the poor in this country which may be insufficient but which is certainly not negative in character.

The next objection of the critics is that protective duties make the rich richer and the poor poorer, thus aggravating the existing inequality of distribution. Their argument is that the duties cause the prices of the goods protected to rise thus injuring the consumers who are mostly poor, while they benefit 'the favoured groups of entrepreneurs, investors, and wage-earners' connected with the industries concerned. Now it must be admitted that it is one of the incidents of industrialisation that is creates a rich entrepreneur class: this is not peculiar to protection, it is inherent in industrialisation itself. On other hand, the 'burden of the consumer' question is not such a simple issue. In the first place, it is not clear that the poorer sections of the society do actually bear a large part of the burden of protection in India; my personal view is that it falls to a greater extent on the *middle* classes who are the principal consumers of imported and protected goods. Apart from this, however, in order to assess the actual injury caused, we have to take into consideration not only the rise in prices (which may indeed be temporary, the period depending upon the measure of protection and the development of the industry), but addition to the incomes of the poor caused by (*i*) increased primary employment in the industry itself and (*ii*) the reactions of this on secondary employment in several other industries and agriculture,[5] which relieve the pressure on the soil. To the extent, (or even more than that), that prices rise as a whole, total consumer purchasing-power increases, so that the harm done to total consumption, which is definitely greater than before, is illusory. What is more, by employing the unemployed and thus bringing about some favourable redistribution, the sum of human happiness is actually increased. Any contrary conclusion is due to the common confusion between the term 'producers' and 'entrepreneurs', in truth by producers we mean here all those, workers and others, who are engaged in industries.

The next contention of the critics is that when protection begins to become effective, the revenue of the Government begins to fall off.[6] Of all the arguments against discriminating protection, this perhaps is the lamest and most slipshod. I do not produce statistics in this connection to disprove what is indeed a fact that during the last few years the revenue from protective duties has fallen. It is, of course, due very largely to a general fall of imports caused by the Depression and the reduced purchasing-power of the people. But the general proposition, that in so far as protection is effective revenue must fall off, must indeed be granted. But the question that arises is: Why should the Government look for revenue in these shaky quarters? And even if they do, why should they not be prepared to adjust their taxation system to the changing fabric of revenue? And is a revenue loss to be regarded as a national loss, in strict theory? At the most, a revenue loss might cause administrative inconvenience, necessitating the imposition of new taxation or the scaling up of the old. Theoretically, it is not even improbable that reduction of duties on some of the 'adult' protected industries would be augmenting the revenue. This can be tried if necessary, but there is no ground whatever for the claim that 'India's tariff policy must primarily be directed by revenue considerations'.[7] On the other hand, we must admit (*i*) that in so far as protection leads to establishment of new industries, it becomes possible to gather more revenue by way of income-tax and excise—both of which can substantially make up for the so-called 'loss,' and (*ii*) that if the national dividend as a whole increases, as it must in a country in which large masses of human and material resources are lying unemployed, these superficial considerations have no bearing on the questions of fiscal policy.

The next important point of the critics of the Indian protectionism is that it has created and will further create 'vested interests' in the country.[8] Now, vested interests and trusts and cartels and such-like are incidents of industrial progress and of changes in organisation. The American, English and German attitudes towards trustification and cartellisation have not been all in the same direction;[9] thus, those who inveigh against these things will have first to get their notions fully clarified as to the end towards which they would wish industrial organisation in this country to progress. They might usefully remember that we can in these, as in many other matters, draw upon the experience of western nations and shape our policies.[10] Vested interests are an excrescence of industrialisation under the capitalist system; you cannot abolish them by abolishing protection; and in so far as protection might have helped industrialisation anywhere, they are the defect of the merit of protection. It is impossible for us to have industries without vested interests; the more important practical issue is, whether we have any means at our disposal to neutralise the harmful influence exercised by them. In modern democracies as well as autocracies, balance is always provided for the overmastering influence of vested interests: in India, as it appears to me, we have a number of mutually neutralising elements which either have been or will be quite adequate to ensure against the domination of Big Business. In the first place, owing to the broad-bottomed franchise of the new Constitution we shall have the representatives of the non-industrialist, consumer population in the legislatures in large number; secondly, foreign interests will be well represented by the 'special responsibilities' of the Viceroy and his various 'discretions'; thirdly, the general surveillance of a foreign Government interested more in agriculture than in industry is also an effective safeguard in this connection; and fourthly, inter-provincial jealousies, which are steadily coming to the forefront (witness, e.g., the ratio controversy, the cotton textiles protection, the Niemeyer Scheme of federal finance, etc.) can be depended upon for certain checks; and lastly, the active presence of an impartial economic judiciary, like the Tariff Board, duly fortified further if necessary as regards constitution and functions, can also be a valuable insurance. The Fiscal Commission had already anticipated this objection and held that the danger of political corruption was not so great in India as in some other countries more or less on these grounds; their hopes will not be belied if the greatest possible publicity is given to the findings of the Tariff Board and if this body is turned into a permanent investigating Commission on the lines of the American Tariff Commission or the Federal Trade Commission. The problem of vested interests is thus neither new nor newly discovered. To deal effectively with that problem moreover, is not beyond our capacities either at present or in the future; 'the power to tax', Chief Justice Marshall used to say, 'involves the power to destroy' and it is this weapon of taxation which among others can be wielded most effectively.

Conclusion

To conclude, in the first place, the theoretical foundations of *laissez-faire* have been found to be inadequate because the assumptions on which they are based, such as that there is full employment, that 'wage-rates tend to adjust themselves to demand and supply conditions in such wise that no involuntary unemployment, other than such as is due to industrial fluctuations, can exist', [11] that cosmopolitan good is the good *par excellence*, that changes in distribution would make no material alteration to international values,—these assumptions cannot be granted. Even the international division of labour, which is the mainstay of Free Trade, is not above reproach, because it is capable of doing permanent harm to a backward country in respect of its production and productive capacity, and because what *tends to be* is not necessarily for the best. So far as India is concerned, her case falls within the category of backward agricultural countries 'wishful to develop manufactures', and possessing cumulative potentialities of natural and human resources. Thus Discriminating Protection of a piecemeal variety hardly meets the requirements of her industries, which, if we are at all to be honest about it, are undoubtedly shouting for a rapid growth. What is needed is a comprehensive visualisation of the industrial problem as a whole and we must also remember that industrialisation is a close interdependence between industries, old and new. The burdens on the consumer and the agriculturist are merely the arguments of crocodiles; there is no loss caused to these interests for which they will not be more than compensated in other ways, owing to increase of employment and owing to internal demand for foodstuffs and raw materials having increased. Moreover, for several years, at any rate, owing to fall of prices of all kinds, the consumers (i.e., people still deriving incomes through employment or otherwise—*not* the unemployed) have gained all along the line. For these reasons, we need have no sympathy for the so-called consumers whose mythical interests seem to dominate our fortunes in fiscal policy. It should be remembered that every fiscal measure is bound to harm some people and benefit others, or harm the same people in some ways and benefit them in others; the function of economists is to deal with each case justly weighing the pros and cons and considering the *tout ensemble* of results and not merely to harp upon one set of such results. Owing to a lack of industrial and commercial development in India, there is in evidence today an increase in destitution and unemployment, which have been caused as much by an increasing maladjustment of the labour supply as by a growing stream of population. At a time when the rest of the world's countries safeguarded their production structures and markets by restrictive measures against a plethora of dumped goods, what had the Government of India done? Our Government was about the only one to have achieved the singular distinction of having done nothing in a world depression which hit agricultural countries the hardest. Our Government was obviously out to maintain *laissez-faire* in all its pristine purity; it would even go to the length of sacrificing Indian currency and fiscal policy on the altar of a false internationalism, lending volunteer services to its cause by refusing to enter into 'a race of competitive depreciation' and to complicate (*sic*) international trade by imposing artificial 'trade barriers'.

Notes

1. Dey, *Indian Tariff Problem*, p. 30.
2. B.N. Adarkar, *Indian Tariff Policy*, pp. 62–63.
3. Pillai, *Economic Conditions in India*, p. 324, supported also by Dr Gilbert Slater in the Introductory Note.
4. And it is this proposition that the critics will have to contest, rather than give a dog a bad name and hang it.

5. The problem is essentially of the same nature as that of the 'Multipliers' of Messrs Keynes and Kahn. See Keynes, *General Theory*, chapter 10, etc. Also P.J. Thomas, 'A Plan for Economic Recovery', in the Conference Number of the *Indian Journal of Economics*, April, 1935.
6. B.N. Adarkar, *op. cit.*, pp. 65–67 and 74–87; Vera Anstey, *Economic Development of India*, p. 389.
7. Vera Anstey, *op. cit.* Italics mine.
8. References to individual writers are unnecessary; free-trade literature is replete with discussions on this point; Indian writers have merely dotted the i's and crossed the t's of Taussig and others.
9. Cf. H. Levy, *The New Industrial System*; Marquand, *Dynamics of Combination*; L. Urwick, *Rationalisation*; Meakin, *The New Industrial Revolution*; and other works by Florence, Robinson and others.
10. The USA, the classical home of vested interests, has also been the land of the most relentless Anti-Trust Laws.
11. Pigou, *A Study in Public Finance*, p. 218.

Select Bibliography

Articles

Adarkar, B.P. 1944. 'Tariffs and Fiscal Policy', *Annals of the American Academy of Political and Social Science*, vol. 233, India Speaking (May), pp. 141–5.

_____. 1935.'The Economic Aspects of the Proposed Indian Constitution', *Economic Journal*, vol. 45, no. 177 (March), pp. 177–83.

_____. 1933. 'The "Fundamental Error" in Keynes's Treatise', *American Economic Review*, vol. 23, no. 1 (March), p. 87.

_____. 1932.'Saving and Usury, A Symposium' (with Edwin Canaan, B.K. Sandwell, J.M. Keynes, and K. Boulding), *Economic Journal*, vol. 42, no. 165 (March), pp. 123–41.

Adarkar, B.P. and S.N. Sen Gupta. 1936. 'The Pareto Law and the Distribution of Income in India', *Economic Journal*, vol. 46, no. 181 (March), pp. 168–71.

Ambedkar, B.R. 1918. 'Small Holdings in India and Their Remedies', *Journal of the Indian Economic Society*, vol. I [Reprinted in V.W. Moon (ed.), *Balasaheb Ambedkar—Writings and Speeches*, vol. 6, Bombay, Government of Maharashtra, 1979, pp. 455–79.]

Ambirajan, S. 1999. 'Ambedkar's Contributions to Economics', *Economic and Political Weekly*, vol. 34, nos. 46–47 (20–26 November), pp. 3280–5.

Bhutani, D.H. 1942. 'The Quality and Perspective of Indian Economic Thought', *Indian Journal of Economics*, vol. 22, no. 3 (January), pp. 250–89.

Brahmananda, P.R. 1995. 'C.N. Vakil's Contributions to Economics: 1920–1950', *Indian Economic Journal*, vol. 42, pp. 1–23.

Chandrasekhar, S. 1944.'Recent Social Science Literature in India', *Annals of the Academy of Political and Social Science*, vol. 233, India Speaking (May), pp. 208–17.

Chatterjee, Atul C. 1943.'Jehangir Cooverjee Coyajee', *Economic Journal*, vol. 53, no. 212 (December), pp. 453–56.

Coyajee, J.C. 1929. 'Monetary Reconstruction in India', *Annals of the American Academy of Political and Social Science*, vol. 145, part II, India (September), pp. 101–14.

Curtis, C.A. 1926. 'Financial Developments in Modern India', *Journal of Political Economy*, vol. 34, no. 6 (December), pp. 785–6.

Das, Rajani Kanta. 1934. 'Child Labour in India', *International Labour Review*, vol. XXVIII, no. 6 and vol. XXIX, no. 1.

——. 1931. 'Woman Labour in India', *International Labour Review*, vol. 24, pp. 376–409 and 536–72.

——. 1925. 'An Opinion on the Suggestions of the Indian Economic Enquiry Committee', *Welfare*, Calcutta.

Dasgupta, Bhanoo B. 1922. 'Recent Banking and Currency Legislation in India', Notes and Memoranda, *Quarterly Journal of Economics*, vol. 37, issue 1 (November), pp. 183–90.

Dubey, Daya Shankar. 1920. 'The Indian Food Problem', *Indian Journal of Economics*, vol. III, part I: pp. 84–106 and part II, pp. 167–80.

Goheen, John, M.N. Srinivas, D.G. Karve, and Milton Singer. 1958. 'Indian Cultural Values and Economic Development: A Symposium', *Economic Development and Cultural Change*, vol. VII, no. 1 (October), pp. 1–12.

Gottileb, M. 1971. 'Mukherjee: Economics Becomes Social Science', *Journal of Economic Issues*, vol. 5 (December), pp. 33–53.

Govindu, Venu Madhav and Deepak Malghan. 2005. 'Building a Creative Freedom: J.C. Kumarappa and His Economic Philosophy', *Economic and Political Weekly*, vol. 40, no. 52 (24–30 December), pp. 5477–85.

Guha, Ramachandra. 1992. 'Prehistory of Indian Environmentalism', *Economic and Political Weekly*, vol. 27, nos 1–2 (4–11 January), pp. 57–64.

Gyanchand. 1934–5. 'The Essentials of Economic Planning in India', *Indian Journal of Economics*, vol. XV, pp. 409–22.

Horne, E.A. 1916. 'Some Family Budgets from Bihar', *Economic Journal*, vol. 26, no. 103 (September), pp. 369–79.

Kale, V.G. 1923. 'Small Industries in India', *Weltwirtschaftliches Archiv* (Journal of the Institute of World Economy and Maritime Commerce, University of Kiel), April. [Source: *http://www.digizeitschriften.de/index.php?id=64&L=2*; accessed 20 March 2008]

_____. 1918–19. 'A Study in Village Economics', *Indian Journal of Economics*, vol. II, no. 4, pp. 462–76.

_____. 1918. 'A Few Observations on the Economics of Education', *Journal of the Indian Economic Society*, vol. I, pp. 151–62.

Kesava Iyengar, S. 1944. 'Industrialisation and Agriculture in India's Post-war Planning', *Economic Journal*, vol. 54, no. 214 (June), pp. 189–205.

_____. 1943. 'Central Banking in Hyderabad', *Economic Journal*, vol. 53, nos 210–11 (June), pp. 274–80.

Keynes, J.M. 1911. 'The Economic Transition in India', *Economic Journal*, vol. 21, no. 83 (September), pp. 426–31.

Krishnamurty, J. 2008. 'The Indian Antecedents of Disguised Unemployment and Surplus Labour', *Indian Journal of Labour Economics*, vol. 51, no. 1 (January–March), pp. 53–62.

_____. Forthcoming. 'Manohar Lal: Scholar, Economist and Statesman', *Modern Asian Studies.*

Madhava, K.B. 1927. 'Analysis of Trade Disputes', *Indian Journal of Economics*, vol. 7, no. 3 (January), pp. 250–76.

Morison, Theodore. 1911. 'A Study in Indian Economics', *Economic Journal*, vol. 22, no. 85 (September), pp. 80–1.

Mukherjee, Radhakamal. 1934. 'The Broken Balance of Population, Land and Water', *Indian Journal of Economics*, vol. 14, pp. 255–6.

Narain, Brij. n.d. 'Development of Indian Industries', *Weltwirtschaftliches Archiv* [Source: *http://www.digizeitschriften.de/index.php?id=64&L=2*; accessed 20 March 2008]

Pillai, P.P. 1923. 'Iron and Steel Industry in India', *Economica,* no. 7 (January), pp. 55–66.

Rao, V.K.R.V. 1938. 'The Problem of Unemployment in India', *Indian Journal of Economics*, vol. 18, no. 4, pp. 627–34.

_____. 1937. 'Earnings of Workers in Larger Industrial Establishments in British India', *Economic Journal*, vol. 47, no. 185 (March), pp. 77–83.

_____. 1933. 'The Indian Balance of Trade (A Further Note)', *Economic Journal*, vol. 47, no. 169 (March), pp. 169–72.

Robinson, Austin. 1935. 'Industrial Organisation in India', *Economic Journal*, vol. 45, no. 180 (December), pp. 771–2.

Saunders A.J. 1926. 'The Indian Economic Conference', *Economic Journal*, vol. 36, no. 141 (March), pp. 133–6.

———. 1917. 'Village Economic Surveys: Madura District, South India', *Economic Journal*, vol. 27, no. 108 (December), pp. 548–58.

Shenoy, B.R. 1934. 'The Interdependence of Price Levels', *Quarterly Journal of Economics*, vol. 48, no. 2 (February), pp. 362–8.

———. 1932. 'An Equation for the Price Level of New Investment Goods', *Quarterly Journal of Economics*, vol. 47, no. 1 (November), pp. 139–49.

Sinha, Dipendra. 1992. 'Institutional Economics of Radhakamal Mukherjee', *Journal of Economic Issues*, vol. 26 (June), pp. 485–92.

Thomas, P.J. 1947. 'The Late Professor V.G. Kale', *Indian Journal of Economics*, vol. 27 pp. 333–34.

———. 1935a. 'A Plan for Economic Recovery', *Indian Journal of Economics*, vol. 15 pp. 447–57.

———. 1935b. 'India in the World Depression', *Economic Journal*, vol. 45, no. 179 (September), pp. 469–83.

Usher, Abbot Payson. 1927. 'Mercantilism and East India Trade', *American Economic Review*, vol. 17, no. 3 (September), pp. 489–90.

Wadia, P.A. 1924. 'The True Basis of Protection', *Economic Journal*, vol. 34, no. 134 (June), pp. 193–9.

Books

Adarkar, B.N. 1940. *The history of the Indian tariff, 1924–39*. Studies in Indian economics, no. 2. Delhi, Manager of Publications.

———. 1936. *The Indian Tariff Policy with Special Reference to Sugar Protection*. Bombay.

Adarkar, B.P. 1944. *Report on health insurance for industrial workers*. Simla, Manager, Government of India Press.

———. 1941. *The Indian fiscal policy*. Allahabad, Kitabistan.

———. 1939a. *The Indian monetary policy*. Allahabad, Kitabistan.

———. 1939b. *The working of protection in India: an interim report*. Allahabad, Allahabad University.

Ambedkar, B.R. 2003. *Ambedkar: Autobiographical notes by B.R. Ambedkar*. Pondicherry, Navayana.

Ambedkar, B.R. 1925. *The evolution of provincial finance in British India; a study in the provincial decentralization of imperial finance*. London, P.S. King & Son.

_____. 1923. *The problem of the rupee, its origin and its solution*. London, P.S. King & Son.

Anstey, V. 1929. *The economic development of India*. London, Longmans, Green and Co.

Arndt, H.W. 1972. 'Development Economics before 1945', in Jagdish N. Bhagwati and Richard S. Eckaus (eds), *Development and Planning: Essays in Honour of Paul Rosenstein Rodan*, London: Allen & Unwin.

Avasthi, A. (ed.). 1997. *Social and cultural diversities: D.P. Mukerji in memorium*. Jaipur, Rawat Publications.

Bandyopadhyay, P. 1957. *Hundred years of the University of Calcutta, a history of the university issued in commemoration of the centenary celebrations*. Calcutta, University of Calcutta.

Banerjea, P. 1929. *Provincial finance in India*. London, Published for the University of Calcutta by Macmillan and Co.

_____. 1922. *Fiscal policy in India*. Calcutta, Macmillan and Co.

_____. 1916. *Public administration in ancient India: A thesis approved by the University of London for the degree of D. Sc. Econ*. London, Macmillan.

_____. 1911. *A study of Indian economics*. First edn. London, Macmillan and Co.

Bayly, C.A. 1983. *Rulers, townsmen, and bazaars: North Indian society in the age of British expansion, 1770–1870*. Cambridge South Asian Studies, 28. Cambridge, Cambridge University Press.

Bengal (India). 1933. *Current economic problems of India*. Alipore, C.R. Battersby at Bengal Govt. Press.

Berkemer, G., T. Frasch, H. Kulke, and J. Lutt (eds). 2001. *Explorations in the History of South Asia: Essays in Honour of Dietmar Rothermund*. New Delhi, Manohar.

Bose, P.K. (ed.). 1981. *Essays in honour of Dr Gyanchand—He that Blazed the Trail*, New Delhi, People's Publishing House.

Bowley, A.L. and D.H. Robertson. 1934. *A scheme for an economic census of India, with special reference to a census of production and re-organization of statistics*. New Delhi, Government of India Press.

Brahmananda, P.R., D.M. Nanjundappa, and B.K. Narayan. 1979. *Indian economic development and policy: Essays in honour of Prof. V.L. D'Souza*. New Delhi, Vikas Publishing House.

Broughton, G.M. 1924. *Labour in Indian industries*. London, H. Milford and Oxford University Press.

Burnett-Hurst, A.R. 1925. *Labour and housing in Bombay: A study in the economic conditions of the wage-earning classes in Bombay*. London, P.S. King.

Calvert, H. 1922. *The wealth and welfare of the Punjab being some studies in Punjab rural economics*. Lahore, Printed by the Civil and Military Gazette.

Chablani, H.L. 1929. *The economic condition of India during the sixteenth century*. Delhi, Oxford Book and Stationery.

——. 1925. *Indian currency and exchange*. London, New York, H. Milford and Oxford University Press.

Chandavarkar, A.G. 1989. *Keynes and India: A study in economics and biography*. Basingstoke, Macmillan.

Chandra, B. 1990. *Ranade's economic writings*. New Delhi, Gian Publishing House.

Chatterjee, A.C. 1908. *Notes on the industries of the United Provinces*. Allahabad, F. Luker, Superintendent, Government Press.

Coyajee, J.C. 1930. *The Indian Currency System, 1835–1926*, Sir William Meyer Lectures. Madras, Thomson and Co.

——. 1924. *The Indian fiscal problem, being a course of seven lectures delivered at Patna university in August, 1923*. Calcutta, Patna University, Patna.

Curjel, D.F. 1923. *Women's labour in Bengal industries*. Calcutta, Superintendent Government Printing, India.

Dandekar, V.M. 1967. *Dhananjaya Ramchandra Gadgil: Making of the man*. Pune, Institute of Politics and Economics, New York, Asia Pub. House.

Dantwala, M.L. 1937. *Marketing of raw cotton in India*. Studies in Indian economics [no. 11]. Bombay, Longmans, Green and Co.

Darling, M. 1928. *The Punjab peasant in prosperity and debt*. Colombia (Missouri), South Asia Books.

Das, R.K. 1941. *History of Indian labour legislation*. Calcutta, University of Calcutta.

——. 1931 *Plantation labour in India*. Calcutta, R. Chatterjee.

——. 1930. *The industrial efficiency of India*. London, P.S. King & Son.

——. 1924. *Production in India; a comparative study in national productivity*. Calcutta, Visva-Bharati bookshop.

Das, R.K. 1923a. *The labor movement in India*. Berlin and Leipzig, W. de Gruyter.

_____. 1923b. *Hindustani workers on the Pacific coast*. Berlin, W. de Gruyter & Co.

_____. 1923c. *Factory labor in India*. Berlin, W. de Gruyter & Co.

Dasgupta, A.K. 1993. *A history of Indian economic thought*. Routledge History of Economic Thought Series. London, Routledge.

Dass, B., S.C. Dutt, M.N. Sarkar, and P.K. Mukherjee. 1940. *The social and economic ideas of Benoy Sarkar*. Calcutta, Chuckervertty Chatterjee.

Datta, B. 1978. *Indian economic thought: Twentieth century perspectives, 1900–1950*. New Delhi, Tata McGraw-Hill.

_____. 1962. *The evolution of economic thinking in India*. Dr P.N. Banerjea Memorial Lectures, 1961. Calcutta, Federation Hall Society.

Deshmukh, C.D. 1974. *The course of my life*. New Delhi, Orient Longman.

Dey, H.L. 1950. *Policy of protection in India; a retrospect*. Poona, D.R. Gadgil.

_____. 1933. *The Indian tariff problem in relation to industry and taxation*. London, G. Allen & Unwin Ltd.

Divekar, V.D. and M. Arumugam. 1977. *Annotated bibliography on the economic history of India, 1500 A.D. to 1947 A.D.* Pune, Gokhale Institute of Politics and Economics.

D'Souza, V.L. 1937. *Economic development of the Mysore state*. Bangalore, Bangalore Press.

Dubey, D.L. 1930. *The Indian public debt (a critical study of the borrowing policy of the government of India in recent times)*. Bombay, D.B. Taraporevala Sons & Co.

Durga Parshad, I. 1932. *Some aspects of Indian foreign trade 1757–1893*. London, P.S. King & Son.

Dutt, S.C. 1934. *Conflicting tendencies in Indian economic thought*. Calcutta, N.M. Ray-Chowdhury & Co.

_____. 1933. *Thirty-five years of Indian economic thought, 1898–1932*. Calcutta, M.M. Moulik.

Father, P. Carty Birthday Celebration Committee. 1941. *Reverend Father P. Carty commemoration volume*. Madras

Flora, G. 1994. *Benoy Kumar Sarkar and Italy: Culture, politics, and economic ideology*. New Delhi, Italian Embassy Cultural Centre.

Gadgil, D.R. 1959. *Origins of the modern Indian business class; an interim report*. New York, International Secretariat, Institute of Pacific Relations.

——. 1955. *Economic policy and development; a collection of writings*. Pune, Gokhale Institute of Politics and Economics.

——. 1924. *The industrial evolution of India in recent times*. London, H. Milford.

Ganguli, B. 1938. *Trends of agriculture and population in the Ganges valley; a study in agricultural economics*. London, Methuen & Co.

Ghose, S.C. 1927. *Organization of railways*. Calcutta, Calcutta University.

——. 1922. *Lectures on Indian railway economics*. Calcutta, University of Calcutta.

——. 1918. *A monograph on Indian railway rates*. Calcutta, Superintendent Government Printing, India.

Ghosh, D. 1946. *Pressure of population and economic efficiency in India*. New Delhi, Indian Council of World Affairs.

——. 1932. *The Ottawa Agreement; a study in imperial preference*. Bombay, Bombay Book Depot.

Gopalakrishnan, P. 1959. *Development of economic ideas (1880–1950)*. New Delhi, People's Publishing House.

Gupta, R.B. 1930. *Labour and housing in India*. Calcutta, Longmans, Green and Co.

Gyanchand. 1939. *India's teeming millions; a contribution to the study of the Indian population problem*. London, G. Allen & Unwin Ltd.

——. 1930. *The essentials of federal finance; a contribution to the problem of financial re-adjustment in India*. London, H. Milford.

——. 1929. *Some aspects of fiscal reconstruction in India*. The Banailli Readership Lectures in Indian Economics, Patna University, 1927–28. Patna, Patna University.

——. 1926. *The financial system of India*. London, K. Paul, Trench, Trubner.

Haridasan, V. 1986. *Dr John Matthai, 1886–1959: A biography*. Cranganore, Trichur District, Kerala, Sunil.

Huque, A. 1939. *The man behind the plough*. Calcutta, Book Co., Ltd.

Iyengar, S.K. 1953. *Economists at home and abroad*. Hyderabad, Director, Indian Institute of Economics.

——. 1951. *Rural economic enquiries in the Hyderabad State, 1949–51*. Hyderabad, Govt. Press.

——. 1927. *Studies in Indian rural economics*. London, P.S. King & Son.

Jagtiani, H.M. 1924. *The role of the state in the provision of railways*. London, P.S. King.

Jain, L.C. 1945. *Indian economy during the war*. The Banaili Readership Lectures. Lahore, Civil and Military Gazette Ltd.

———. 1941 *The working of the protective tariff in India*. Delhi, University of Delhi.

———. 1933a. *A Reserve Bank for India*. Lahore, Uttar Chand Kapur.

———. 1933b. *The monetary problems of India*. London, Macmillan and Co.

———. 1929. *Indigenous banking in India*. London: Macmillan and Co.

Jathar, G.B. and S.G. Beri. 1930. *Indian economics; a comprehensive and critical survey of the economic problems of India*. London, H. Milford.

Jevons, H.S. 1917. *The consolidation of agricultural holdings in the United Provinces*. Allahabad.

———. 1915. *Economics in India, inaugural lecture*. Allahabad, Pioneer Press.

Kale, V.G. 1931. *Problems of world economy*. Madras, Thompson & Co., University Printers.

———. 1929. *Economics of protection in India*. The Banaili Readership Lectures delivered at Patna university in 1928. Poona, Aryabhushan Press.

———. 1918. *Introduction to the study of Indian economics*. Poona, Aryabhushan Press.

———. 1912. *Indian industrial and economic problems*. Madras, G.A. Natesan.

Karve, D.G. 1941. *Historical and economic studies, published on the occasion of the Silver Jubilee of the Historical and Economic Association of the Fergusson College, Poona*. Poona, D.G. Karve.

———. 1936. *Poverty and population in India*. London, H. Milford and Oxford University Press.

Keatinge, G.F. 1921. *Agricultural progress in western India*. London, Longmans, Green and Co.

———. 1912. *Rural economy in the Bombay Deccan*. London, Longmans, Green and Co.

Keer, D. 1962. *Dr Ambedkar, life and mission*. Bombay, Popular Prakashan.

Kellock, J. 1926. *Mahadev Govind Ranade, patriot and social servant*. Calcutta, Association Press (YMCA).

Kelman, J.H. 1923. *Labour in India: A study of the conditions of Indian women in modern industry*. London, G. Allen & Unwin.

Kuber, W.N. 1973. *Dr Ambedkar: a critical study*. New Delhi, People's Publishing House.

Kumarappa, J.C. 1992. *Essential Kumarappa: A collection of his thoughts and writings on Gandhian economics*. Hyderabad, Academy of Gandhian Studies.

_____. 1945. *Why the village movement? (A plea for a village centered economic order in India)*. Wardha, C.P., All India Village Industries Association.

Latifi, A. 1911. *The industrial Punjab: A survey of facts, conditions and possibilities*. Bombay, Published for the Punjab government by Longmans, Green and Co.

Lindley, M. 2007. *J.C. Kumarappa: Mahatma Gandhi's economist*. Mumbai, Popular Prakashan.

Lokanathan, P.S. 1946a. *India's post-war reconstruction and its international aspects*. New Delhi, Indian Council of World Affairs.

_____. 1946b. *Industrialization*. Oxford Pamphlets on Indian Affairs, no. 10. London, G. Cumberlege.

_____. 1935. *Industrial organization in India*. London, G. Allen & Unwin.

_____. 1929. *Industrial welfare in India*. Madras, Methodist Pub. House.

Lokanathan, P.S. and Saigal. 1947. *Industrial Labour in India*. New Delhi, Indian Council of World Affairs.

Madan, B.K. 1939. *India and imperial preference; a study in commercial policy*. London, H. Milford and Oxford University Press.

Madan, G.R. 1966. *Economic thinking in India*. Delhi, S. Chand.

Mann, H.H., D.L. Sahasrabuddhe, N.V. Kanitkar, and V.A. Tamhane. 1917. *Land and labour in a Deccan village*. London, H. Milford and Oxford University Press.

Matthai, J. 1915. *Village government in British India*. London, T.F. Unwin.

Mehta, A. 1966. *The economic revolution of our time*. Prof. Brij Narain Memorial Lectures, 1965. Chandigarh, Panjab University Publication Bureau.

Mehta, J.K. 1932. *The elements of economics mathematically interpreted*. London, G. Routledge.

Mishra, K. 1996. *V.K.R.V. Rao, his life and times*. New Delhi, Vikas Publishing House.

Moon, V. (ed.). 1979. *Dr Babasaheb Ambedkar, writings and speeches*. Bombay, Education Department, Government of Maharashtra.

Mujeeb, M. 1972. *Dr Zakir Husain: a biography*. New Delhi, National Book Trust, India.

Mukherjee, Radhakamal. 1951. *The Indian working class*. Bombay, Hind Kitabs.

Mukherjee, Radhakamal. 1938. *The regional balance of man, an ecological theory of population*. Madras, University of Madras.

_____. 1938. *The changing face of Bengal, a study in riverine economy*. Calcutta University Readership Lectures. Calcutta, The University of Calcutta.

_____. 1936. *Le migrazione asiatiche*. Rome, Tipografia Failli.

_____. 1933. *Land problems of India*. London, Longmans, Green and Co.

_____. 1916. *The foundations of Indian economics*. London, Longmans, Green and Co.

Mukerjee, Radhakamal and H.L. Dey. 1939. *Economic problems of modern India*. London, Macmillan and Co.

Mukhtar, A. 1935. *Trade unionism and labour disputes in India*. Bombay, Longmans, Green and Co.

_____. 1930. *Factory labour in India*. Madras, Annamalai University.

Myles, W. 1925. *Sixty years of Punjab food prices, 1861–1920*. Lahore, Board of Economic Inquiry.

Narain Brij. 1946. *Economic structure of free India*. Lahore, Indian Book Co.

_____. 1944a. *Indian economic problems: Pre-war, war and post-war*. Lahore, Atma Ram & Sons.

_____. 1944b. *Curve fitting for students of economics*. Delhi and Lahore, S. Chand & Co.

_____. 1939. *India before and since the crisis*. Allahabad, Indian Press.

_____. 1935. *Tendencies in recent economic thought; lectures delivered as Sir Kikabhai Premchand Reader, 1934, to the University of Delhi*. Delhi, University of Delhi.

_____. 1929. *Indian economic life, past and present*. Lahore, Uttar Chand Kapur & Sons.

_____. 1919. *Essays on Indian economic problems*. Lahore, The Panjabee (electric) Press.

Narain Brij, S.R. Sharma, F. Pelsaert, and P.V.D. Broecke. 1957. *A contemporary Dutch chronicle of Mughal India*. Calcutta, Susil Gupta.

Niyogi, J. 1929. *The evolution of the Indian income tax*. London, P.S. King.

Panandikar, S.G. 1933. *Industrial labour in India*. Bombay, Longmans, Green and Co.

_____. 1926. *The wealth and welfare of the Bengal Delta, comprising the districts of Mymensingh, Dacca, Bogra, Pabna, Faridpur, Bakarganj, Tippera and Noskhali*. Calcutta, Calcutta University Press.

_____. 1921. *Some aspects of the economic consequences of the war for India*. Bombay.

Pillai, P.P. 1925. *Economic conditions in India*. London, G. Routledge.

Prahlad Kumar, and J.K. Singh. 2006. *Economics of J.K. Mehta: a peep into Mehtanomics*. New Delhi, Deep & Deep Publications.

Prasad, J. 1923. *Bibliography of economic books relating to India*. Allahabad, Department of Economics, University of Allahabad.

Presidency College (Calcutta). 1956. *Centenary Volume 1955: Presidency College, Calcutta*. Alipore, West Bengal Government Press.

Qureshi, A.I. 1934. *The farmer & his debt; being a study of farm relief in Australia, New Zealand and South Africa, with suggestions for India*. London, The Indian Rural Reconstruction League.

Rajkumar, P.V. 1978. *Economics is not all: Thoughts and tributes: Dr B. Natarajan 67th birthday commemoration volume*. Madras, Institute of Techno Economic Studies.

Ranade, M.G. 1982. *Essays on Indian economics: a collection of essays and speeches*. New Delhi, Publications Division, Ministry of Information and Broadcasting, Government of India.

Ranadive, B.T. 1930. *Population problem of India*. Calcutta, Longmans, Green and Co.

Ranga, N.G. 1968. *Fight for freedom, autobiography of N.G. Ranga*. Delhi, S. Chand.

———. 1930. *The economics of handloom. (Being a study of the social and economic conditions of handloom weavers of South India.)* Bombay, Taraporewala Sons.

———. 1926a. *Economic organization of Indian villages*. Andhra economic series, 1. Bezwada, the Vani Press.

———. 1926b. *The handloom weaving industry*. Madras.

Rao, S.L. (ed.). 2002. *The partial memoirs of V.K.R.V. Rao*. New Delhi, Oxford University Press.

Rao, V.K.R.V. 1940. *The National income of British India, 1931–1932*. London, Macmillan.

———. 1939. *An essay on India's national income, 1925–1929*. London, G. Allen & Unwin Ltd.

Rao, V.K.R.V. and C.N. Vakil. 1931. *Taxation of income in India*. Calcutta, Longmans, Green and Co.

Rawlley, R.C. 1919a. *The silk industry and trade; a study in the economic organization of the export trade of Kashmir and Indian silks, with special reference to their utilization in the British and French markets*. London, P.S. King & Son.

Rawlley, R.C. 1919b. *Economics of the silk industry: A study in industrial organisation*. London, P.S. King & Son.

Ray, P. 1934. *India's foreign trade since 1870*. London, G. Routledge.

Ray, P.C. 1895. *The poverty problem in India; being a dissertation on the causes and remedies of Indian poverty*. Calcutta, Thacker, Spink & Co.

Rege, D.V. and S.R. Deshpande. 1945. *Report on an enquiry into conditions of labour in India*. India, Labour Investigation Commitice.

Roy, T. 2000. *The economic history of India, 1857–1947*. New Delhi, Oxford University Press.

Saha, K.B. 1930. *Economics of rural Bengal*. Calcutta, Chuckervertty Chatterjee.

Sanyal, N. 1930. *Development of Indian railways*. Calcutta, University of Calcutta.

Sapre, B.G. 1927. *Essentials of Indian economics*.

Sarkar, B.K. 1938. *Studies in applied economics and world-economy*. Calcutta, Chuckervertty Chatterjee.

_____. 1937. *Social insurance: legislation and statistics: a study in the labour economics and business organization of neo-capitalism*. Calcutta, Calcutta Publishers.

_____. 1936. *The problem of correlation between exchange rates and exports: an analysis of Indian statistics in its bearings on economic theory: a paper for the 20th Indian Economic Conference, Agra, December 31, 1936–January 2, 1937*. Calcutta, Calcutta Oriental Book Agency.

_____. 1934a. *Imperial preference vis-à-vis world-economy in relation to the international trade and national economy of India*. Calcutta, N.M. Ray-Chowdhury & Co.

_____. 1934b. *Indian currency and reserve bank problems*. Calcutta, N.M. Ray-Chowdhury & Co.

_____. 1934c. *Imperial preference vis-a-vis world economy in relation to the international trade and national economy of India*. Calcutta, N.M. Ray-Chowdhury & Co.

_____. 1933a. *Economic planning for Bengal*. Calcutta.

_____. 1933b. *Indian currency and reserve bank problems (1926–33)*. Calcutta, N.M. Ray-Chowdhury & Co.

_____. 1926. *Economic development. Snapshots of world movements in commerce, economic legislation, industrialism and technical education*. Madras, B.G. Paul & Co.

Sarkar, J. 1917. *Economics of British India*. Calcutta, Sarkar.

Sarma, S.K. 1911. *Indian monetary problems*. Madras, Law Printing House.
Shah, K.T. 1949. *National Planning Committee: Report*. Bombay, Vora.
——. 1941. *Industrialisation of the Punjab*. Lahore, Printed by the Superintendent, Government Printing Punjab.
——. 1929. *Federal finance in India*. Bombay, D.B. Taraporevala & Sons.
——. 1923. *Trade, tariffs & transport in India*. Bombay, National Book Depot.
——. 1921. *Sixty years of Indian finance*. Bombay, Printed at the Bombay Chronicle Press.
Shah, K.T. and K.J. Khambata. 1924. *Wealth & taxable capacity of India*. Bombay, D.B. Taraporevala Sons & Co.
Shah, K.T., P.J. Thomas, J.C. Kumarappa, Datar Singh, and J.C. Coyajee. 1942. *The economic background*. Oxford Pamphlets on Indian Affairs, no. 3–double pamphlet. London, New York, Bombay, etc. H. Milford and Oxford University Press.
Shah, N.J. 1924. *History of Indian tariffs*. Bombay, Thacker & Co.
Shirras, G.F. 1923a. *Report on an enquiry into the wage and hours of labour in the cotton mill industry*. Bombay, Printed at the Government Central Press.
——. 1923b. *Report on an enquiry into working class budgets in Bombay*. Bombay, Printed at the Government Central Press.
——. 1920. *Indian finance and banking*. London, Macmillan and Co., Limited.
Singh, B. 1957. *The frontiers of social science: In honour of Radhakamal Mukerjee*. London, Macmillan.
Sinha, S.K. 1994. *Contribution of C.N. Vakil to Indian economic planning*. New Delhi, Deep and Deep.
Slater, G. 1936. *Southern India, its political and economic problems*. London, G. Allen & Unwin.
——. 1918. *Some south Indian villages*. London, H. Milford and Oxford University Press.
Soni, H.R. 1932. *Indian industry and its problems*. London, Longmans, Green and Co.
Sovani, N.V. 1981. *Indian economics, the old and the new paradigms*. Prof. V.G. Kale memorial lectures, 1980. Pune, University of Poona.
Spengler, J.J. 1971. *Indian economic thought; a preface to its history*. Durham, N.C., Duke University Press.

Subba Rao, N.S. 1935. *Some aspects of economic planning: Being Sir William Meyer lectures, 1932–33, University of Madras*. Bangalore, Bangalore Press.

Subrahmanya Aiyar, G. 1903. *Some economic aspects of British rule in India.* Madras, Swadesamitran Press.

Thakurdas, P., J.R.D. Tata, and G. Birla. 1944. *A plan of economic development for India*. Bombay, Printed by S. Ramu, at The Commercial Printing Press.

Thomas, P.J. 1963. *Mercantilism and the East India trade*. London, Cass.

_____. 1939. *The growth of federal finance in India, being a survey of India's public finances from 1833 to 1939*. London, H. Milford and Oxford University Press.

Thomas, P.J. and K.C. Ramakrishnan. 1940. *Some South Indian villages: A resurvey*. Madras, University of Madras.

Thomas, P.J. and N. Sundararama Sastry. 1940. *Commodity prices in South India, 1918–1938*. Madras, Univ. of Madras.

_____. 1939. *Indian agricultural statistics (an introductory study)*. Madras University economics series, no. 3. Madras, University of Madras.

Thorat, S. 1998. *Ambedkar's role in economic planning and water policy*. Delhi, Shipra Publications.

Thorat, S. and Aryama. 2007. *Ambedkar in retrospect: Essays on economics, politics, and society*. New Delhi, Rawat Publications in association with Indian Institute of Dalit Studies.

Vakil, C.N. 1974. *Poverty and planning*. Westport, Conn., Greenwood Press.

_____. 1925. *Financial developments in modern India, 1860–1924*. Bombay, D.B. Taraporevala Sons & Co.

_____. 1923. *Our fiscal policy*. Bombay, D.B. Taraporevala Sons & Co.

Vakil, C.N. and M.C. Munshi. 1934. *Industrial policy of India, with special reference to customs tariff*. Calcutta, Longmans, Green and Co.

Vakil, C.N., S.C. Bose, and P.V. Deolalkar. 1931. *Growth of trade and industry in modern India; an introductory survey*. Calcutta, Longmans, Green and Co.

Visvesvaraya, M. 1934. *Planned economy for India*. Bangalore, Bangalore Press.

Wacha, D.E. 1915. *Commerce and statistics; being a reprint of four papers read and written at various times*. Bombay, D.B. Taraporewalla, Sons & Co.

Wadia, P.A. and G.N. Joshi. 1925. *The wealth of India*. London, Macmillan and Co.

Wattal, P.K. 1934. *The population problem in India; a census study*. Bombay, Bennett, Coleman & Co.

———. 1923. *The system of financial administration in British India*. Bombay, Times of India.

Zachariah, B. 2005. *Developing India: An intellectual and social history, c. 1930–50*. New Delhi, Oxford University Press.

Reports

Great Britain. 1928. *Report of the Royal Commission on Agriculture in India*. London, H.M. Stationery Office.

India. 1950. *Report of the Fiscal Commission, 1949–50*. Delhi, Manager of Publications.

———. 1922. *Report of the Indian Fiscal Commission, 1921–22*. Simla, Superintendent, Government Central Press.

India, and C.G. Todhunter. 1925. *Report of the Indian Taxation Enquiry Committee, 1924-25*. Madras, Printed by the Superintendent, Government Press, Calcutta, Government of India, Central Publication Branch.

Royal Commission on Indian Currency and Finance (Great Britain). 1926. *Report of the Royal Commission on Indian Currency and Finance with Appendices, Minutes of Evidence and Index*. London, H.M. Stationery Office.

Royal Commission on Labour in India, and J.H. Whitley. 1931. *Report of the Royal Commission on Labour in India*. London, H.M. Stationery Office.

Index